TIM BURTON

INTERVIEWS

CONVERSATIONS WITH FILMMAKERS SERIES
PETER BRUNETTE, GENERAL EDITOR

Photo credit: Photofest

TIM
BURTON
INTERVIEWS

EDITED BY KRISTIAN FRAGA

UNIVERSITY PRESS OF MISSISSIPPI / JACKSON

www.upress.state.ms.us

The University Press of Mississippi is a member of
the Association of American University Presses.

Manufactured in the United States of America

∞

Library of Congress Cataloging-in-Publication Data

Burton, Tim, 1958–
    Tim Burton : interviews / edited by Kristian Fraga.— 1st ed.
      p. cm.— (Conversations with filmmakers series)
    Includes index.
    ISBN 1-57806-758-8 (cloth : alk. paper) — ISBN 1-57806-759-6
(pbk. : alk. paper)
      1. Burton, Tim, 1958– —Interviews. 2. Motion picture producers
and directors—United States—Interviews. I. Fraga, Kristian. II. Title.
III. Series.

    PN1998.3.B875A3   2005
    791.4302'33'092—dc22   2004065125

British Library Cataloging-in-Publication Data available

CONTENTS

INTRODUCTION

"Tim Burton." The name alone conjures images of gothic landscapes, demonic clowns, and the melancholy sweetness of a loner struggling to find his way in an unaccepting world. Like Alfred Hitchcock before him, Tim Burton has become a mythic persona known as much for his physical appearance, alternately described as endearingly passe, dork chic, or disheveled, as for his highly stylized films. These films, full of extreme and symbolic imagery, have become part of our cultural landscape.

From *Pee-Wee's Big Adventure* (1985) to *Tim Burton's Corpse Bride* (2005), Burton's films have been able to transcend both genre and explanation. The ideas and themes that appear in his work, as well as the interviews in this volume, are both universal and timeless. Like any good fairytale, his pictures, upon first glance, reach people on an emotional level rather than on an intellectual one. Because of this, Burton is one of only a handful of filmmakers, among them Woody Allen, Martin Scorsese, Stanley Kubrick, David Lynch, and Spike Lee, who have had the rare opportunity to make personal films within the Hollywood studio system. However, the same factors that have helped turn Burton's personal films into big box office are the very same "weaknesses" that many in the more academic circles of cinema feel have rendered Burton more of a visual opportunist than a complete filmmaker.

On the heels of the first screening of *Batman Returns* for Warner Bros. executives, Burton was asked by writer David Breskin if he felt that because of the extreme nature of his films there was a danger of them being looked at as nothing more than visual candy. Burton's answer was quite revealing. "No, it's not, even if it may be perceived that way, and often is. Everything has quite a deep foundation, otherwise how could you really do something? The process is too difficult and it's too painful to not have some deeply rooted feelings in it." In many ways the box office success of his pictures have hurt Burton's position as a personal filmmaker. Because he and his work have been branded "Hollywood," it can be argued that his movies have quite often not been examined in their proper context. This could account for the discrepancy between Burton's lackluster critical reception and his spectacular box office success. Burton's career serves as a fascinating study of how a director who approaches filmmaking on an intimate and, shall we say, more European nature manages to become a major studio player. For Tim Burton, filmmaking has never been about dollars and cents, but rather about clarity and sense.

Throughout this volume you will hear Burton repeatedly talk about filmmaking as a form of self-discovery. In the Breskin interview he is very candid about making-films-as-therapy and the cathartic nature of his work. "People don't realize, because of the surface way the films look and the cartoonish nature of them, that the only thing that keeps me going through a movie is that these characters mean something to me."

Right off the bat, no pun intended, Marc Shapiro for *Starlog Magazine* introduces us to the thirty-year-old wunderkind as he puts the finishing touches on his soon-to-be-released second feature film, *Beetlejuice*. What is interesting about this interview, and the one that follows by David Edelstein for *Rolling Stone*, is that we get a basic foundation covering much of Burton's early work including his short films; *Vincent* and *Frankenweenie*, which will be talked about more in depth in later interviews, and, of course, his first feature film, *Pee Wee's Big Adventure*.

Key aspects of Burton's personality and career emerge in these early interviews: his defiance of the studio system ("I'm for anything that subverts what the studio thinks you have to do"), the genre-bending nature of his pictures ("It's hard to describe this film as just one thing . . . "), his unique approach to narrative structure ("I was intrigued that there was no story"), and his early days at Disney ("Remove part of your brain and become a zombie factory worker").

We clearly see a filmmaker who is interested in themes and ideas and, at the end of the day, directs pictures because they *mean* something to him. Pay particular attention to the last two paragraphs of the *Starlog* interview. From his "unkempt hair" to his somewhat prophetic statement about his choice in material one day getting him "into trouble," we gain an early glimpse at the Tim Burton who will emerge over the next two decades as one of cinema's most unique voices.

While the back-to-back box office successes of *Pee-Wee's Big Adventure* and *Beetlejuice* introduced the world to Tim Burton, the 1989 release of *Batman* made him a household name. Alan Jones's *Cinefantastique* interview with Burton focuses on the creative aspects of bringing the Caped Crusader to the big screen. Along with the director, Jones talks to a number of filmmakers Burton collaborated with on this picture. One of the more interesting aspects of this particular interview is *Batman* production designer Anton Furst talking about his relationship with Burton. Both he and Burton discuss the mutual respect they have for each other as both filmmakers and friends. Furst's eventual suicide is a painful loss for Burton and a subject that comes back, indirectly, throughout this volume. It isn't until later interviews, the 1997 *Premiere* and *Starlog Magazine* pieces, both found in this volume, that we get a direct indication of the impact Furst's death had on Burton, in particular during the making of the Batman sequel.

By the end of the summer of 1989, Burton is a full-blown "player" in the industry. One can see the shift in his career as he gains more creative control over his pictures. With the release of *Edward Scissorhands* in 1990, Burton cements his signature style into the minds of filmgoers around the world and his Hollywood legend is all but secure.

Edward Scissorhands is full of visual layers that offer a glimpse into the personal world of Tim Burton. On the most basic level one could read Edward Scissorhands as Tim Burton; lonely, misunderstood, and longing to touch and create in an environment more inclined to label and destroy. He infuses Edward with a purity and essence of goodness that is symbolic and in many ways extreme.

The elegant simplicity of Johnny Depp's portrayal of Edward and the classical structure of the narrative allows audiences to identify with and ultimately understand the character on a base level. By using the elemental structure of the fairytale as a template, Burton creates his most personal film by tapping into universal themes.

Throughout David Edelstein's 1990 profile of the young director for *Mirabella* we see a Burton who is open about his troubles growing up in Burbank, or as he puts it, "the pit of hell," with parents who really never understood him. "There's something about suburbia, it's really a place to hide. Or people use it as a sort of mask of normalcy." His distant relationship with his parents, in particular his father, is a thread that runs throughout his films and the interviews in this volume. This is a situation he clearly isn't comfortable discussing, and for the most part, he shies away from it until his 2001 profile in *Playboy*. With the release of *Big Fish* in 2003 Burton deals with the issue head on in what might be his most revealing film.

From Edelstein's piece we learn about how important Vincent Price and his Edgar Allan Poe films were to a young Tim Burton. They were not mere excursions, allowing Burton to escape from the drudgery of suburban life, but rather a release that was necessary on many levels. "Embracing death and the catharsis of 'Oh my God, I'm going to die' and *The Fall of the House of Usher* and *The Raven* and Edgar Allan Poe and Vincent Price helped me to live."

Edward Scissorhands is a personal film created by a director invested in making intimate pictures anchored by the most fantastic situations. Burton perfectly sums up his deeply personal approach to filmmaking when he tells Edelstein, "It's why you struggle as a child and you draw and want to create. There is an impulse to be seen. For yourself: what you are. It's always scary for me to show movies. I actually hate it; I feel very, very vulnerable. Because if you weren't a verbal person, you weren't this and that, you wanna let that be the thing people see you through. And so when that doesn't happen—and it doesn't, they see maybe success or failure but they don't see you—it gets further and further away from you, and it's just sad."

Edward Scissorhands is the movie that, in many ways, establishes the Burton aesthetic. Returning for this picture are key collaborators: production designer Bo Welch (*Beetlejuice, Batman Returns*), concept artist Rich Heinrichs (who worked on all of Burton's films from *Vincent* to *Planet of the Apes*), and Danny Elfman, composer for all of Burton's films except *Ed Wood*. The Burton/Elfman relationship has reached a level of global association akin to the famed Hitchock/Herman and Spielberg/Williams connections. Burton credits Elfman's music for being as much responsible for the success, in terms of capturing the feelings and emotions of all his pictures (save *Ed Wood*) since *Pee-Wee's Big Adventure*.

Scissorhands also marks the first time Burton collaborates with members of what will become his extended creative family. Director of photography Stefan Czhapskey would go on after *Scissorhands* to photograph *Batman Returns* and *Ed Wood*, arguably two of Burton's most beautiful and visually dynamic films. Caroline Thompson, the screenwriter of *Scissorhands*, is also responsible for writing Burton's two feature-length stop-motion animated features, *Tim Burton's The Nightmare Before Christmas* and *Tim Burton's Corpse Bride*. As head of Tim Burton Productions, Denise Di Novi would produce *Edward Scissorhands* and *Batman Returns*. After stepping down as head of the company, she would go on to produce for or with Burton, *Ed Wood*, *Tim Burton's The Nightmare Before Christmas*, *James and the Giant Peach*, and *Cabin Boy*.

Finally, *Edward Scissorhands* signaled the beginning of one of the most fruitful relationships of Burton's professional career. He and actor Johnny Depp would team up again for *Ed Wood*, *Sleepy Hollow*, *Charlie and the Chocolate Factory*, and *Tim Burton's Corpse Bride*. Many credit their successful collaboration to Depp's uncanny ability to take on the role of Burton's onscreen alter ego. For Burton, a director who externalizes the internal struggles of his character with his extreme imagery and use of costumes, make-up, and masks (Beetlejuice, Batman, Joker, Catwoman, Edward Scissorhands, Ed Wood, etc.), Depp's chameleon-like nature as an actor makes him a perfect fit. "I love actors who like to transform . . . it's exciting to see that. And I really get a lot of energy out of somebody like him who, you know, doesn't care how he looks, is willing to do anything."[1]

With the production of *Batman Returns*, Burton begins one of the most demanding periods of his career as well as one of the most difficult times in his life. With the mixed reaction to the film upon its release (critics celebrated its darkness; parents rebelled), the suicide of Anton Furst, the end of his first marriage, and the instability within his own production company, Burton begins a descent into what he later describes as an "Alison and Wonderlandy"[2] hole.

Hints of Burton's internal and external struggles can be perceived in the 1992 *Starlog* interview by Marc Shapiro. We get insight into the making of *Batman Returns* and his reasons for going back to Gotham City after four years of vowing never to do a sequel. Burton, noted by Shapiro as being semi-serious, does open up to some degree when asked about his frame of mind during the making of the picture. "If you had been a fly on the wall, you would have seen a morose, depressed person. . . . I was moodier than I usually am on a movie, and I think part of that came from the fact that I was afraid doing a second Batman movie was going to weigh on my mind."

Certainly, directing the follow-up to one of the biggest hits of all time was "weighing" on Burton's mind, but it isn't until David Breskin's aforementioned lengthy interview, that we have a clear picture of an artist struggling to maintain a purity and sense of self in an industry known for destroying those very values. Burton is candid about the inherent conflict and duality in keeping a genuine and truly personal perspective in Hollywood, a world that is all about facade. "You see people turning into the most frightening creatures. . . . The whole situation perverts you. And it's a mistake to think that it doesn't." This interview covers Burton's career from *Vincent* to *Batman Returns* and gives us an indepth look into Burton's creative process. It also sets up a number of questions that are discussed, to varying degrees, in later interviews.

Batman Returns garnered some of the director's best reviews and grossed over 260 million dollars worldwide, but the future direction of Tim Burton's career was debated in many circles. Burton responded to his critics with one of his most unique and inspired works to date, *Tim Burton's The Nightmare Before Christmas*. This picture ushered in a quantum leap in the art of stop-motion animation and was the first Disney movie to be released using this technique.

Henry Selick, a friend of Burton's from the early Disney days and one of the top stop-motion animators in the business, was selected to direct the picture. It was he who oversaw the multimillion-dollar undertaking over its glacial three-year production period, and he who deserves credit for bringing this movie to life. However, this can never be mistaken for anything other than pure Tim Burton. From the visuals down to the music, songs, and lyrics written by Danny Elfman, it is a testament to

Burton's visual signature that a picture he did not direct could so easily fit into the aesthetic and capture the spirit of his overall body of work.

Disney was eager to team up with their prodigal son and as David Hoberman, then president of Walt Disney Pictures and Touchstone, put it, "This was an opportunity for us to be in business with Tim Burton and to say, 'We can think outside the envelope. We can do different and unusual things.' "[3] Not too bad for a kid dismissed by the very same studio ten years earlier.

"Initially . . . I was going to direct this picture . . . I tried to get it going as a short film, a TV special, Home Shopping Network, anything that would take it, but I couldn't even give it away back then." Burton's recollection of the studio turning its back on his project is remembered very much the same way by Selick. "I thought that people, especially kids, would love his work the way they loved Charles Addams." He tells Mimi Avins in her 1993 *Premiere Magazine* profile of the film "But nobody recognized that at Disney. They thought, *Oh, this is just too weird.*"

The possessory credit that appears in the title of the picture (and his next stop-motion animated opus over a decade later) is a clear indication of the market value of the director's name. *Tim Burton's A Nightmare Before Christmas* would turn out to be a triumph for the filmmaker both artistically and financially. However, it would also be his last box office success for a number of years.

With the studios clamoring for a piece of the big money business known as TIM BURTON, the director set his sights on the world of Z filmmaking and schlock science fiction. His fascination with the "low end" of filmmaking would yield two distinct pictures with varying degrees of success.

"I have no conception of what is cheesy, and what isn't . . . The lines to me are now completely blurred. I have no idea between good and bad anymore. That will be for others to decide." It is fitting that Burton would confess these feelings to Lawrence French as he put the finishing touches on *Ed Wood*, his black and white bio-pic of Hollywood's legendary "worst" director of all time Edward D. Wood Jr. Considered by many to be Burton's finest effort—certainly it is his most critically accepted picture—it was, however, his first box office disappointment.

Lawrence French's interview for *Cinefantastique* offers a number of interesting insights into not only the production of *Ed Wood*, but also the way Burton plays the Hollywood game. His decision to follow up the big budget machinery of *Batman Returns* with the smaller scale production of *Ed Wood* is telling on many levels. Burton's personal connection to the material and willingness to go against the grain, in terms of style and execution, is a clear indication that his desire to take a more "independent" approach to filmmaking was in effect during the production of *Ed Wood*.

Burton has claimed that neither he nor anybody else in Hollywood has a clue as to what makes a hit movie. "I'm equally surprised if a movie does well or badly." For him, that quality of the unknown is part of the energy and excitement that pushes him to make a picture in the first place. Even Burton, however, must have known that a black-and-white bio-pic, a comedy no less, about an obscure filmmaker is not a combination that easily equals box office success. It is a credit to his artistic sensibilities and his clout within the industry that not only was this picture made, but also for the first time, the critics and Hollywood as a whole took notice of Tim Burton the *filmmaker* and not just the hit maker.

On the heels of *Ed Wood*, one of his most complex and structured pictures, Burton would next produce one of the wildest and most unwieldy movies of his career. *Mars Attacks!*, inspired from a line of little-known Topps bubble gum cards depicting graphic images of martians blowing up planet earth and its inhabitants, would leave American moviegoers and critics dumfounded and have Hollywood executives scratching their heads wondering what to make of the visionary director.

Mars Attacks! is all about Burton's approach to an emotional cinema rather than an intellectual one. His choice of material stems more from a concern with understanding the self and responding to emotions than from a desire to make "commercial" pictures in an effort to solidify his place in the industry. His movies are a product of an internal process to grasp what's going on in the world around him and deal with how it affects him. Case in point, his explanation to Christine Spines in her 1997 interview for *Premiere Magazine* of the impetus behind *Mars Attacks!*. "It was during the Gulf War . . . when the media seemed to have taken it to another level—wars having titles and theme music—and I found it kind of disturbing. I felt like these characters were just a good cathartic shakeup of that kind of thing."

Burton's decision to make *Mars Attacks!* is a perfect illustration of a director responding to material based on imagery. The movie is a tone poem, as Burton constructs a narrative to support the visuals, not the other way around. According to Burton, "Movies are abstractions until they've been made—and that's the beauty of them."

The "tooney" nature of Burton's work has time and again overshadowed the deeper subtext that is always brimming at the surface of his films. Granted, little green martians chasing Danny DeVito and Tom Jones with ray guns is enough to zap any form of serious criticism, and I, in no way, claim that Burton ever intended *Mars Attacks!* to be a movie with a "message." But it is a mistake to dismiss Burton's pictures as mere fluff based on surface imagery.

Mars Attacks! in many ways serves as an exclamation point to the career of an artist who is every bit a product of his upbringing. In much the same way a Martin Scorsese or Steven Spielberg film reflects the environment and psychology of their respective youth, Tim Burton's movies offer a similar unique perspective into his formative years. His films capture the mythological themes and campy over-the-top beauty of earlier larger than life pictures such as the Poe films starring Vincent Price or the stop-motion epics of Ray Harryhausen. As much as these films have influenced Burton's singular vision, his preoccupation with "childlike" impulses have often come at the expense of a defined narrative structure and logical character development. "Growing up as part of the television generation, I probably veer toward bad taste. I like to think of myself as liking certain art pieces that aren't considered good taste. But you go with your background, it's hard to shake whatever roots you have. I always try to turn bad taste into good taste—but that gets very messy."[4] Burton's take on the situation, while rather simple, raises a number of questions.

Given Burton's aesthetic and particular tastes, should his films be judged according to a defined conventional dramatic structure? The criticism that a Tim Burton film is more concerned with visuals and colorful characters than with story is an interesting take on the work of a director who operates on the level of pure cinema. His movies are *about* the visuals and how they define and reveal the nature of his characters. To separate the imagery from the narrative, which are virtually one and the same, is to reduce his films to a predetermined template they will never fully fit.

If there is any doubt about where Burton's priorities lie in terms of what drives his movies, all one needs to do is study the names of each of his pictures. In all the films he has directed, the titles are either simply named after one of the main characters (*Vincent, Frankenweenie, Beetlejuice, Batman, Edward Scissorhands, Ed Wood, Big Fish, Corpse Bride*), the main character in his current escapade (*Pee-Wee's Big Adventure, Batman Returns, Charlie and the Chocolate Factory*), or a place or location (*Mars Attacks!, Sleepy Hollow, Planet of the Apes*). For Burton, the story is what links the characters and the worlds they inhabit, not strictly what the picture is about.

Burton is candid about his relationship to the screenplay, "I couldn't tell you a good script if it hit me in the face." In his earlier interviews he's a bit cavalier and quick to acknowledge that story structure isn't his strong suit. However, by the Breskin interview in 1991, he's clearly becoming a bit leery of the whole issue. When asked whether his "problem" with narrative is in fact a problem, he answers, "Well, I feel that less and less. Because now it's become redundant . . . maybe things will become more abstract." By the time of the *Playboy* interview in 2001, Burton had clearly decided how to handle the criticism. "When people come up and hand me scripts I always want to say, Hey why are you handing me a script? Have you read any reviews of my films? Every reviewer says my scripts are terrible!"

With the release of *Sleepy Hollow* in the fall of 1999 Burton would regain his box office touch and create a picture replete with his signature gothic imagery and operatic sensibilities. Once again drawing from the movies that inspired him as a youth, the Hammer Horror Pictures and Mario Bava's *Black Sunday*, Burton puts his spin on one of America's true mythological tales, Washington Irving's "The Legend of Sleepy Hollow."

Burton's energy and enthusiasm for bringing the images of *Sleepy Hollow* to life are captured perfectly in his interview with Stephen Pizzello for *American Cinematographer*. This piece focuses on his aesthetic choices in the making of the picture and offers an interesting look at Burton's creative process.

"I always like a good fairy tale, or any story that has symbolic meaning. . . . I was particularly drawn to the idea that Ichabod Crane is this guy w——— s inside his own head, while his nemesis has no head at all! Th——— aposition was interesting to me; it really worked on a symbolic, ——— subconscious level."

Chi——— r Nashawaty's cover article for *Entertainment Weekly* brings us int——— iting room with Burton, as once again he deals with the stress ———ing his film to the masses. In this interview Burton is candid ab——— struggles the year before with *Superman Lives* and how that le——— *Sleepy Hollow*. "That was so extremely painful. I had sketche——— leetings upon meetings. After *Superman*, I was happy to chop peoples' heads off in *Sleepy Hollow*. It was cathartic."

It is not surprising that following box office misfires such as *Ed Wood* and *Mars Attacks!* that Burton would turn to seemingly more commercial fare such as *Sleepy Hollow*. It is clear from the interviews up to this point that he is a shrewd player in the high stakes game of Hollywood, probably more so than he would like to let on, and fully understands the old industry axiom, a director is as good as his last hit. It's also clear that at this point in his career he was a filmmaker in flux.

On the heels of the *Superman Lives* fiasco and before embarking on *Sleepy Hollow* Burton published *The Melancholy Death of Oyster Boy and Other Stories*. The book is a collection of illustrated short stories that could only come from the mind of Tim Burton. One character in particular, Stain Boy, would go on to be the title character of a series of animated shorts, written and directed by Burton. He also served as a conduit for Burton to release his personal and creative frustrations during the time of *Superman Lives*.

"Stain Boy is one of my favorite characters, and in a way he's probably the perfect symbol of what that whole Superman experience that year—truthfully that's pretty much how I felt. If anybody wants to know what that year was like, then just read that, that's the best description of it."[5] says Burton.

The box office success of *Sleepy Hollow* once again solidified Burton as a hit maker in the eyes of the industry. With his next picture, Burton would take on another story of mythic proportions, but instead of dealing with the colonial past, he would set his sights to the not-so-distant future.

Planet of the Apes would go on to be Burton's second highest grossing picture behind *Batman*. Much like the production of his first blockbuster, this film would go through the same issues of script wrangling during shooting, an incessant rumor mill churned by avid fans (this time mostly on the internet), and the studio's focusing more on the toys and marketing than on the actual film. Burton laments, "Sometimes I feel like the film gets in the way of the merchandising. There were people over in Taiwan making *Planet of the Apes* swords before we'd even shot the thing."

In the 2001 *Premiere* and *Playboy* interviews, Burton reveals himself to be a bit leery of the whole "blockbuster" mentality of filmmaking. The script issues were certainly a problem felt by both the director and his stars. Tim Roth, who played the evil ape commander Thade, summed it up in the *Premiere* piece. "I read the first script, and then it was constant change, so I would just read what was happening with my character in the morning, while I was in makeup. . . . I have no idea what's been going on, which will be good when I see the film."

In the *Playboy* interview by Kristine McKenna, Burton opens up about issues that were first raised a decade earlier in the Breskin article. We learn more about his family and how that relationship has progressed, hear what Burton perceives to be his strengths and weakness as a filmmaker, his feelings on being a public figure, and how being a studio filmmaker has affected him on a personal level. What's interesting about this interview is that we get a sense that Burton has become much more comfortable in being Tim Burton, the man and the public persona. There is a maturity and sense of understanding of both his creative and personal life that we see for the first time.

We now get a glimpse of both an artist and a man, perhaps not having figured it all out, but at least accepting a certain amount of responsibility and exuding a sense of security about where he comes from and the impact his roots have had on his art. "I wouldn't change anything, because the more pain you endure when you're young, the richer your adult life will be. . . . If you're lucky, you'll develop a creative outlet to exorcize those feelings."

This was never more true than with *Big Fish*, Burton's tenth studio picture as director. *Big Fish* serves as yet another example of Burton escaping from the blockbuster to a more personal kind of filmmaking.

This movie may very well be the clearest window into some of his innermost feelings.

Big Fish is a fairytale about the complexities of everyday life. Through a series of different adventures, similar in some respects to the dramatic structure of *Pee-Wee's Big Adventure*, we follow the exploits of Edward Bloom, played by both Ewan McGregor and Albert Finney, and witness the tall-tales that become the whole of his life experience. It is a movie that defies simple categorization as Burton performs a juggling act between subtle shifts in tone and style. Perhaps the picture has best been described by the director himself. "*Big Fish* is about what's real and what's fantastic, what's true and what's not true, what's partially true and how, in the end, it's all true."[6]

Working from a screenplay by John August, Burton, along with *Planet of the Apes* cinematographer, Philippe Rousellot, creates one of the most visually rich pictures of his entire filmography. The economy and precision of the camera work in *Big Fish* should finally put to rest any lingering criticism of Burton's inability to use the camera in telling his stories.

At the heart of the picture is the father-son relationship between Edward and his son William, played by Billy Crudup. It would be much too simplistic to narrow it all down and say *Big Fish* is about Tim Burton and his father, but the personal relevance of the themes and characters in this picture can't be overlooked. Burton himself clearly makes the connection, "My father had been ill for a while. . . . I tried to get in touch with him, to have, like in this film, some sort of resolution, but it was impossible."[7]

Perhaps in life it was impossible for Burton to reconcile his relationship with his father. However, much like William Bloom, through the power of storytelling (filmmaking), he may ultimately find the strength and to some degree an understanding of the unique connection he and his father shared. "I went back to thinking about my father, and as bad a relationship as I had, early on it was quite magical. . . . It's important to remember that. I forgot that for too long."[8]

Interestingly, two months before the release of *Big Fish*, Burton became a father himself for the first time, when girlfriend Helena Bonham-Carter, who plays multiple roles in *Big Fish*, gave birth to Billy Burton on 4 October 2003.

On 19 November 2003, Burton attended a screening of *Big Fish* at the American Museum of the Moving Image. The screening was the culmination of the museum's two-week retrospective entitled "Tim Burton's Big Adventure." After the screening Burton spoke with David Schwartz, chief curator of film at the museum, and fielded questions from the sold-out audience. The transcript of that evening has been included as the final interview of this volume.

Because Burton is talking shop in front of a live audience, there is a certain energy and lightness that is unique to this interview. Burton's humor certainly comes out, and he's a man who, contrary to popular belief, seems comfortable if somewhat guarded in front of a large audience.

Schwartz, for the most part, avoids probing into the director's personal life and this is probably for the best considering Burton's unique answer to the question about his relationship with his father. While informative, Burton is clearly not too interested in opening up about his personal life in front of a few hundred strangers.

In this interview we go behind the scenes of *Big Fish* as Burton talks about, among other things, the visual inspiration behind the look of the picture, how he has developed as a filmmaker, how others perceive his work, and what he thinks about some of his earlier pictures.

At the start of this interview Burton talks about the script of *Big Fish* and how screenwriter John August helped focus the material to create a dramatic structure not found in the book *Big Fish* by Daniel Wallace. On this picture, Burton is working with one of the best scripts of all his films, and after *Planet of the Apes*, he is clearly relieved to have a screenplay that "everybody liked" including the studio. "It's amazing all the other stuff you go through when you don't have what should be the number one element right off the bat."

In this last interview, Burton talks briefly about his next picture as director, *Charlie and the Chocolate Factory*, starring Johnny Depp and scheduled for release in the summer of 2005. When asked if the project was a go, Burton responds, "Well, we've got a tie-in with McDonald's, so I guess it's real."

Burton has indicated his picture will not be an Apes-like reimagining of *Willy Wonka & the Chocolate Factory*, the 1971 musical staring Gene Wilder, but rather an adaptation of the source material, the book by Rohald Dahl. "I remember the story. It was, in a way, my story: misfit boy has a dream, sticks with it and gets lucky," says Burton. "I always like that Charlie was rather grim."9

Tim Burton, like personal filmmakers such as Woody Allen, Oliver Stone, Martin Scorsese, or Francis Ford Coppola, uses his films to explore the issues that consume him, not only as an artist, but also as a man. Certainly, he deals with these issues in a much more stylistic, and, for lack of a better word, "tooney" way than the filmmakers listed above. However, similar to Scorsese re-creating the mean streets of his youth or Stone piecing together the incidents and events of a decade that forever shaped his life, Tim Burton, too, is on a personal journey with each picture. A journey every bit as introspective and far reaching as any filmmaker working today. The candid interviews collected in this volume make clear that Tim Burton, over the past two decades, has become one of the most distinctive voices in modern day cinema.

In keeping with the standards set by the University of Mississippi Press for its *Conversations with Filmmakers* series, the interviews selected for this volume have not been edited for content and have only been altered to italicize the titles of films, books, and music. Because of this, you will find an inherent repetition of information from article to article. For example, Tim Burton's rise from lowly Disney animator to Hollywood's hottest young director is often repeated throughout the volume. However, in some respects, Burton's answers become more layered through the repetition of questions, and because of this, one is able to get a more complete picture based on his fractured statements. Seeing these interviews in chronological order, one can't help but notice the irony of learning about an individual, so famous for being inarticulate, through the power of his own words—certainly, a paradox Tim Burton could truly appreciate.

A quick thanks to Bird, Indy, Riaz, David, Bean, Teba, Sep, "T", Father, Sikes, Gus, The Talented, and the rest of the gang at Sirk. Walter for being there every step of the way, Anne and Shane for bringing it all together, the interviewers and publications who graciously allowed us to reprint these interviews, and to Sal for being a true teacher and friend.

This book is dedicated to my muse *Jeunnifer*, who is as sweet, misunderstood, and full of magic as any of Burton's creations.

KF

Notes

1. Charlie Rose interview, November 15, 1999
2. "Tim Burton's Hollywood Nightmare," by David Edelstein in *Vanity Fair* (November 1994)
3. "Puppetmaster," by Lawrence French in *Cinefantastique* (December 1993)
4. "Spaced Invaders," by Steve Goldman in *Empire Magazine* (March 1997)
5. *Burton on Burton* (revised edition), edited by Mark Salisbury (Faber & Faber, 2000)
6. "Drawn to Narrative," by Lynn Hirschberg in *New York Times Magazine* (November 2003)
7. "The Vision Thing," by Mark Salisbury in *Premiere Magazine* (February 2004)
8. Ibid.
9. "Drawn to Narrative," by Lynn Hirschberg in *New York Times Magazine* (November 2003)

CHRONOLOGY

1958   Timothy William Burton is born in Burbank, California, on August 25.

1976   Eighteen-year-old Burton receives a scholarship to California Institute of the Arts, founded by Walt Disney.

1979   Burton is hired by Disney Studios on the strength of his Cal Arts short, *Stalk of the Celery Monster*.

1981   Burton's first Disney assignment is *The Fox and the Hound*. Burton later says, "My foxes looked like road kill." He is reassigned in a design capacity to *The Black Cauldron*, released in 1985.

1982   Burton directs *Luau*, a low-budget independent film, which is never released. He writes, designs, and directs the stop-motion animated short, *Vincent* and later directs a re-imagining of *Hansel and Gretel* with an all Asian cast for the Disney Channel. Both projects are all but dismissed by the studio.

1984   Burton directs the live-action black and white short, *Frankenweenie*. The film is buried by Disney after the ratings board deems the picture too intense for young children. It's finally released on video, along with *Vincent*, in 1992. After starring in *Frankenweenie*, Shelley Duvall signs Burton to direct "Aladdin and His Wonderful Lamp," for her Showtime Series, *Faerie Tale Theatre*. Shot on video, the production features James Earl Jones and Leonard Nimoy.

1985   At age twenty-six, Burton directs his first studio feature film, *Pee-wee's Big Adventure*. Made for $6 million the movie grosses $45 million domestically. This picture marks the beginning of his famed collaboration with music composer Danny Elfman. He also directs "The Jar," an episode of NBC's *Alfred Hitchcock Presents* and designs animation for an episode of Steven Spielberg's *Amazing Stories*, entitled "Family Dog."

1988   Burton scores his second consecutive box office hit with *Beetlejuice*, starring Michael Keaton, Gena Davis, and Alec Baldwin.

1989   *Batman*, directed by Burton and starring Jack Nicholson and Michael Keaton, goes on to shatter box office records and becomes a cultural phenomenon. Burton marries German artist Lena Gieseke and forms Tim Burton Productions with producing partner Denise Di Novi.

1990   Twentieth Century Fox releases *Edward Scissorhands*, Burton's most personal film. His fourth feature film as a director, his first as a producer, goes on to become one of the biggest hits of the Christmas season. *Scissorhands* also marks the first collaboration between Burton and actor Johnny Depp. Burton develops and executive produces *Beetlejuice* as an animated television series and has a cameo appearance in Cameron Crowe's *Singles*. He directs the as-yet-to-be-released documentary about Vincent Price, *Conversations with Vincent*.

1991   Burton sets up Skellington Productions in San Francisco and begins production on *Tim Burton's The Nightmare Before Christmas*. This will be the first stop-motion animated feature produced by Disney.

1992   *Batman Returns* opens to big box office but is criticized by many as too dark and overtly violent. Burton's marriage ends and Denise Di Novi, while continuing to produce for Burton, steps down as the head of Tim Burton Productions. Burton makes an uncredited and unseen cameo as a corpse in a coffin in friend Danny DeVito's *Hoffa*.

1993   *Tim Burton's The Nightmare Before Christmas* is released. Directed by Henry Selick, based on characters created by Burton, the picture is a hit with audiences and critics. Burton teams up with

Steven Spielberg and co-produces *Family Dog* as an animated series for Amblin Entertainment.

1994 Burton directs *Ed Wood*, his most critically acclaimed picture. It is also his first box office disappointment. *Cabin Boy*, produced by Burton and Di Novi, dies at the box office and is grilled by the critics.

1995 Burton produces the third Batman picture, *Batman Forever*, directed by Joel Schumacher.

1996 The Burton-directed *Mars Attacks!* baffles filmgoers and critics alike upon its release. Burton and Di Novi produce Henry Selick's live-action/stop-motion adaptation of Roald Dahl's *James and the Giant Peach*. This will be the last film Burton and Di Novi produce together.

1997 Burton spends a year developing the ill-fated *Superman Lives*. His first book, *The Melancholy Death of Oyster Boy & Other Stories* is published.

1998 Burton directs the French television commercial, *Hollywood Gum*.

1999 Burton teams up with actor Johnny Depp for the third time in the box office hit *Sleepy Hollow*. Rick Heinrichs, longtime Burton friend and collaborator, wins an Academy Award for his production design on the picture.

2000 Burton writes and directs six episodes of his animated internet series, *Stainboy*. He also directs two commercial spots for Timex—*Kung Fu* and *Mannequin*.

2001 Upon its release, *Planet of the Apes* becomes Burton's second-highest grossing film but is dismissed by the critics.

2003 On October 4 Burton and girlfriend Helena Bonham-Carter have their first child, Billy Burton. Two months later Columbia Pictures releases Burton's tenth feature film as director, *Big Fish*. From November 8 through November 16 the American Museum of the Moving Image runs "Tim Burton's Big Adventure" a retrospective of his films. They also open "Tim Burton Drawings," a gallery exhibiting a number of the director's selected drawings. Dark Horse releases *Tim Burton's Tragic Toys for Girls and Boys*, a merchandising line based on the characters from *The Melancholy Death of Oyster Boy & Other Stories*.

2004   For his work on *Big Fish* Burton is nominated for a David Lean
        Award for Direction by the British Academy of Film and
        Television Arts (BAFTA). Later the same year he goes into
        production on *Charlie and the Chocolate Factory* starring Johnny
        Depp as the eccentric chocolatier Willy Wonka.

2005   Warner Brothers releases *Charlie and the Chocolate Factory* and
        the stop-motion animated feature *Tim Burton's Corpse Bride*,
        co-directed and produced by Burton.

FILMOGRAPHY

As Director

1982
LUAU
Director, Producer, and Screenplay: **Tim Burton** and Jerry Rees
Music: Kent Halliday, featuring Jan and Dave
Cast: Mike Gabriel (Bob), Susan Frankenberger (Arlene), Terrey Hamada (Princess Yakamoshi), Jow Raft, Jay Jackson, Brian McEntee, Harry Sabin, Jerry Rees, Cynthia Prince (surfers), John Musker, Ben Burgess, Rick Heinrichs, Brick Newton, George Sukara, Ed Sommert, Gale Muster, Sue Kroser (businessmen), Phil Young (Kahuna), Randy Cartwright (IQ), **Tim Burton** (The Supreme Being/Mortie), Louis Take, Rosalie Lauzisero, Kathleen A. Sabin, Meredith Jackson, Rebecca LoDolo, Amy Sabin, Darrell Van Citters

1982
VINCENT
Distributed by Buena Vista Distribution Co., Inc.
Producer: Rick Heinrichs
Director, Screenplay, and Design: **Tim Burton**
Technical Director: Stephen Chiodo
Cinematography: Victor Abdalov
Music: Ken Hilton
Sculpture and additional design: Rick Heinrichs
Animation: Stephen Chiodo
Cast: Vincent Price (narrator)
16mm, Black and White
5 minutes

1982
HANSEL AND GRETEL
Executive Producer: Julie Hickson
Director: **Tim Burton**
Screenplay: Julie Hickson, based on the story by Jacob Ludwig Carl Grimm
and Wilhelm Carl Grimm
Cast: Michael Yama (Gretel), Jim Ishida (Hansel)
16mm, Color
45 minutes

1984
FRANKENWEENIE
Distributed by Buena Vista Distribution Co., Inc.
Walt Disney Presents
Producer: Julie Hickson
Director: **Tim Burton**
Screenplay: Lenny Ripps, based on an original idea by **Tim Burton**
Cinematography: Thomas Ackerman
Editor: Ernest Milano
Music: Michael Convertino, David Newman
Associate Producer: Rick Heinrichs
Art Director: John B. Mansbridge
Cast: Shelley Duvall (Susan Frankenstein), Daniel Stern
(Ben Frankenstein), Barret Oliver (Victor Frankenstein), Joseph Maher
(Mr. Chambers), Roz Braverman (Mrs. Epstein), Paul Bartel (Mr. Walsh),
Sofia Coppola as "Domino" (Ann Chambers), Jason Hervey (Frank
Dale), Paul C. Scott (Mike Anderson), Helen Boll (Mrs. Curtis)
35mm, B&W (shot on color stock)
25 minutes

1984
ALADDIN AND HIS WONDERFUL LAMP
Episode of *Faerie Tale Theatre*
A Platypus Production in association with Lion's Gate Films
Producer: Bridget Terry, Fredric S. Fuchs
Executive Producer: Shelley Duvall
Director: **Tim Burton**

Screenplay: Mark Curtiss, Rod Ash
Music: David Newman, Michael Convertino
Production Design: Michael Erler
Cast: Valerie Bertinelli (Princess Sabrina), Robert Carradine (Aladdin), James Earl Jones (genie of the lamp and genie of the ring), Leonard Nimoy (evil magician), Ray Sharkey (grand vizier), Rae Allen (Aladdin's mother), Joseph Maher (sultan), Jay Abramowitz (Habibe), Martha Velez (lady servant), Bonnie Jeffries, Sandy Lenz, and Marcia Gobel (the three green women), John Salazar (servant)
Color Video
47 Minutes

1985
PEE-WEE'S BIG ADVENTURE
Warner Bros., Aspen Film Society-Shapiro
Producer: Robert Shapiro, Richard Gilbert Abramson
Director: **Tim Burton**
Screenplay: Phil Hartman, Paul Reubens, Michael Varhol
Cinematography: Victor J. Kemper
Editor: Billy Weber
Music: Danny Elfman
Production Design: David L. Snyder
Cast: Paul Reubens (Pee-wee Herman), Elizabeth Daily (Dottie), Mark Holton (Francis), Diane Salinger (Simone), Judd Omen (Mickey), Irving Hellman (neighbor), Monte Landis (Mario), Damon Martin (Chip), David Glasser, Gregory Brown, Mark Everett (BMX Kids), Daryl Roach (Chuck), Bill Cable, Peter Looney (policemen), James Brolin (himself, as Pee-wee), Morgan Fairchild (herself, as Dottie)
35mm, Color
95 minutes

1985
THE JAR
Episode of Alfred Hitchcock Presents
Director: **Tim Burton**
Teleplay: Michael McDowell, based on Ray Bradbury's original teleplay
Music: Danny Elfman

Cast: Griffin Dunne, Fiona Lewis, Laraine Newman, Paul Bartel
35mm, Color
23 minutes

1988
BEETLEJUICE
Warner Bros., The Geffen Company
Producers: Michael Bender, Larry Wilson, Richard Hashimoto
Director: **Tim Burton**
Screenplay: Michael McDowell, Warren Skaaren, from a story by
Michael McDowell, Larry Wilson
Cinematography: Thomas Ackerman
Production Designer: Bo Welch
Art Director: Tom Duffield
Music: Danny Elfman
Editor: Jane Kurson
Visual Effects Supervisor: Alan Munro
Visual Effects Consultant: Rick Heinrichs
Cast: Alec Baldwin (Adam Maitland), Geena Davis (Barbara Maitland),
Jeffrey Jones (Charles Deetz), Catherine O'Hara (Delia Deetz), Winona
Ryder (Lydia Deetz), Sylvia Sidney (Juno), Robert Goulet (Maxie Dean),
Glenn Shadix (Otho), Dick Cavett (Bernard), Annie McEnroe (Jane),
Michael Keaton (Betelgeuse), Patrice Martinez (receptionist),
Simmy Bow (janitor), Maurice Page (Ernie)
35mm, Color
92 minutes

1989
BATMAN
Warner Bros.
Producers: Jon Peters, Peter Guber
Director: **Tim Burton**
Screenplay: Sam Hamm and Warren Skaaren, from a story by Sam Hamm;
based on characters created by Bob Kane
Cinematography: Roger Pratt
Production Design: Anton Furst
Supervising Art Director: Les Tomkins

Music: Danny Elfman, songs by Prince
Editor: Ray Lovejoy
Cast: Jack Nicholson (Joker/Jack Napier), Michael Keaton (Batman/Bruce Wayne), Kim Basinger (Vicki Vale), Robert Wuhl (Alexander Knox), Pat Hingle (Commissioner Gordon), Billy Dee Williams (Harvey Dent), Michael Gough (Alfred), Jack Palance (Carl Grissom), Jerry Hall (Alicia)
35mm, Color
126 minutes

1990
EDWARD SCISSORHANDS
Twentieth Century Fox
Producers: Denise Di Novi, **Tim Burton**
Director: **Tim Burton**
Screenplay: Caroline Thompson, based on a story by **Tim Burton** and Caroline Thompson
Cinematography: Stefan Czapsky
Production Design: Bo Welch
Music: Danny Elfman
Make-up effects: Stan Winston
Editor: Richard Halsey, Colleen Halsey
Cast: Johnny Depp (Edward Scissorhands), Winona Ryder (Kim), Dianne Wiest (Peg), Anthony Michael Hall (Jim), Kathy Baker (Joyce), Robert Oliveri (Kevin), Conchata Ferrell (Helen), Caroline Aaron (Marge), Dick Anthony Williams (Officer Allen), O-Lan Jones (Esmeralda), Vincent Price (the inventor), Alan Arkin (Bill)
35mm, Color
105 minutes

1992
BATMAN RETURNS
Warner Bros.
Producers: Denise Di Novi, **Tim Burton**
Director: **Tim Burton**
Co-producer: Larry Franco
Screenplay: Daniel Waters, based on a story by Daniel Waters and Sam Hamm; based on characters created by Bob Kane

Cinematography: Stefan Czapsky
Production Design: Bo Welch
Art Director: Rick Heinrichs
Music: Danny Elfman
Editor: Bob Badami and Chris Lebenzon
Cast: Michael Keaton (Batman/Bruce Wayne), Danny DeVito (The
Penguin/Oswald Cobblepot), Michelle Pfeiffer (Catwoman/Selina Kyle),
Christopher Walken (Max Shreck), Michael Gough (Alfred Pennyworth),
Michael Murphy (Mayor), Cristi Conway (Ice Princess),
Andrew Bryniarski (Chip), Pat Hingle (Commissioner Gordon),
Vincent Schiavelli (organ grinder), Steve Witting (Josh, Shreck image
consultant), Jan Hooks (Jen, Shreck image consultant), John Strong
(sword swallower), Rick Zumwalt (tattooed strongman), Anna Katarina
(poodle lady), Paul Reubens (Tucker Cobblepot, the Penguin's father),
Diane Salinger (Esther Cobblepot, the Penguin's mother)
35mm, Color
126 minutes

1994
ED WOOD
Touchstone Pictures
Producers: **Tim Burton**, Denise Di Novi
Director: **Tim Burton**
Co-producer: Michael Flynn
Screenplay: Scott Alexander, Larry Karaszewski, based on the book
Nightmare of Ecstasy by Rudolph Grey
Cinematography: Stefan Czapsky
Art Director: Okowita
Editor: Chris Lebenzon
Original music: Howard Shore
Production Design: Tom Duffield
Cast: Johnny Depp (Ed Wood), Martin Landau (Bela Lugosi), Sarah
Jessica Parker (Dolores Fuller), Patricia Arquette (Kathy O'Hara), Jeffrey
Jones (Criswell), G. D. Spradlin (Reverend Lemon), Vincent D'Onofrio
(Orson Welles), Bill Murray (Bunny Breckinridge), Mike Starr (Georgie
Weiss), Max Casella (Paul Marco), Brent Hinkley (Conrad Brooks), Lisa
Marie (Vampira), George "The Animal" Steele (Tor Johnson), Juliet

Landau (Loretta King), Clive Rosengren (Ed Reynolds), Norman Alden
(Cameraman Bill), Leonard Termo (Make-up man Harry), Ned Bellamy
(Dr. Tom Mason)
35mm, B&W
127 Minutes

1996
MARS ATTACKS!
Warner Bros.
Producers: **Tim Burton** and Larry Franco
Director: **Tim Burton**
Screenplay: Jonathan Gems, based on the trading card series by Len
Brown, Woody Gelman, Wally Wood, Bob Powell, Norman Sauders
Cinematography: Peter Suschitzky
Art Direction: John Dexter
Editor: Chris Lebenzon
Original Music: Danny Elfman
Production Design: Wynn Thomas
Cast: Jack Nicholson (President Dale/Art Land), Glenn Close
(First Lady Marsha Dale), Annette Bening (Barbara Land), Pierce
Brosnan (Professor Donald Kessler), Danny DeVito (Rude Gambler),
Martin Short (Press Secretary Jerry Ross), Sarah Jessica Parker (Nathalie
Lake), Michael J. Fox (Jason Stone), Rod Steiger (General Decker),
Tom Jones (himself), Lukas Haas (Richie Norris), Natalie Portman
(Taffy Dale), Jim Brown (Byron Williams), Lisa Marie (Martian girl),
Sylvia Sidney (Grandma Florence Norris), Pam Grier (Louise Williams),
Jack Black (Billy Glenn Norris), Ray J (Cedric Williams), Paul Winfield
(General Casey), Brandon Hammond (Neville Williams), Jerzy
Skolimowski (Dr. Zeigler), O-Lan Jones (Sue Ann Norris), Christina
Applegate (Sharona)
35mm, Color
105 Minutes

1999
SLEEPY HOLLOW
Paramount Pictures, Scott Rudin Productions, Mandalay Pictures,
American Zoetrope

Producers: Scott Rudin, Adam Schroeder
Co-producers: Kevin Yagher, Andrew Kevin Walker (uncredited)
Director: **Tim Burton**
Screenplay: Andrew Kevin Walker, based on *The Legend of Sleepy Hollow*
by Washington Irving; screen story by Andrew Kevin Walker and
Kevin Yagher
Cinematography: Emmanuel Lubezski
Art Direction: Ken Court, John Dexter, Andy Nicholson
Editor: Chris Lebenzon
Original Music: Danny Elfman
Production Design: Rick Heinrichs
Cast: Johnny Depp (Constable Ichabod Crane), Christina Ricci (Katrina
Anne Van Tassel), Casper Van Dien (Brom Van Brunt), Miranda
Richardson (Lady Van Tassel/the Western Woods Crone), Michael
Gambon (Baltus Van Tassel), Marc Pickering (Young Masbeth),
Christopher Walken (Hessian Horseman), Michael Gough (Notary
James Hardenbrook), Christopher Lee (Burgomaster), Jeffrey Jones
(Reverend Steenwyck), Lisa Marie (Lady Crane), Richard Griffiths
(Magistrate Samuel Phillipse), Ian McDiarmid (Dr. Thomas Lancaster),
Steven Waddington (Killian), Casper Van Dien (Brom Van Brunt),
Alun Armstrong (High Constable), Mark Spalding (Jonathan Masbath),
Jessica Oyelowo (Sarah, the servant girl), Tony Maudsley (Van Ripper)
Peter Guinness (Ichabod's father) Nicholas Hewetson (Glenn), Orlando
Seale (Theodore), Sean Stephens (Thomas Killian), Gabrielle Lloyd
(Dr. Lancaster's wife), Robert Sella (Dirk Van Garrett), Sam Fior (young
Ichabod Crane), Tessa Allen-Ridge (young Lady Van Tassel), Cassandra
Farndale (young Crone)
35mm, Color
105 Minutes

2000
STAINBOY (Internet Animated Series)
Flinch Productions
Producers: **Tim Burton**, Michael Viner
Director: **Tim Burton**
Writer: **Tim Burton**
Original Music: Danny Elfman (theme), Jason Wells

2001
THE PLANET OF THE APES
Twentieth Century Fox, The Zanuck Company
Producer: Richard D. Zanuck
Director: **Tim Burton**
Screenplay: William Broyles Jr., Lawrence Konner, Mark Rosenthal,
based on the novel by Pierre Boulle
Cinematography: Phillipe Rousselot
Art Direction: Sean Haworth, Philip Toolin
Production Design: Rick Heinrichs
Music: Danny Elfman, "Rule the Planet" remix by Paul Okenfold
Editor: Chris Lebenzon, Joel Negron
Special Make-up: Rick Baker
Visual Effects and Animation: Industrial Light and Magic
Cast: Mark Wahlberg (Captain Leo Davidson), Tim Roth (General Thade),
Helena Bonham Carter (Ari), Michael Clark Duncan (Colonel Atar),
Paul Giamatti (Limbo), Estella Warren (Daena), Cary-Hiroyuki Tagawa
(Krull), David Warner (Senator Sandar), Kris Kristofferson (Karubi),
Erick Avari (Tival), Glenn Shadix (Senator Nado), Lisa Marie (Nova),
Luke Eberl (Bim), Evan Parke (Gunnar), Freda Foh Shen (Bon),
Chris Ellis (Lt. General Karl Vasich), Anne Ramsay (Lt. Col. Grace
Alexander), Andrea Grano (Major Maria Cooper), Michael Jace
(Major Frank Santos), Michael Wiseman (Specialist Hansen),
Eileen Weisinger (Leeta)
35mm, Color
124 Minutes

2003
BIG FISH
Columbia Pictures, The Zanuck Company, Jinks/Cohen Company
Producers: Bruce Cohen, Dan Jinks, Richard D. Zanuck
Director: **Tim Burton**
Screenplay: John August, based on the novel by Daniel Wallace
Cinematography: Philippe Rousselot
Production Design: Dennis Gassner
Art Direction: Roy Barnes, Jean-Michael Ducourty, Robert Fechtman,
Jack Johnson, Richard L. Johnson

Editor: Chris Lebenzon
Original Music: Danny Elfman
Cast: Albert Finney (Edward Bloom), Ewan McGregor (Young Edward Bloom), Billy Crudup (William Bloom), Jessica Lange (Sandra Bloom), Alison Lohman (Young Sandra Bloom), Helena Bonham Carter (Jenny/the Witch), Steve Buscemi (Norther Winslow), Danny DeVito (Amos), Robert Guillaume (Dr. Bennett), Marion Cotillard (Josephine), Matthew McGrory (Karl the giant), Ada Tai (Ping), Arlene Tai (Jing), Deep Roy (Mr. Soggybottom), David Denman (Don Price), Missi Pyle (Mildred), Loudon Wainwright III (Beaman)
35mm, Color
125 minutes

2005
CHARLIE AND THE CHOCOLATE FACTORY
Warner Bros., Village Roadshow Pictures, The Zanuck Company, Plan B Productions
Producers: Brad Grey, Richard D. Zanuck
Director: **Tim Burton**
Screenplay: John August, based on the book by Roald Dahl
Cinematography: Philippe Rousselot
Production Design: Alex McDowell
Editor: Chris Lebenzon
Original Music: Danny Elfman
Cast: Johnny Depp (Willy Wonka), Freddie Highmore (Charlie Bucket), Jordan Fry (Mike Teavee), Annasophia Robb (Violet Beauregarde), Julia Winter (Veruca Salt), Philip Wiegratz (Augustus Gloop), Helena Bonham Carter (Mrs. Bucket), David Kelly (Grandpa Joe), Missi Pyle (Ms. Beauregard), Harry Taylor (Mr. Gloop), Ty Dickson (Oompa Loompa), Christopher Lee (Willy Wonka's father), Noah Taylor (Father Bucket), James Fox (Mr. Salt)
35mm, Color

2005
TIM BURTON'S CORPSE BRIDE
Warner Bros., Will Vinton Studios, Tim Burton Animation Co.
Producers: **Tim Burton**, Alison Abbate

Directors: **Tim Burton**, Michael Johnson
Screenplay: Caroline Thompson, Pamela Pettler
Cinematography: Pete Kozachik
Production Design: Alex McDowell
Art Direction: Nelson Lowry
Editor: Jonathan Lucas
Original Music: Danny Elfman
Cast: Johnny Depp (Victor), Helena Bonham Carter (Corpse Bride),
Emily Watson (Victoria), Albert Finney, Richard Grant, Joanna Lumley,
Christopher Lee
35mm, Color

As Producer Only

1989
BEETLEJUICE (Animated Television Series)
Nelvana/NBC Television
Developed by **Tim Burton**
Executive Producers: David Geffen and **Tim Burton**

1993
TIM BURTON'S THE NIGHTMARE BEFORE CHRISTMAS
Touchstone Pictures
Producers: **Tim Burton**, Denise Di Novi
Co-producers: Kathleen Gavin, Jeffrey Katzenberg (uncredited)
Director: Henry Selick
Screenplay: Caroline Thompson, based on story and characters by
Tim Burton, adaptation by Michael McDowell
Cinematography: Pete Kozachik
Art Direction: Barry E. Jackson, Deane Taylor
Editor: Stan Webb
Original music, lyrics, and score: Danny Elfman
Visual Consultant: Rick Heinrichs
Cast: Danny Elfman (Jack Skellington's singing voice), Chris Sarandon
(Jack Skellington's speaking voice), Catherine O'Hara (Sally), William
Hickey (Dr. Finklestein), Glenn Shadix (Mayor), Paul Reubens (Lock),

Catherine O'Hara (Shock), Danny Elfman (Barrel), Ken Page (Oogie
Boogie), Ed Ivory (Santa "Sandy Claws" Claus), Susan McBride (Big Witch)
35mm, Color
76 minutes

1993
FAMILY DOG (Animated Television Series)
Amblin Entertainment, Nelvana Limited, Universal TV, Warner Bros.
Television
Director: Chris Buck
Producer: Chuck Richardson
Executive Producer: **Tim Burton**, Steven Spielberg, Dennis Klein
Music: Danny Elfman
Visual Effects: Ian Gooding
Character design: **Tim Burton** (uncredited)
Cast: Martin Mull (Skip Binsford), Molly Cheek (Bev Binsford), Danny
Mann (Family Dog), Zak Huxtable Epstein (Billy Binsford), Cassie Cole
(Buffy Binsford)
30 minutes, Color

1994
CABIN BOY
Touchstone Pictures/Buena Vista
Producer: **Tim Burton**, Denise Di Novi
Director: Adam Resnick
Screenplay: Adam Resnick, from a story by Chris Elliott and Adam
Resnick
Cinematography: Steve Yaconelli
Art Direction: Daniel A. Lomino, Nanci Roberts
Original Music: Steve Bartek
Production Design: Seven Legler
Editor: Jon Poll
Cast: Chris Elliott (Nathanial Mayweather), Ritch Brinkley (Captain
Greybar), James Gammon (Paps), Ricki Lake (Figurehead), Brian
Doyle-Murray (Skunk), Brion James (Big Teddy), Melora Walters (Trina),
David Letterman (old salt in fishing village), Andy Richter (Kenny),
I. M. Hobson (Headmaster Timmons), Alex Nevil (Thomas), David H.

Sterry (Lance), Bob Elliot (William Mayweather), Edward Flotard (limo driver), Jim Cummings (voice of cupcake), Ann Magnum (Calli), Russ Tamblyn (Chocki), Mike Starr (Mulligan)
35mm, Color
80 minutes

1995
BATMAN FOREVER
Warner Bros.
Producer: **Tim Burton**, Peter MacGregor-Scott
Director: Joel Schumacher
Screenplay: Lee Batchler, Janet Scott Batchler, Akiva Goldsman, from a story by Lee Batchler and Janet Scott Batchler; based on characters created by Bob Kane
Editor: Dennis Virkler
Cinematography: Stephen Goldblatt
Art Direction: Christopher Burian-Mohr, Joseph P. Lucky
Original Music: Eliot GoldenthaL
Production Design: Barbara Ling
Cast: Val Kilmer (Batman/Bruce Wayne), Tommy Lee Jones (Two-Face/Harvey Dent), Jim Carrey (The Riddler/Edward Nygma), Nicole Kidman (Dr. Chase Meridian), Chris O'Donnell (Robin/Dick Grayson), Michael Gough (Alfred Pennyworth), Pat Hingle (Commissioner James Gordon), Drew Barrymore (Sugar), Debi Mazar (Spice), Elizabeth Sanders (Gossip Gerty), Rene Auberjonois (Dr. Burton)
35mm, Color
122 minutes

1996
JAMES AND THE GIANT PEACH
Walt Disney Productions/Buena Vista
Producers: **Tim Burton**, Denise Di Novi
Director: Henry Selick
Co-producers: John Engel, Brian Rosen, Henry Selick
Screenplay: Karey Kirkpatrick, Jonathan Roberts, Steve Bloom, from the book by Roald Dahl
Cinematography: Peter Kozachick (animation), Hiro Narita (live action)

Art Direction: Kendal Cronkhite, Blake Russell, Lane Smith
Editor: Stan Webb
Original Music: Randy Newman
Production Design: Harley Jessup
Cast: Simon Callow (Grasshopper), Richard Dreyfuss (Centipede),
Jane Leeves (Ladybug), Joanna Lumley (Aunt Spiker), Miriam Margolyes
(The Glowworm/Aunt Sponge), Pete Postlewaite (old man), Susan
Sarandon (Spider), Paul Terry (James), David Thewlis (Earthworm),
Steven Culp (James's father), Susan Turner-Cray (James's mother)
35mm, Color
79 Minutes

TIM BURTON

INTERVIEWS

Explaining *Beetlejuice*

MARC SHAPIRO / 1988

Beetlejuice has gone through a great many changes. A change of title from *Beetle Juice* to *Beetlejuice* (makes sense) and an unresolved spring release date to a definite April opening are the most noticeable. But these changes pale by comparison to those the marketing people are going through trying to find a cubbyhole for this comedy/ horror/ fantasy film.

And it's not just the power-lunch types who are drawing a blank. Even Michael McDowell, who wrote the script with Warren Skaaren, won't bet the farm on just what *Beetlejuice* is.

"I don't see it as a horror film at all," says McDowell. "I'm almost afraid to say what it is."

Then, there's the film's director, Tim (*Pee-wee's Big Adventure*) Burton, who offers his own clear-as-mud explanation.

"Well, it's kind of intellectual and kind of stupid," he admits. "It's not really a flatout anything."

You get those kinds of explanations with Tim Burton, vague in the extreme and honestly confused. Burton, this day, appears even more confused and vague than usual, and with good reason: He has just crawled out of an all-day stint in the editing room making still more adjustments to *Beetlejuice's* final cut. Also, with the go-ahead for the long-awaited *Batman: The Movie* slated for a July start, Burton has been spending his nights storyboarding and fine-tuning, with screenwriter Sam Hamm the final shooting script.

From *Starlog Magazine*, 130 (May 1988), 42–47. Reprinted by permission.

"It's funny," says Burton, propping his feet up on his office desk. "I couldn't get anything going for the longest time after *Pee-wee*. Now, it's candle-at-both-ends time."

Burton's *Beetlejuice* burn, budgeted at $13 million and filmed in 10 weeks in Los Angeles and Vermont locations, is a battle royal between good ghosts and bad mortals told from the point-of-view of the recently deceased Adam and Barbara Maitland. The pair's ideal ghostly existence in their Vermont home is interrupted by the sale of said abode to the Deetz's: Charles, Delia, and daughter Lydia. When the Deetz family's earthly habits get on their nerves, the Maitlands strike back supernaturally. However, when the Deetz's get hip to the spiritual happenings, the dead darlings call on the aid of a spirit named Beetlejuice to exorcise the human family once and for all.

Beetlejuice stars Michael (*Gung Ho*) Keaton, Geena (*The Fly*) Davis, Alec (*Knots Landing*) Baldwin, Jeffrey (*Howard the Duck*) Jones, Catherine (*SCTV*) O'Hara and Winona (*Lucas*) Ryder. The film seems a throwback to the classic 1930s *Topper* movies with a touch of *The Exorcist* thrown in for good measure. But that doesn't seem to encourage Burton who claims he is dreading the day when he has to sit down with the marketing people.

"It's hard to describe this film as just one thing. It has elements of horror but it's not really scary and it's funny but not really a comedy," confesses the director. "*Beetlejuice* is one of those movies that just does not fit *any* place."

But while Burton can't pigeonhole his creation, he does acknowledge that McDowell's script came along just in time to keep him from being a one-hit wonder.

The success of *Pee-wee's Big Adventure* in 1985 made Burton the hot new kid on the block. Unfortunately, in seeking out new film worlds to conquer, he also found that he was already being stereotyped.

"Nearly every script I was offered had the word 'Adventure' somewhere in the title," he says. "One project fell through and *Batman* was still on hold. I was freaking out until the script for *Beetlejuice* came along."

Beetlejuice, by middle-level budgeted film standards, is a special effects monster. The likes of Alan Monroe, Robert Short, and Chuck Gaspar contribute such schtick as headless corpses running around and a staircase rail that turns into a snake. Most of the effects were done live on the set, locking Burton and company into that aspect of rigid production. However, the director did find a way to liven up the acting side.

"Many of the cast come from an improvisational background, so I felt it would serve to balance the movie if much of what the actors did was created on the spot. We didn't throw out Michael's script. We just embellished it a lot," laughs Burton.

The director also has a good laugh at his approach to doing the film's FX. Much in the tradition of the Large Marge character in *Pee-wee*, *Beetlejuice*'s effects, claims Burton, are not "up to Industrial Light & Magic standards."

Says Burton, "We went big and more personal with them. What people will see are effects that are, in a sense, a step *backward*. They're crude and funky and also very personal."

Those qualities have also been the trademark of Tim Burton's career to date. Born within spitting distance of the Walt Disney Studios, Burton landed a job in that company's animation department after graduation from the prestigious California Institute of the Arts. In that capacity, he was instrumental in the creation of the features *The Fox and the Hound* and *The Black Cauldron*.

Unfortunately, between 1981 and 1984, Burton was caught up in the shifting political climate at Disney that saw his first three directorial efforts go right from his camera into oblivion. The first, an animated martial arts version of *Hansel and Gretel*, aired once on the Disney Channel on Halloween night. Burton followed with *Vincent* a stop-motion short about a boy's fondness for imitating Vincent Price (narrated by Price himself), which made sporadic appearances at film festivals and captured an award at the Chicago Film Festival. Burton's first step into live-action work was *Frankenweenie*, a tribute to director James Whale's *Frankenstein* that chronicles a boy's (Barret Oliver) attempts to bring his dead dog back to life.

All three efforts were distinguished by childlike views of a darkly perverse universe and the fact that Disney chose not to give audiences, movie or television, much of a look at them.

"*Vincent* and *Frankenweenie* going unreleased has been a constant source of frustration to me," explains Burton. "Disney owns both films.

I can't even get a copy of them. I would think the people at Disney would at least find a slot for *Frankenweenie* with one of their features."

At one point, *Frankenweenie* was scheduled to be paired with a re-release of *Pinocchio* but negative feedback at a test screening caused studio heads to change their minds.

"They claimed the film was too violent," observes Burton. "The only violence in that is when the dog gets run over by a car and that is done off-camera. I don't understand it, but I guess I'll have to accept it."

Burton's luck changed for the better when his first offer to direct a feature was that quirky, offbeat fantasy *Pee-wee's Big Adventure*. The character of Pee-wee Herman had already been established in other media by creator/comedian Paul Reubens, but that didn't prevent Burton from making his presence felt.

"There was a lot of spontaneity involved in making *Pee-wee* and I was flying by the seat of my pants much of the time," says Burton. "There was such a mutual belief by Pee-wee and myself in the character that what he did was never questioned. What we did was thrust people into his world. We said, 'This is Pee-wee, believe him or not.' We tried to make people understand the character by making him as colorful as possible and setting him up in an atmosphere where he was comfortable. It was a very cut-and-dried movie; people either liked it or they didn't."

While juggling *Beetlejuice* and *Batman* chores, Burton recently returned to his cartoonist roots by teaming up with *Beetlejuice* writer McDowell for "Oyster Boy," a lyrical fantasy story for the forthcoming second volume of *Taboo*, a horror comic anthology.

"Doing 'Oyster Boy' was fun because it allowed me to get back into a less pressure-packed situation for a while," says Burton. "The idea of getting back to drawing something simple and not having delusions of huge amounts of money being on the line was refreshing."

Meanwhile, back in his Gotham City lair, Burton is finally hatching his plans for the much-delayed *Batman*. The film, scripted by Sam Hamm and slated to begin shooting in July, borrows from all phases of the Batman saga, according to Burton.

"There will be elements of the comic-book character, some of the intensity of Frank Miller's *The Dark Knight Returns* and a bit of the humor of the TV series. One thing this movie will *not* be is a major special effects movie. There will be FX, but they will be more natural and physical. You may see Batman swinging out over Gotham City on his bat-rope, but there will be nothing exploding out of his stomach," says Burton.

Casting for *Batman* is being angled in the direction of unknowns which, to a large extent, was also the situation with *Beetlejuice.*

"With the possible exception of Michael Keaton, nobody in Missouri is going to be super-familiar with these people. That works to the film's advantage, though, because *Beetlejuice* has an odd tone to it that's not conducive to having one star," the director explains. "The roles in the film are pretty much equal. Everybody plays a part in telling the story and that's why the film works."

What did not always work were the numerous special FX. Doing them live was a noble intent, but Burton chuckles when he recalls how "intent didn't mean a damn thing when we couldn't get that damn tombstone to crumble on cue.

"This was the first time I dealt with a full-blown special effects film," relates Burton, "and it sure made my life difficult at times. The intent was to do them quick, funky, and fun. You can only take that so far when you've got 90 adults standing around on a set getting pissed off because a mechanical hat isn't doing what it's supposed to do. Much of the stuff we did worked live, but 'Let's do it in post-production' was a phrase you heard frequently on this show."

Burton claims that *Beetlejuice,* much like his stints on *Pee-wee's Big Adventure* and the remake of "The Jar" for the modern *Alfred Hitchcock Presents,* has added to his coming-of-age as a director.

"I've had fun dealing with the actors on this film and that's a hard thing to admit because it hasn't always been the case. Because of my animation background, I basically was in the position of having to deal with my craft on a non-verbal level. *Pee-wee* forced me into the verbal world and dealing with flesh and blood people.

"*Beetlejuice* has been a continuation of that growing process for me. I've been dealing with actors who are both fun people and who have a real feel for this movie. It sure helps in the confidence department."

Burton is not thinking beyond *Beetlejuice* ("a Tim Burton kind of movie") and the pending start of *Batman* in terms of upcoming projects. "I don't want to take just anything for the sake of saying, 'I'm working.' I've got to like what I'm doing."

The director runs his fingers through his already unkempt hair. "You know, it's really weird," mutters Tim Burton. "I can't figure why it is I constantly respond to things on an intellectual level that are basically so stupid. I know it's ultimately going to get me into trouble but there doesn't seem to be any way around it.

"When I get around material like *Beetlejuice*. I'm hooked."

Mixing *Beetlejuice*

DAVID EDELSTEIN/1988

It's hard to imagine someone being instantly in sync with Pee-wee Herman, but in 1984, when twenty-six-year-old Tim Burton was asked to direct his first feature, *Pee-wee's Big Adventure,* he brought something special to the party: a passion for wacko individualists. "I believed Pee-wee," Burton says, without a trace of irony. "So I thought, 'Let's just go through the movie and believe him, whatever he does.' I love extreme characters who totally believe themselves. That's why I had fun with Betelgeuse."

Betelgeuse, played by Michael Keaton, is the anarchic superspook of *Beetlejuice*, which Burton has directed like a cheerfully indulgent parent—he lets his little monsters run wild, to the exclusion of pace, point, and structure. This isn't your standard, slick ghost comedy—the plot chases its own tail, and the jokes are a blend of the brainy and the infantile. The picture, a whatzit, has provoked its share of bewildered reviews. The fat guy and the other one didn't like it, and *The New York Times* said it was for people who think a shrunken head is funny.

Luckily for Burton, *millions* of people think a shrunken head is funny, especially when it sits on top of a full-sized body and stares out of bulging, doleful eyes. *Beetlejuice* grossed about $32 million in its first two weeks, and Burton has relaxed and made the most of his movie's addled reception.

"I've been enjoying the bad reviews," he says ebulliently. "These bland newscasters, they have to say the word *Beetlejuice,* and they have to show a clip—and I don't care what anybody says, it makes me wanna

From *Rolling Stone*, 2 June 1988: 50–53, 76. Reprinted by permission of the author.

see the movie. It's really funny. It's like you're watching some hallucination, like somebody's putting something else behind them that they don't know about. It was like the feeling I got when I saw Andy Warhol on *The Love Boat.*"

Burton, a former animator, thrives on weird juxtapositions—they're the key to his genius. His style is dork chic: he wears shapeless, oversize jackets, and his hair is shoulder length. Under heavy lids, he has sad, spacey eyes. He's the sort of guy who uses words like "nutty" without ironic emphasis, who pronounces something "great, great, great—like, so *cool*" and then, to illustrate a point, casually sketches a bizarre creature with a second head coming out of its mouth.

Amiable and unpretentious, he has a whiff of stoned melancholy about him, like someone who thinks too much and makes sense of too little. And that's where he nestles his movies, in that twilight zone between the humdrum and the flabbergasting. If the two don't quite gel, so much the better—and funnier.

"The things that interest me the most are the things that potentially won't work." Burton says. "On *Beetlejuice,* I could tell every day what was gonna work and what wasn't. And that was very invigorating. Especially when you're doing something this extreme. A lot of people have ragged on the story of *Beetlejuice,* but when I read it, I thought, 'Wow! This is sort of interesting. It's very random. It doesn't follow what I would consider the Spielberg story structure.' I guess I have to watch it more, because I'm intrigued by things that are perverse. Like, I was intrigued that there was *no story.*"

Beetlejuice is a haunted-house comedy turned inside out: its heroes are a pair of attractive, lovable ghosts driven bats by ghoulish people. When they can't take any more, they call in the title character, a "bio-exorcist." As played by Michael Keaton, with frazzled hair, rotted teeth and fungoid cheeks, the scuzzy con man blasts the movie into slapstick heaven—he's sleaze-ball wizard.

Until his entrance, the picture has been funny in spurts but something else, too: goggle-eyed, a little sad. At the start, a couple (Alec Baldwin and Geena Davis) are killed in a freak accident; as ghosts, they learn they must remain in their rustic New England home for 125 years. Into their afterlives come the new owners: a screechingly tasteless sculptor (Catherine O'Hara); her geeky husband (Jeffrey Jones); and their sweet but morbid daughter (Winona Ryder), who dresses like a witch to express her inner weirdness. The ghosts aren't malicious—they just hate seeing their cozy domicile turned into a Soho house of horror. So they do things like sever their own heads—while the living, who can't see them, remain oblivious.

If you've ever felt out of place, you'll plug into the ghosts' awkwardness—and into Burton's dopey, matter-of-fact surrealism. Aside from Betelgeuse (the spelling has been simplified for the title), no one quite fits in. The afterlife isn't grand and Spielbergian but a mangy series of typing pools and waiting rooms, in which you have to take a number to see your caseworker. Next to you sit horribly mutilated people in the state they were in when they bit the big one, but used to it now, so they're blasé, as if they weren't charred or squashed.

When Burton first read Michael McDowell's script, he thought he could have written it himself—it carried his trademark blend of the outlandish and the matter-of-fact. In *Pee-wee's Big Adventure*, for instance, the trucker Large Marge turns toward the camera and her eyes balloon out of her skull; then they retract and she goes on talking, as if nothing unusual had happened. And in *Beetlejuice*, Keaton's head spontaneously gyrates on its shoulders; when it stops, he asks, slightly peeved, "Don't ya' hate it when that happens?"

The deadpan style resembles the great Warner Bros. cartoons, and the best gags are like jack-in-the-boxes—they zoom out of the screen and then snap back in. The disorientation is exhilarating. In *Beetlejuice*, Burton deftly blurs the line between a large model of the New England town (in which Betelgeuse, bug size, makes his home), "real life" and the afterlife. Bo Welch, who designed the sets, describes it as "a hierarchy of reality that leads you into unreality. Tim would encourage me to push that border. I'd go a certain distance, and he'd say, 'Let's go further,' and I'd go, 'Arrghhh!' and then be thrilled when we did it."

Burton lets his actors push that border, too. Catherine O'Hara at last has the sexy confidence she had on every episode of *SCTV* and considers *Beetlejuice* the closest she has come to her *SCTV* experience. Under bright-red hair, her blue eyes give her an otherworldly derangement; in a celebrated set piece, she rises at a stuffy dinner party and—against her will—leads her guests in a spastic dance to the banana-boat song "Day-O." "The idea was, we were possessed by Harry Belafonte's recording," says O'Hara, giggling. "We tried to get that our bodies were really into it but that *we* were trying to get out."

The scene is a prime example of Burton's Inconstant: it's as if the little incongruities formed a chain reaction and mushroomed—a comic atom bomb. "The first time I saw an audience react to it, I got, like, frightened," says Burton. "I got chills, I was truly terrified. I don't know why. I guess it's the power."

"I think Tim must be very secure," says O'Hara. "He knows what he wants, but he's also open to ideas." Take, for instance, Burton's collaboration with Michael Keaton. Keaton last had this gonzo edge as the enterprising morgue attendant in Ron Howard's *Night Shift* (1982) but settled down into more mundane roles. His last four movies have been disappointments, and he wasn't up for another.

"I turned down the role because I didn't quite get it, and I wasn't looking to work," says Keaton. In the original script, Betelgeuse was underwritten, vaguely Middle Eastern and more evil. But Burton wanted to change the tone and invited Keaton to come up with his own shtick. "I went home and thought, 'Okay, if I would do this role, how would I do it?' " Keaton says. "You clearly don't create him from the inside out. Meaning, what motivates this guy—his childhood or whatever. You work from the outside in."

Keaton really gets going when he talks about Betelgeuse, the way he must have when he wandered around his house for hours, trying out bits. "It turns out the character creates his own reality," he says. "I gave myself some sort of voice, some sort of look based on the words. Then I started thinkin' about my hair: I wanted my hair to stand out like I was wired and plugged in, and once I started gettin' that, I actually made myself laugh. And I thought, 'Well, this is a good sign, this is kind of funny.' Then I got the attitude. And once I got the basic attitude, it really started to roll."

And what was the attitude?

"It's multi-attitudinal. The attitude is 'You write your own reality, you write your own ticket. There are no bars, I can do anything I want and under any rationality I want. . . .' "

He stops himself from analyzing it too much. "At some point," he says, "you show up on the set and just go *fuckin' nuts*. It was *rave* acting. You rage for twelve or fourteen hours; then you go home tired and beat and exhausted. It was pretty damned cathartic. It was rave and *purge* acting."

"The thing I love about Michael is that he *gets into it,*" says Burton. "He'd say some funny thing that wasn't in the script, and we'd get ideas from that. I enjoyed working that way. My animation background—you sit around with a bunch of guys and talk about what would be a good idea to do. The whole cast was like that. It was this hallucination we were all involved in. We knew what we were doing, but we didn't know what we were doing."

"Credit to the cast," says Keaton. "Everybody said, '*We're in this.*' Everybody agreed to go along with this experiment. This picture is not without faults, but I'll tell ya, I feel very good about being part of a project that has broken some rules and is at the very least innovative, imaginative, creative—just plain funny."

Like Keaton, defenders of *Beetlejuice* are the first to admit its flaws. But since when do great comedies have to be seamless? As its biggest champion, Pauline Kael, wrote in *The New Yorker,* "The best of W.C. Fields was often half gummed up, and that doesn't seem to matter fifty-five years later. With crazy comedy, you settle for the spurts of inspiration, and *Beetlejuice* has them . . . enough . . . to make this spotty, dissonant movie a comedy classic."

The comedy classicist has an unlikely home town—Burbank, or "the pit of hell," as Burton calls it. "Probably his out-of-place-ness comes from growing up there," says Bo Welch. "It's in the middle of the movie business, but it's so mundane that it forces your imagination to work overtime." As a kid, Burton loved to draw, put on shows, and play pranks—like the time he covered his brother in fake gore and pretended to hack him up with a knife. (A neighbor phoned the police; Burton still shivers when he talks about it.)

From college at Cal Arts he landed a plum job with Walt Disney Studios. "They were trying to train new animators," he says. "All the old guys had retired, so what was left in charge was these second-stringers. They were older; they were bitter that they weren't the ones that were in the limelight. So a lot of things besides creativity leaked in. What drove me nuts is, here you are at Disney—'Best animation in the world,' they say. 'A dream come true.' And on the other hand, they say, 'Remove part of your brain and become a zombie factory worker.' The split that it created drove people nuts. So you either succumb to it or you leave.

"Classic example: I was at Disney, I was in animation for a year, I was totally freaked, I was so bored. They liked my designs, so they said, 'Why don't you do some for *The Black Cauldron?* Great, great, go wild.' So I spent months, I came up with everything under the sun. One thing I thought was really creepy: it had these birds and their heads would be like hands with eyes; instead of beaks there'd be hands grabbing you.

"Finally, they brought in this other guy, Andreas, that you would consider classic Disney—cutesy little animals and stuff. And it was, 'Your stuff's a little, kinda out there, Tim, but we want to get you together with this guy—maybe the two of you can come up with, like, Disney but, like, a little different.' By the end of two weeks, we didn't get along—he was doing his thing and I was doing mine. He'd take my drawings and try to translate 'em. So finally the producer comes in and says, 'Tim, here's a graph. T - - - - - - * - - A. This is Andreas and this is you. We wanna go somewhere right about here in terms of the style.'

"From that I moved into live action," Burton says.

In 1984, Burton directed a live short for Disney called *Frankenweenie*, the story of a boy who brings his dog back to life. The movie was meant to accompany *Pinocchio*, but the ratings board found it disturbing and slapped it with a PG rating; when Disney was shaken up in 1984, the film got lost in the shuffle. (The company still hasn't released it and won't even give Burton a copy.)

Frustrated by Disney's inaction, Burton was liberated by a friend at Warners, who screened *Frankenweenie* for Pee-wee Herman and his producers. "It was the easiest job I ever got," says Burton of *Pee-wee's Big Adventure*. "I had a much more difficult time getting that busboy job six months earlier." In spite of horrible reviews, the daft little sleeper grossed $45 million domestically.

In August, Burton will begin shooting in London his most expensive picture: *Batman*, a $20 million action comedy that promises to go way beyond the comic books and TV show. In keeping with his taste for incongruity, Burton wants "to get a little more real with it" than you'd expect. "There's tension and insanity," he says. "We're trying to say this guy is obviously nuts, but in the most appealing way possible. I go back to what I thought comic books gave people. People love the idea that once they dress up, they can become somebody else. And here you have a human being in what I would consider the most absurd costume ever created.

"The villain is the Joker, the coolest of all. And also the flip side of Batman. Here you got a guy [Batman] who is rich, and something bad happened to him, and instead of getting therapy, he fights crime. But it's still kinda schizophrenic—it's something he questions in his own mind. And the Joker, something happened to him, too, but he'll do or say *anything*, which is another fantasy that all of us have—it's total freedom. So you've got two freaks. It's so great."

The split is pure Burton: one unhappy character dresses up to express something but still feels hopelessly out of place in the real world; another, an extremist, creates his or her own demented reality. Burton clearly identifies with the former, but the latter—Pee-wee, Betelgeuse, the Joker—charges him up, inspires him to dazzling heights.

Both types have attempted to impose their personalities on a void— which is sort of how Burton grew up, as an awkward, artistic kid in Burbank. Maybe that's why he's drawn to any organic expression of character, no matter how clumsy. As a child he was moved by bad movies, the kind it's trendy to laugh at. "There's a lot of weird stuff in them—somebody had an *idea*. It went really wrong, and yet you can see somebody's strange mind. I love that."

Hollywood tends to quash such self-expression—it lives by formulas. But Burton slipped through the net, and he's hopping with joy. "If *Beetlejuice* turns out to be successful, I will be so happy," he says, "and so *perversely* happy. I'm for anything that subverts what the studio thinks you have to do."

Batman

ALAN JONES / 1989

There's a story *Batman* director Tim Burton likes to tell. In 1978 Burton was still in school and was attending a big comic book convention in San Diego. The event was held just a few months before Richard Donner's big budget *Superman* movie was due to open and a Warner Bros. press officer was there to give a slide show presentation featuring scenes from the production.

"The ballroom was packed with people," said Burton. "All eyes were glued to the screen with this poor Warner guy trying to keep it all under control. Suddenly, one fan stood up and screamed, 'Superman would never change into his costume on a ledge of a building. I'm going to boycott this movie and tell everyone you are destroying the legend!' Intense applause followed as he stormed out of the hall. Wow, I thought. And from that moment on I always knew in the back of my mind the enormous problems facing anyone taking on a film version of a comic book hero.

The newly-married Burton faced more than his fair share of vitriol from vociferous comic book fans during the making of his multi-million dollar *Batman*, which opened to thunderous boxoffice for Warner Bros. on June 23. Burton developed the *Batman* script with Sam Hamm at Warners after being assigned to the project when his *Pee-wee's Big Adventure* turned out to be a surprise hit for the studio. Before Hamm, Julie Hickson, who produced Burton's Disney shorts, *Hansel and Gretel* and *Frankenweenie*, had written a 30 page treatment.

From *Cinefantastique* 20:1/20:2 (1989) 48+. Reprinted by permission.

"I wasn't working on it full-time," said Burton. "I'd just meet Sam on weekends to discuss the early writing stages. We knocked it into good shape while I directed *Beetlejuice*, but as a 'go' project it was only green-lighted by Warners when the opening figures for *Beetlejuice* surprised everybody—including myself!"

The *Batman* project had been languishing at Warners for nearly ten years. Producers Mike Uslan and Benjamin Melniker had negotiated the film rights from D.C. Comics in 1979. Several months later Melnicker had swung a development deal with Peter Guber's Casablanca Film Works, based at Warner Bros. Melnicker and Uslan are credited as executive producers on the film, which is produced by Guber and his partner Jon Peters.

Uslan and Melniker hired screenwriter Tom Mankiewicz and patterned their production after *Superman* (1978), also scripted by Mankiewicz. The project was announced in late 1981 with a budget of $15 million. Set in the near future, Mankiewicz's script followed the *Superman* formula, concentrating on Batman's origins, including the murder of his parents. After a phenomenally successful run in *Detective Comics* in 1939, the character's origin had been outlined in a two-page introduction in the first issue of *Batman*, written by Bill Finger and drawn by Bob Kane, published in early 1940. That issue also introduced The Joker in its lead story, and killed him off in the issue's final strip "The Joker Returns." But Kane had second thoughts and redrew the strip's final panel to keep Batman's primary nemesis going in over two hundred stories.

Though Burton and screen-writer Sam Hamm are credited with turning the direction of *Batman* away from the campy TV series of the '60s back to the dark, *noirish* Kane and Finger originals, that direction was actually the stated intention of Uslan and Melniker. "The project has to be done right," said Uslan in late 1983, when their version of *Batman* was being readied for a summer 1985 release on a budget of $20 million. "The film must be about the creature of the night and capture the spirit of what Batman was originally about and what the comic, by and large, has reverted to in the last couple of years."

Uslan had worked part-time for D.C. Comics in the early '70s on a program that taught kids how to read using comic books. He later wrote *Batman* stories for D.C. Comics while a law student at Indiana

University in the mid-'70s. "It was a lifelong ambition come true," said Uslan, "to write a couple of issues of *Batman*. I began then to think, wouldn't it be great to do a definitive *Batman* movie totally removed from the TV show, totally removed from camp; a version that went back to the original Bob Kane/Bill Finger strips."

The Joker was the main menace in the Mankiewicz version, which also pitted Batman against "normal" street crooks, and introduced Robin only at the very end. Directors associated with the project's development included Joe Dante and Ivan Reitman. Uslan wanted an unknown to play Batman and his cast wish-list included William Holden as Commissioner Gordon and David Niven as Alfred, Bruce Wayne's faithful butler.

But the Uslan/Melniker *Batman* would have been very different from the darkly poetic vision Burton finally realized, as Uslan's 1983 description of their idea of the Batcave illustrates. "When you see it in the film, it'll be the Batcave that appeared in the comics: the mechanical dinosaur, the giant penny, The Joker's giant playing card." Though Mankiewicz's script improved on the character's comic book origins— the comic's inspiration for the costume, young Bruce Wayne seeing a bat flying through his bedroom window was dropped—the script never licked the problem of making the comic book elements believeable in screen terms.

"The very first *Batman* treatment I read was remarkably similar to *Superman*," said Burton. "It had the same light, jokey tone, and the story structure followed Wayne through childhood to his genesis as a crimefighter. I found it all rather disturbing because, while that route was probably fine in the case of *Superman*, there was absolutely no exploration or acknowledgement of the character's psychological structure and why he would dress up in a bat suit. In that respect, it was very much like the television series."

Burton was wrestling with the comic's psychological aspects, trying to move the story-line in a positive direction, when he first met Hamm. "Sam was a big comic book fan and he knew exactly what to do with the script." Burton credited the success of Frank Miller's *The Dark Knight*, a graphic novel that explored the psychology of Batman in dark, *noirish* films, with helping sell Warners on the psychological approach and leap back to the original comics that he and Hamm wanted to take.

"The success of the graphic novels made our ideas far more accept-able," said Burton. "The movie doesn't wallow in darkness, but without becoming a psychological tone poem, it addresses all the issues without hammering you over the head. *The Dark Knight* works on the comic page—it seems to be a direct response to all the light-heartedness that had gone before—but it was far too dark stylistically for movie pur-poses. I think the movie is funny without being campy at the expense of the material. The tone is more consistent than in any other film I've made."

When Hamm got sidelined by last year's writer's strike, Warners brought in Warren Skaaren to help prepare the film's final shooting script. And during filming, Burton did further rewrites with an uncred-ited Charles McKeown. It was during those rewrites that the plot point was added, making The Joker the killer of young Bruce Wayne's parents, an element not found in the comics that had earlier been part of both the rejected Mankiewicz script and Hickson treatment.

Though it didn't fit the mold of the *Batman* he wanted to make, Burton said he was a big fan of the '60s TV series starting Adam West. It was the first TV show Burton said he could recall running home to watch. "I loved it," said Burton, who was only seven years old when the show debuted in 1966. "I still do, although I would never say I was ever a fanatic. But, I'm not from the hate school who thinks it's blasphe-mous to Bruce Wayne's memory and against everything he stood for."

Burton said he knew that in making *Batman* he would face the ire of comic book fans, "passionate about the minutest details," but said he was equally aware of the pull of fans of the TV show, "a far larger group because it was more in the public eye." Burton saw his dilemma as a "no win situation" and decided to follow his instincts, come what may.

"The good thing about this movie is if you liked the TV show it shares a similar flavor," said Burton. "I decided to take the movie in the direction I felt was right and remain unshaken by anything that would eventually happen. I was so clear about the course I was taking because what attracted me to the project in the first place were Batman and The Joker—my favorite characters. Like all great larger-than-life images, they can be explored any number of different ways. There is just as much room for the TV show and *The Dark Knight* as there is for my movie. Why shouldn't there be?"

Still, Burton and nearly everyone connected with the film was surprised by the vociferousness of the comic book brigade's up in arms
protest over the casting of Michael Keaton as Batman, first suggested by
producer Jon Peters. Burton has long tired of defending his controver-
sial creative decision and merely sighs when the subject is brought up.
"There's nothing more to say apart from how comfortable I feel about
Michael's contribution," said Burton. "The fan reaction is a surface
response. The moment you mention Keaton he immediately brings to
mind *Mr. Mom* and *Nightshift*—the comedy/romance sit-com-type picture. Obviously I knew from the beginning that wasn't the road I would
ever take. If I had been afraid of that argument, I wouldn't have asked
Michael to do it in the first place. I looked at actors who were more the
fan image of Batman, but I felt it was such an uninteresting way to go."

According to the *Los Angeles Times*, other actors considered for the
Batman role included Mel Gibson, Bill Murray, Charlie Sheen, and
Pierce Brosnan. Burton said he chose Keaton for his acting ability.
"Michael is very good," said Burton. "*Clean and Sober* proved it. He's
funny/dramatic in a way which added to what I was trying to achieve.
Taking someone like Michael and making him Batman supported the
whole split personality idea. The most interesting aspect I perceived in
the story—what it was really about—has now been underscored.
Michael's personality tunes into those differences, making him the perfect choice. He has a lot going on inside him, there's an explosive side;
he has a temper and a great amount of anger—that was exactly the
Bruce Wayne character, not some unknown, handsome, strong hunk."

Also behind Burton's choice of Keaton as Batman was the fact that
Jack Nicholson had been cast first as The Joker. Said Burton, "I kept
imagining the reviews and hearing the response in my head, 'Well,
Jack's great, but the unknown so-and-so is nothing special!' Michael is
more straightforward here than he's ever been in any movie. If people
have problems with him, then they'll have problems with the movie.
But is that my problem? He's a part of the whole. He doesn't call attention to himself, and he's not doing anything but fitting seamlessly into
an ensemble cast. Certain actors are so strong, they are often better
than the material. Michael has the back-up strength of a great script.
When you see the film, he's an actor playing a part that fits in exactly
with what I envisioned. End of story. What is all the drama about?!"

The budget of *Batman* was price-tagged in the *Los Angeles Times* by producer Jon Peters at $35 million, plus $5 million in interest charges. Burton said he hadn't kept track of the film's cost and honestly didn't know the final figure. "All I cared about was the tight, tough schedule," he said. "We did go over budget, but nothing that wasn't really anticipated with a project this size. I was willing to listen regarding certain cuts they wanted made. I'm not the type of person who has to rigidly stick to the script. And when I saw the rough cut, I'm happy to say every scene we shot has made it into the movie."

At Pinewood, the production sprawled across the studio's 95-acre backlot, taking up most of its 18 sound stages. "Sean Young's replacement by Kim Basinger was the first problem we encountered," said Burton. "We were lucky not to lose more time. We had decent weather. Shooting at night didn't cause anything untoward to happen. Overall, we didn't do too badly."

Batman was filmed at Pinewood not so much for economy, but because Burton had always wanted to work in Britain. "To be honest, I wanted to get out of the States because of all the hype, hoopla, and controversy the film was attracting," he said. "It was happening in England too, but to a far lesser degree. I didn't need any extra distractions and coming here pretty much removed the stress level in that area so I could focus on the movie. There are only two places you can make a movie like this—Los Angeles or London. In many ways the craftsmen and artists are better in Britain. Even though the dollar was iffy, I'm glad I decided to base operations at Pinewood. It wouldn't have been cheaper in L.A., just more problematic."

Pivotal to the *Batman* look is the work of production designer Anton Furst, renowned for his elaborate sets on films like *High Spirits, Full Metal Jacket*, and *The Company of Wolves*. Furst had been recommended to Burton by effects supervisor Derek Meddings. The designer needed no introduction to Burton, who had sought him out originally to work on *Beetlejuice*. But Burton had been told that Furst wasn't available for *Batman*, due to his commitment on Neil Jordan's *High Spirits*, so another production designer had already been assigned by Warners.

"Burton had been told I couldn't do the film, but he doggedly wouldn't believe it," said Furst. "Tim had wanted me to do *Beetlejuice*, but after two exhausting years working with Stanley Kubrick on *Full Metal*

Jacket, I didn't feel in any position to take on a new film. Tim had seen *The Company of Wolves* and had always wanted to work with me. I remember he flew from Los Angeles to San Francisco when he knew I was about to stay with friends there. He wanted to approach me before I travelled on to L.A. in case someone else got me first. Tim is really singleminded when there's something he feels strongly about. *Batman* he felt strongly about so I replaced the original choice of designer. I wish I'd done *Beetlejuice* now, rather than *High Spirits!*"

Furst budgeted *Batman* while he finished work on the filming of Neil Jordan's ghost story comedy. "The spectacular thing about Tim is he has this extraordinary ability to get onto the pulse of a movie and define its atmosphere and general spirit," said Furst. "He is quite amazing in his observations. That spirit is one of the reasons why I'm sure Warners backed such a young director in the first place. They know he's got something, and even if they don't quite know what it is, they're willing to go along with it. I found his spirit contagious, and we do have a lot in common. We both wear black, for example. There was an instant affinity between us.

"I don't think I've ever felt so naturally in tune with a director," continued Furst, "conceptually, spiritually, visually, or artistically. There was never any problem because we never fought over anything. I often wanted his advice, but when I came up with four ideas in four different directions, he'd always choose the one I liked most. He was in America when I had to make certain decisions over the Batmobile, so I faxed over numbered designs even though the one I liked was rather radical. When I called him he said, 'I've got the one in front of me.' And of course it was the same one. It was always the same one."

Furst stressed that his collaboration with Burton worked so well because they both agreed on the same philosophy of moviemaking. "When we first met, we both independently mentioned how sick we were of the ILM school of film-making," said Furst. "You can't stun with effects anymore, you have to go back to basics. We both agreed the best special effect we could ever remember seeing was the house in *Psycho* because it registers such a strong image. Impact, that's what films are about—not effects. I felt much better after that conversation, knowing he was totally uninterested in camera tricks and the clever, clever approach.

"Texture, attitude and feelings are what [Burton] is a master at," continued Furst. "He's good at getting to the bottom line, or what he terms, 'the broadstroke.' What do we really need out of this shot? We don't want details or the icing on the cake. What do we have to put across? Tim is good at paring down to the lowest common denominator and then embellishing on that because detailing is easy. This takes a lot of intelligence and he's good at articulating this and following those ideas through. The producers always went along with him because he could always articulate why he was doing something."

"Anton is the best in his field," said Burton about his design collaborator. "It's always important for me to work with people I like in these important capacities. Since my background is in illustration and design, it's the one area I'm very critical about. I have a tendency to bully departments if I'm not getting what I want. Working with someone who has real artistic talent and a strong input is a nice luxury. It excites me, and it's important for me to like them as friends. Anton's creative spark and the affinity we had went beyond a working relationship. We constantly talked back and forth; threw concepts around and discussed our thoughts openly."

Burton and Furst came up with a look for Gotham City—actually identified as New York City in the comics from May 1939 to December 1940—that can only be described as "retro high-tech." Burton abhored the term. "I shiver at that description!" he said. "If people say Gotham City looks like *Blade Runner*, I'll be furious!" Reading the film's reviews, Burton must be positively livid then, because most critics likened its architecture to Ridley Scott's effort, but also to Terry Gilliam's *Brazil*.

"So few great movie cities have been built," said Burton. "*Metropolis* and *Blade Runner* seem to be the accepted spectrum. We tried so hard to do something different although people tend to lump things in categories. We conceptualized Gotham City as the reverse of New York in its early days. Zoning and construction was thought of in terms of letting light in. So we decided to take that in the opposite direction and darken everything by building up vertically and cramming architecture together. Gotham City is basically New York caricatured with a mix of styles squashed together—an island of big, tall cartoon buildings textured with extreme designs."

Crucial to Burton's Gotham City concept was that nothing look new. "Anton textured it beautifully to keep the operatic feel intact," said Burton. "All the sets are an extention of an opera staging, and I think Anton has been very successful with my brief of timelessness. *Batman* is similar to *Beetlejuice* in that regard—it has a timeless quality with contemporary references making it believable within its own context of reality. I couldn't film any other way although it's dangerous to describe something as timeless because the tendency is to go overboard and make it too stylized. No-one feels anything but removed if you do that."

To create the Gotham City sets on Pinewood's backlot, Furst had a $5.5 million construction budget. "A third of that money you can't see as a lot went below the ground," said Furst. "On the backlot we had to pile drive into the ground to secure the set which had to withstand gale force winds. Imagine if we'd had a winter like the year before when a hurricane hit? It would have been a nightmare. That happened on *Superman* when the set was blown away. Concrete pads up to ten-feet deep with metal tubing cemented in meant the set was built to last. We weren't told to make it last for all the proposed *Batman* sequels. But we were filming through a winter, and it was cheaper in the long run to build it properly."

Furst paced out the Pinewood lot looking through a standard medium-wide camera lens to determine the height to build the Gotham Citystreet set to give Burton maximum latitude. Everything was built 40-feet high, with the Cathedral 10-feet taller, so Burton could shoot freely without resorting to models or matte paintings. Only one main street was afforded by the budget, so Furst designed an alleyway in the back, and bridges over the set to provide Burton with a variety of perspectives.

"My job is to give the director as many variations on views as I can," said Furst. 'It was important to lock in the geography early on because we had to have Gotham Square, a big parade going down the main street with the Batwing crashing into the Cathedral. These were strong parameters to lock down so the shots could be planned well in advance."

Helping to combat the comic book fan backlash against their production was Warners' decision to hire artist Bob Kane, one of Batman's creators, as the project's creative consultant. "Hiring Kane was a very intelligent move," said production designer Anton Furst. "He loved what we were doing. We sent over sketches constantly and he kept sending back these little drawings with notes attached saying, 'Well done boys.' He came over once to visit the set and when he was shown around, he was totally awe-inspired. Very clever, because when it comes to the American media, just to have it sanctioned by the creator makes it very difficult for the [audience] to complain. If Kane goes on record saying his concept has been brilliantly interpreted, the ardent fans buckle down. He must have a massive copyright merchandising deal so it's also in his interest."

Kane had envisioned actor Jack Nicholson in the role of his Joker as far back as 1980, when he drew a likeness of the character over a still of the actor from *The Shining*. "Kane thinks our Joker is better than the original in his strip," said Furst. "Very early on Bob kept saying, 'Get Jack Nicholson. He is The Joker. Get the man!' "

Nicholson's hiring for the role of The Joker was credited by Anton Furst as a turning point for the production. "Getting Jack was very important for the movie," said Furst. "It was so fucking obvious. I don't think there was ever a part more tailor-made for him. If he turned the part down, Tim and I both agreed we would never feel the same about the picture. As soon as he said yes, there was this great motivating force behind the movie because everyone knew that ingredient was dead right. And he fulfilled all expectations. When you have an actor with that sort of charisma, it heightens everyone else's performance and sets a standard level they all had to rise to. It was mainly because of Jack that the adrenaline ran so high."

Called in to do Nicholson's makeup as The Joker was Nick Dudman, makeup supervisor on George Lucas' *Willow*, who trained under the tutelage of English makeup master, Stuart Freeborn. Dudman was approached by Furst early in preproduction before Nicholson had been signed. "I met Burton and Anton at a time when nobody knew whether *Batman* was a 'go' project or not," said Dudman. "Burton told me there were two aspects to *Batman* that really scared him. One was Batman's cloak, which under no circumstances could look like an old tea cloth. And the other was the look of The Joker. He didn't want him to look like an actor simply wearing white makeup."

Batman began its twelve-week shoot in mid-October last year at Pinewood Studios, outside London. Though rumors were rampant during filming that Nicholson and Burton weren't getting along—and that Nicholson was trying to pressure Warner Bros into replacing the director—Burton said Nicholson's improvisational style jibed closely with his own. "Jack had a clear idea of the character and played around within those boundaries," said Burton. "I actually prefer improvisation, although preferably with on-page guidelines. He's a textbook actor who's very intuitive. He gets to know the character and then has quite a lot of fun with it. He'd always question how much he should laugh as The Joker and at one point, asked me if he could go really nuts in a scene. But that comes only when both have a clear idea of the proper approach to take. He wouldn't have asked me that if he didn't feel we were in tune with each other.

"It's not a campy performance at all," said Burton about Nicholson's acclaimed performance as The Joker. "Jack is absolutely brilliant at going as far as you can go, always pushing to the edge, but still making it seem real. He's less broad here than in *The Witches of Eastwick*. You can't play it too broad when you have white skin and green hair. He understood when it was time to bring his performance down."

In the *Batman* comics, The Joker was a lab assistant who decided to stage a million-dollar robbery. When he dives in a pool of chemical waste to escape Batman, he discovers that his hair has turned green, his skin white, with his red lips spread permanently into a fiendish grin. The Joker's product-tampering victims in the film borrow imagery from the comics where his use of poison left victims with a horrified, mocking grin.

For his role as The Joker, Nicholson had what was known as an "off-the-clock" agreement. His contract specified the number of hours he was entitled to have off each day, from the time he left the studio to the time he reported back for filming. "Nicholson had to leave at a certain point each night—allowing time for us to clean him up—for it to be worth bringing him in the next day," said Dudman. "Anything over two and a half hours in the makeup chair was silly because he would only be on the floor for four hours. Although it was a crippling schedule, we got it down to two hours in all—90 minutes to get everything on and colored up, 20 minutes for the wig placement, and 10 minutes to re-touch and finish."

Dudman said it was a joy to work with Nicholson. "Having Jack around was great," said Dudman. "He's such an amusing person. He made it a pleasure to go to work." And there were fringe benefits. "When he didn't work, neither did we," said Dudman. "As Jack didn't like working weekends or too many days in a row, we always had breathing space to catch up. The prosthetics had specific foam densities and had to be absolutely flawless, so there was a lot of waste. Having extra days to review how many sets and back-ups we had was an added luxury."

Dudman said Nicholson was a great kidder on the set. "I'm a terrible giggler," said Dudman, "so I had to leave the floor several times. But he could be amusing one second and the next turn on the evil with one subtle expression. And the quality wasn't lost through overuse of makeup. My initial terror was always that the makeup would sabotage what he was trying to produce, causing him endless frustration. Jack is one of the top actors in the world. Apart from Dustin Hoffman in *Little Big Man*, I can't think of another celebrity who has consented to a total face change. He told me he wanted to play someone behind a mask, just to get an idea of what it was like. Luckily, we got him at a time he was prepared to experiment. I can see why he spent a lot of time thinking about playing The Joker. It was a brave move."

Did Burton feel Nicholson was integral to the funding of *Batman*, as has been suggested? "That's hard to say," pondered the director. "My recollection is that Warners said yes before anyone was signed. Warners definitely wanted to make the movie and an actor of Jack's caliber only helped raise the level of perception a few more notches."

Anti-Keaton comic book protesters also took to task Bob Ringwood's superhero costume design for the film because it incorporated fake muscles, cloak-cum-wings, and a rather large cod-piece. "The idea was to humanize Batman," said Burton about the design of Batman's costume. "He dresses like this for theatrical effect. We had to find a psychological basis for his dress code. You can't just do, 'Well, I'm avenging the death of my parents—Oh!, a bat's flown in through the window. Yes, that's it. I'll become a Batman!' That's all stupid comic book stuff and we don't explore it at all. He dresses up as a bat because he wants to have an amazing visual impact. It all gets away from the fact he's just being a simple vigilante, something I always loathed about the character. He's creating an opera wherever he goes to provoke a strong, larger-than-life reaction. He switches identities to become something else entirely, so why wouldn't he overdo it?"

As for the costume's enlarged cod-piece, Burton sees nothing wrong with injecting a little sex into the comic imagery. "Aren't comics always about sex anyway?" he said. "Teens like them because they tune in to sexual fantasy at the exact time they're going through puberty. Bob's design was less an outfit, more a complete body suit. It isn't tights and underwear worn on the outside, but a complete operatic costume to overstate the image Batman has of himself. Nor is it *Robocop* inspired. We don't make as much of it as the comic fans have—it's just an image-conscious costume."

Robin, Batman's sidekick, isn't in the finished film, though Burton and Hamm included the character in the shooting script. Burton made the decision to drop Robin shortly before filming began because he felt the character's introduction slowed the movie's pace. "We could never get Robin in before the last third of the movie," said Burton of the script dynamics. "By that time we just wanted to get on with the story rather than introduce somebody else new in tights, simply because the comic lore dictated it. Luckily, when I made the decision to cut him out entirely—something that made everyone nervous—that comic book issue was published where the fans voted to kill off Robin. The timing was very helpful in convincing Warners Robin didn't matter."

Like *Beetlejuice*, the supporting cast of *Batman* is very "off the wall," a penchant that is becoming one of the director's trademarks. "I love a certain kind of casting," said Burton. "Jack Palance was the only person who could possibly portray Nicholson's boss. He is one of the few living actors who had the emotional weight and authority to counterpoint Nicholson's strong character. Jerry Hall [Palance's girlfriend] doesn't play herself, although you know she's a famous model. Half the time she's wearing a disfiguring mask and a lot of power is registered as a result of blurring her real life with her character role. People will read that and say, 'Campy, campy, campy." But it isn't that at all. I think it's strong since she's a recognizable figure as a model, therefore it becomes much more resonant. I'm so happy with that sort of trade-off casting."

The Palance and Hall roles, as well as Robert Wuhl as newspaper reporter Alexander Knox, were ones created especially for the script.

From the comics, Burton cast Pat Hingle as Police Commissioner Gordon, a friend of Bruce Wayne's who is unaware of his associate's crime fighting alter ego. By the film's end, Gordon introduces the comic's famed Batsignal searchlight as a means of calling the crime-fighter. Alfred, Wayne's faithful butler wasn't introduced in the comics until May 1943, but, played by suberb English character actor Michael Gough, is in on Batman's film origins from the beginning.

Batman's comic book girl-friend is played by Kim Basinger, who replaced originally cast Sean Young after she broke her leg early in the filming. "The Vicki Vale character went from brunette to blonde—an interesting switch which didn't phase me as much as I thought it would," said Burton. "Incidentally, Kim isn't producer Jon Peter's girl-friend. She didn't get the part through favoritism. That was yet more of the salacious gossip we've had to put up with. We sued an English tabloid newspaper over that report."

Music for *Batman* was composed by Danny Elfman, who scored Burton's *Pee-wee's Big Adventure* and *Beetlejuice*. Whereas Burton used Harry Belafonte calypsos on the soundtrack of *Beetlejuice*, *Batman* features the more contemporary songs of Prince, almost universally panned by critics and audiences alike, as being out of place in the film.

"*Batman* doesn't have as blatant a soundtrack as, say, *Top Gun*," said Burton in defense of Prince. "The songs in the film I would call scored source pieces. They are integrated seamlessly into the soundtrack. Prince worked with Elfman to ensure the songs didn't stand out when, for example, the radio is switched on. Our eyes are not on high volume soundtrack sales." Asked why he wasn't daring enough to include the *Batman* TV theme somewhere, Burton just shrugged.

Batman is heavy on the special visual effects, supervised by Oscar-winner Derek Meddings and his Shepperton Studios-based Meddings Magic Camera Company. The film's mechanical effects were supervised by John Evans, with whom Meddings worked on *Moonraker*. For a director whose filmic oeuvre is heavy on the effects work, Burton has a refreshingly nonchalant attitude about their use, which is probably why his films utilize effects so well. "I don't like relying too heavily on effects," said Burton. "In *Beetlejuice* I treated this area very matter-of-factly, using them like a bridge between two shots. That's my overall attitude—integrate them into the narrative rather than make them stand out."

Warners is said to be so confident about *Batman*'s smash boxoffice potential that a sequel is already in the works. Names like Robin Williams as The Riddler and Danny DeVito as The Penguin have been mentioned in conjunction with a second adventure supposedly to shoot next May. Warners bought the $2 million Gotham City set on Pinewood's backlot to use on two future productions, and are protecting their investment behind 24-hour guard dog fences. "The set is costing $20,000 a week to keep up because of scaffolding hire charges," said Furst. "So when they get around to making a sequel, it probably would have cost Warners only $1/4 million to resume it, as opposed to building it from scratch. Even the cost of renovation on top probably means it was worth keeping the set up."

Burton said there was no point talking about sequels until his movie's performance at the boxoffice can be analyzed. "I don't want anything to do with a sequel anyway," said Burton. "Sequels are only worthwhile if they give you the opportunity to do something new and interesting. It has to go beyond that, really, because you do the first for the thrill of the unknown. A sequel wipes all that out, so you must explore the next level. I don't rule out anything if the challenge is exciting."

With a rash of comic book heroes about to hit the big screen, the onus is on *Batman* to prove the trend is a worth while investment. And Burton feels good about that. "*Batman* was the toughest job I've ever had to do," he said. "Actually, that isn't saying much because I had to work in a restaurant once, which was far harder!

"It was tough from the point of having no time to regroup after the script revisions," he continued. "I never had time to think about them. I always felt like I was catching up. I worked six days a week and exhausted myself because I feared I wasn't doing a good job. I was afraid my mental condition wasn't right for me to be making this movie, and even now I have amnesia about certain times during the shooting. But it's the movie I wanted to make and it's true to the spirit of why I wanted to do it in the first place. It's something new and original, not a copy of anything that's gone before. It has a spirit of its own that has transferred to the screen. And isn't that what you want when you go to the movies?"

Odd Man In

DAVID EDELSTEIN/1990

Tim Burton has no idea how people will take his new movie, *Edward Scissorhands*, a fairy tale about a freshly made boy (Johnny Depp) whose creator (Vincent Price) drops dead before giving him hands. Instead, Edward has large shears attached to his wrists to be able to touch and feel; moved to caress the cheek of his dead "father," he tenderly slices it open.

Burton says the film is about not being able to touch, to communicate. It's about being at odds with your own body, doomed to misrepresent yourself and, in turn, to be miserably misperceived. And the movie, he worries, might be misperceived, too. It's not a comedy, a romance, or a drama—although it has all three elements. There are no easy handles.

Burton's three other features, *Pee-wee's Big Adventure*, *Beetlejuice*, and *Batman*, were huge hits, but a lot of critics detested them, and Burton has little sense of how anything he makes will be received—especially this, his most personal film. He half expects to be rejected for his awkward self-expression; meaning to caress, he may discover he has . . . sliced.

It's odd to find him now, the boy with all the blockbusters, so bereft. He's rich, he's newly married, he has his own Gap ad. His movies are dizzyingly playful, deadpan in spirit yet full of springing jack-in-the-boxes. In person, however, the man behind the curtain is a sad child.

Like his films, Burton, thirty-two, is antic with a droop. He's tall but so slim and wilting that he seems shorter; he's also as pale as a cave

From *Mirabella*, December 1990, 31+. Reprinted by permission of the author.

dweller. Clearly the model for his current protagonist, he has a mop of bedraggled hair and large, puttyish features; when he removes his circular black glasses, there's another layer—heavy lids—over hollow, dolorous eyes that only rarely meet yours. His clothes conceal him, too: today, in his office at Warner Hollywood he wears an oversized shirt over a black T-shirt reading, "Alien Sex Fiend." He's not indifferent to appearance: this is how he presents himself.

To quote him is not to get him right; you miss the air of stoned melancholy, the spastically gesticulating hands and the sentences that stop and restart and that you have to complete for him. You also miss his strange and frequent cackle, which comes at morbid moments and makes him sound like a punk Phyllis Diller.

Burton would be out of place anywhere, and his awareness of that suffuses his work, which is set in a peculiar twilight zone between the matter-of-fact and the flabbergasting. In his early animated short, *Vincent*, the tormented young hero (who resembles Burton) staggers through imaginary dark corridors pretending he's Vincent Price in a Poe film. In *Beetlejuice*, his novice ghosts don sheets to make themselves terrifying, but look, instead, merely hopeless. Even Bruce Wayne (Michael Keaton) is poignantly absurd in his black Batman getup—with those tall, pointed ears framing that solemn face. *Batman* was the first cult blockbuster and those in its cult love what others liked least: its melancholy spirit and depressed superhero.

"Sad, sad," says Burton, grinning. "What's great about [the costume] is it's the visual representation of the internal side of people. That's what I love. People putting on sheets or a bat costume to have some effect. It's a boldly sad statement. It's like a pathetic, last ditch attempt before death. This is it, in a way."

Many people missed that dimension of Keaton's Batman; they found him distant. Burton—who thinks the success of *Batman* had little to do with his work, who thinks that no one could even *see* the movie through the hype—was left stung and bewildered. And when that happens, he wraps himself in his childhood alienation like a cape.

He was born in Burbank, "the pit of hell," and raised by parents who didn't get him in the least. Still don't. (What's with this kid?) It was drawing that liberated Burton. Enchanted by Dr. Seuss, he'd continue the art on the bottom of the page. And, as *Vincent* recounts, he'd find release in Vincent Price movies, responding with all his heart to the oversensitive hero/villain.

"Embracing death and the catharsis of 'Oh my God, I'm going to die' and *The Fall of the House of Usher* and *The Raven* and Edgar Allan Poe and Vincent Price helped me to live," he says. "That's why I think all that [morbid imagery] in heavy metal is valuable. I don't subscribe to the idea that it causes death. All you have to do is look at the parents."

Although he now directs Price instead of fantasizing about him, Burton's romance with death endures. His house is full of Mexican Day of the Dead figurines; and his movies make you laugh at your own dread of dying, turning the afterlife—as in *Beetlejuice*—into a mangy series of waiting rooms where you take a number and sit.

Burton relishes that perversity: he's for anything that subverts studio formulas. And while he tightly controls the look of his films, he loves to let the story go, to let events present themselves. "A lot of people think that's bad editing," he says, aware that his work can seem shapeless. "But I prefer to let it out and not try to create some kind of trendy or hot editing. I'm not that type of person."

When I suggest to Burton that editing doesn't express him the way other parts of the process do, he muses that after a shoot ends, it's like breaking up with someone—he edits in a depression, which somehow gets incorporated into the film.

Burton mentions his depressions so often that I finally ask him if he is, in fact, a manic-depressive. "I'm a happy-go-lucky manic-depressive," he answers, almost cheerfully. "It does get very deep and dark for me, and it gets scary at times when I feel I can't pull out of it. But I don't consider myself negative-negative. I'm positive-negative. When things get really bad, the final straw is to laugh. That's my release. Seeing those pointed ears, y'know."

Not everyone responds to those pointed ears, but Burton hopes audiences who didn't get *Batman* will find *Edward Scissorhands* more emotionally transparent. "Sometimes people see the image and don't go any further," he says. "This is the first time I feel like the image is also the feeling."

Edward is the ultimate isolated teen. Alone, he dwells in his Gothic mansion on a hill until an Avon lady (Dianne Wiest) discovers him and brings him down into suburbia, where he meets her cheerleader daughter (Winona Ryder). When the suburbanites welcome him, he shows his gratitude by doing what he can: he sculpts their hedges into eccentric topiary. All is bliss until they turn on him.

The movie, says Burton, is about "growing up in the kind of neighborhoods where on the surface you're immediately accepted. When you go to another country, people are leery of you and it takes them time to get to know you. Here it's 'Oh hi, how ya doin'?' and it's a very surface thing that gets kinda peeled away."

The neighborhood was brought to life by designer Bo Welch, who— along with Danny Elfman, composer of the puckish yet impassioned scores—is both a close collaborator and friend. Welch could not be less like Burton. A surfer with a degree in architecture, he's tanned and golden-haired and diffident. His girlfriend is former SCTV fave Catherine O'Hara, whom he met on Beetlejuice. He loves the graphic sharpness of Burton's films and the way Burton encourages him to push the boundaries of reality for the sake of a feeling.

In Burton's office, the pair recount their journey into the suburban heart of darkness. As we talk, Burton pulls out the book Suburbia, a deadpan piece of anthropological grotesquerie by photographer Bill Owens, and leafs through it, eager to show that this culture is indeed insane, but also beautiful, with a weird integrity.

In the book, which inspired the look of the film, people pose in front of their garages or in paneled rooms and explain their lifestyles. "There's one comment I love," says Burton, reading aloud, " 'I find a sense of freedom in the suburbs. You assume the mask of suburbia for outward appearances, and yet no one knows what you really do.'

"That's what's so incredible about it," Burton goes on. "Because you're so close to people and yet—this is the way I grew up feeling— you have no idea what they're really about. And it can change at any moment. You're never so close and distant from people at the same time. There's something about suburbia, it's really a place to hide. Or people use it as sort of a mask of normalcy."

"There's also a very secure feeling," says Welch, who redesigned a Florida suburb for the movie, "a calm and soothing feeling about that kind of block, where everybody sits in their garages and looks at each other's open garages."

"I always wonder why some people see things as weird and some people don't," says Burton, counting himself in the first camp. "Some people feel like an alien: you look at almost anything and it seems strange to you. I grew up with the resin grapes and the raised bullfighter on black velvet painting . . . and I could never in a million years . . . I had no feeling for why they had this in their house, what it meant.

"You have stuff in your house, it means something to you, it means *some*thing to you, doesn't it? Something personal. Doesn't anything . . . if somebody either gives you something . . . or it has some bizarre little personal . . . isn't it weird that there are things floating on your wall and 'Mom, why is that on the wall?' "

"No reason," answers Bo, for Mom.

"It's not even like they like it," Tim goes on, breathless, still distressed. "I never got a sense my parents even liked what they . . . it's like some bizarre alien force came in the middle of the night and put things on the wall and took their brain out and asked them not to question it."

"People decorate for some unexplained reason just to decorate," concludes Welch. "It has no bearing on anything."

Welch explains that for *Edward Scissorhands* he shrunk the windows of the houses "to be a little less friendly, a little more masklike and to heighten the hiding-in-suburbia feeling." He and Burton also came up with a four-color scheme for the houses: "sea-foam green, dirty flesh, butter and dirty blue." Welch took out existing neighborhood greenery and replaced it with his own, so that Edward could shape it into, say, a thirty-foot dinosaur or a man bowling. "It has a carnival feel," says Welch, "a happy feel. Edward brings out life in what's there in suburbia."

On the hill is the mansion, full of colossal gizmos and dark passageways—a perfect correlative for Edward's inner world. "I love the way it came out," says Welch. "The mansion is monochromatic, suburbia is garish; the mansion is huge and dark, in suburbia the rooms are small and bright. This is all through Edward's eyes. You should have a feeling of seeing this world for the first time." The way Burton, alien-in-residence, sees it.

Burton is married now. He met and fell in love with a twenty-five-year-old German student while in England for *Batman*. But he doesn't radiate domestic bliss. He finds Hollywood "redundant" and is leery of neighbors. "When you get these people with very tanned skins and

Beverly Hills mansions coming up to you and saying, 'You must be incredibly happy,' how would that make you feel?" He cackles. "Very uneasy, wouldn't it? It certainly doesn't make you feel comfortable . . . you start to become like the Batman character—'I'm gonna go live in a cave, just completely live in my interior world.' "

Listening to him, you realize that the amiable director still fancies himself a misperceived monster, "ugly on the outside, beautiful on the inside." But the feeling, he points out, is not unique to him. "Everybody in the whole world has been misperceived. In school, you wanted something to come across this way and it didn't come across. That's always very sad, and I think when a lot of people grow older they cut that off and some people don't . . .

"It's why you struggle as a child and you draw and want to create. There is an impulse to be seen. For yourself: what you are. It's always scary for me to show movies. I actually hate it; I feel very, very vulnerable. Because if you weren't a verbal person, you weren't this and that, you wanna let that be the thing people see you through. And so when that doesn't happen—and it doesn't, they see maybe success or failure but they don't see you—it gets further and further away from you, and it's just sad . . ."

When I protest that some people, myself included, respond to his movies exactly as he intends, he replies, sympathetically, "You were probably tortured in school."

Now he's quick to scale down expectations for *Edward Scissorhands*. "It's not a big movie. It doesn't have . . . it's quieter on a certain level."

More lyrical? I ask. More moving camera? More Spielberg?

"The camera moves a little more but don't worry, it's still clunky. There's still a few shaky camera moves. It's still got that same depressed . . ." Burton trails off.

He has a way of bringing down the room, our boy. You almost forget that in a while he'll go back to his cave and sketch some pitiful creature or useless gizmo and it will be so sad, he'll have to laugh.

Tim Burton

DAVID BRESKIN/1991

Tim Burton, like his work, is a wonderful mess. He's falling-apart
funny and completely alienated; he's morbid and ironic; he's the
serious artist as goof-ball flake. A self-described "happy-go-lucky
manic depressive," he's like a bright flashlight in a very dark place: the
grim factory of Hollywood. Burton is a true visionary. Our culture
usually doesn't use that word for people whose visions look like
cartoons and go down like dessert, but Burton is spitting in the eye of
our culture anyway, while simultaneously celebrating it. That's the
fabulous, odd thing about his work: he's angrily spitting something sweet.

Tim Burton was born in Burbank, California, in 1958, and has
lived near Hollywood all his life. He has a brother and two parents,
from whom he's always felt distant. Growing up, he did feel close to
Edgar Allan Poe and Vincent Price and many monsters from many
bad movies. He also took sanctuary in the confines of his own
imagination; for him, drawing was a refuge. Burton's first vehicle
of public acceptance was a garbage truck: in ninth grade, he won first
prize in a contest to design an anti-littering poster, and his work
graced the refuse trucks of Burbank for a year. Wanting a career for
which he wouldn't need too much schooling, he studied animation
at the California Institute of Arts. Upon graduation, he went to work
for Disney.

Unhappy on the animation assembly line, Burton eventually won
some measure of freedom within the Disney kingdom, directing his first

Originally published in *Inner Views: Filmmakers in Conversation*. Boston: Faber and Faber,
1992, 326–64. Reprinted by permission of author.

animated short, *Vincent*, in 1982. With narration by Vincent
Price, this five-minute, black-and-white piece of stop-frame animation,
heavy on German Expressionist sensibility, chronicled the miserable
life and liberating fantasies of a seemingly normal but deeply disturbed
suburban boy, quite like young Tim. A kung fu *Hansel and Gretel* with
an all-Asian cast followed, to everyone's dissatisfaction. Then came
Frankenweenie, a half-hour exploration of the Frankenstein myth come
to the suburbs, starring Shelley Duvall, Daniel Stern, and a monster/dog
named Sparky. This lovable little mutt of a movie, which announced
the outsider-in-town theme Burton would later develop in *Edward
Scissorhands*, was buried by Disney until 1992, when they released a
home video version.

Burton's first full-length feature, *Pee-wee's Big Adventure*, was
an inventive, well-modulated romp built around the singular,
screechy talents of Paul Reubens, aka the prepubescent, grey-suited,
rouge-cheeked Pee-wee Herman. The critics paid little attention,
but the picture did great business. Next, Burton enlarged his
visual signature on the campy, surreal *Beetlejuice*, a black laugh
of a ghost story. Starring Geena Davis, Alec Baldwin, and Michael
Keaton in a comic tour de force, the film was an over-the-top
lob into the irrational, a cherry bomb tossed into the grey
classroom of mortality. It didn't all coalesce (how could it?) but
when it worked, Burton's pie-in-your-face existentialism worked
like magic. The critics paid little attention, but the picture did
fabulous business.

Never particularly a fan of comic books or cartoons, Burton was
nonetheless chosen to direct *Batman*, one of those blockbuster
properties that had been in development forever, with the studio
executives clustered around it in dumb wonder, like cave men around
their first fire. Burton went deep into the myth, and deep into the
dark, and produced a flawed but fascinating pop epic. The movie had
a grand, rotten urban texture and a brooding tone. It was weighty
but not ponderous, and it was great fun—here Jack Nicholson had
the comic turn—but the fun was somewhat submarined by awkward
action, narrative glitches, and inappropriate music by Prince. The
critics paid all sorts of attention, and the picture did historic business.
This gave Burton the freedom to direct *Edward Scissorhands*, a

profoundly personal project he'd first conceived as a teenager. A simple fairy tale gift-boxed in a sophisticated design package, the story concerned a castle-bound boy with shears for hands, who's plucked from the fortress of his solitude by an angelic Avon lady and thrust into the banal wonders of suburbia. Yearning and sentimental, the movie felt like Burton's ache, and was affectingly played by a cast that included Dianne Wiest, Winona Ryder, and Johnny Depp.

After waffling for some time, Burton decided to do the inevitable *Batman* sequel. (A sequel to *Beetlejuice* had also been proposed, and turned down.) He tried *Batman Returns* largely for the chances to take a whack at some new characters and to take the myth more in his own direction, exercising a control which the overwhelming success of the first movie brought him and which his added experience would naturally provide.

The first *Batman* film also brought him his wife, Lena Gieseke, a German painter, whom he met while filming in London and married in February of 1989. In addition to directing major motion pictures, Burton draws constantly and paints occasionally. A coffee-table book of his art is in the planning stage, as are some children's picture books he plans to author. He's also shot a documentary about Vincent Price, and is developing a full-length animated feature, *Nightmare Before Christmas*.

I spoke with Burton twice in March of 1991, in his production company office at Warner's Hollywood lot. Before our first session, he was in the midst of preparing *Batman Returns* to show to studio executives—he said he'd "rather show it to aliens"—and he was even more nervous than usual. Burton talks with his hands cutting the air, covering his face, pulling his hair. He struggles to make sense of himself, starting four or five sentences for every one he finishes, and dicing his words into bits. Indeed, he's been called "famously inarticulate" by the *Washington Post*. (I've chosen clarity in favor of interview verité in the editing and punctuation of our conversation, in hopes that what you lose in the *way* he thinks—his vegematic style of verbalization—you gain in actually understanding *what* he thinks.) The fact is, English seems like a foreign language for Burton: he thinks visually. Everything he says carries with it the burden of translation.

Session One

BRESKIN: *Why do think you are a director?*

BURTON: I never wanted to be. I never felt, I am going to be a director. It probably has more to do with having an idea and just wanting to control it a little bit. I've always kind of quietly had ideas and controlled them, maybe not in a demonstrative way. It really has to be that impulse. And I just lucked into movies. I started in animation, but I couldn't sustain that—because of my attention span. I have enough of an attention span for live-action movies, and enough of a temperament to work it out. And it's funny, there's this wonderful thing of having an idea and not being completely in control—in dealing with outside elements, which you have to do in movies, which I find quite exciting. The things that happen that are out of your control are quite energizing.

BRESKIN: *Is that tension, between what you can control and what you can't, the juice for you?*

BURTON: Yeah. Yeah! I think it becomes absurd and it becomes surreal. You are thrust, just in the nature of making a film, into a surreal situation, where there's a lot of passion. And I find that attractive. I think that's why I've always enjoyed Fellini films—he shows the beauty and surrealism behind the scenes, things you go through that people don't see. That's quite energizing.

BRESKIN: *Isn't the impulse to art, to draw, for you, an attempt to control your world?*

BURTON: Sure. I am very interiorized, and very private. I've never verbalized that aspect of working. I've chosen, and I choose, to protect it, in an intuitive way and not an intellectual way. So I'm kind of cagey about what I intellectualize.

BRESKIN: *Does the intellectualizing alienate you from your inspiration?*

BURTON: Yeah, because you are bombarded by outside elements: media, reviews, people. That's why I find myself interiorizing *more*. I don't want to hear what it is I do or I don't do, or start to analyze that too much. I feel my strength in my enjoyment is very private and interior. That's really the only thing I enjoy about it. And I try to protect that to some degree.

Everybody has a different way of thinking. And my way is with a certain amount of intellectualization of the themes, but there's a cut-off point—where I have a strong enough idea of what's going on, and then I cut it off and just try to deal with it intuitively. It's just your own barometer. I look at certain things—actors on the set—and I have my barometer of belief in what they are doing. 'Cause oftentimes when you are dealing with stupid-*looking* things, and all the sets look kind of ridiculous, you have to find that line of belief. I hate it where things just look ridiculous and people act funny, so it's just your own barometer. So I'm very cagey about it.

BRESKIN: *Let me stop you right there, because "cageyness" implies a kind of consciousness of what to reveal and what not to reveal, as opposed to a built-in censor.*

BURTON: Yeah. [Pause.] I guess the cageyness has to do with kind of fighting outside things. It's very hard to be in all of this—you really do have to fight to keep a certain kind of clarity. You see people turning into the most frightening creatures. I remember when I first got into this, and I'd see somebody yelling and screaming and bursting their blood vessels and I'd go, "Whoa! What's that guy's problem? Why he is reacting so strangely?" But being in it for a while, you tend to understand why. The whole situation perverts you. And it's a mistake to think that it doesn't. And I think it's a constant struggle to try to maintain what it is that you're doing, or what you're trying to do, and to keep that as simple as possible.

BRESKIN: *So the warding off is a self-protective measure?*
BURTON: It is, I think. It certainly feels that way to me.

BRESKIN: *David Lynch indicated that one of the reasons he never pursued psychoanalysis or therapy was that he was afraid it would block his creative process.*
BURTON: That can be interesting. I went through that process a little bit, and I completely *unraveled.* [Laughs.] There's so much about yourself and other people that's interesting, but I just unraveled

too quickly! I had a therapist who was very good, and they'll tell you that one of their main concerns is not to let you unravel as you're recovering.

BRESKIN: *They want to let you hold onto your defenses until you have some new things to hold on to.*
BURTON: Exactly! And I just dived right in and immediately went to the bottom level of antidepressants and everything. I couldn't handle it. So I understand it. It's a true balancing act. Your mind plays funny tricks on you all the time.

BRESKIN: *How did the "shrinkage" relate to your work?*
BURTON: [With a Brooklyn accent, as an old-time director.] "Well, luckily I was in between pic-chahs!" [Laughs.] I was just a ball of yarn there. There are times in your life when you feel stuck. And I was wanting to burst through something, what it was I didn't know. Depression. Throughout my life, some form and level of depression has always hung over me. And I don't think it's bad necessarily, but sometimes when it gets bad—and there have been a few points—it keeps you kind of stuck.

BRESKIN: *How long did you stick with it, before it became intolerable?*
BURTON: A couple of years. I had a couple of shrinks. I had one guy, he didn't talk to me the whole time. [Manic laugh.] It was hilarious. *That* was my problem: I never spoke to anybody. So I found the perfect therapist, who just sat there for an hour and didn't speak. It was like being in any other relationship—I didn't say a word. So it was redundant in a way. He checked his watch every now and then. It was weird. We didn't say anything to each other. Maybe we were speaking Vulcan-style.

BRESKIN: *In the past, you've brought up making-films-as-therapy a number of times, both as a metaphor, and almost literally in the case of* Vincent—*that it was therapy for you to make that film.*
BURTON: People don't realize, because of the surface way the films look and the cartoonish nature of them, that the only thing that keeps me going through a movie is that these characters mean something

to me. My process is that I look at all these characters and get a *feeling* out of them that I find to be very meaningful. And thematic, to me. That's the only way for me to approach it. I could never approach it like it's just a funny movie or it's a weird-looking movie.

BRESKIN: *It's not candy.*

BURTON: No, it's not, even if it may be perceived that way, and often is. Everything has quite a deep foundation, otherwise how could you really do something? The process is too difficult and it's too painful to not have some deeply rooted feelings in it. I wouldn't actually do it, I'm not proficient enough at it; I don't have that thing that some people have, that allows them to move from one picture to another, and be a very good director, and keep moving. Each thing to me is like the *last* thing: it's all very big and tragic and cathartic. "This is the next and last picture"—I really go through that quite grandly, in my own way.

BRESKIN: *Do you ever fear that because the superficial characteristics of your films are so strong—the surfaces are so brilliant, the edges are so sharp—the audience will be blinded to the elements underneath?*

BURTON: I believe that one hundred percent. I have found that to be true on everything I've done. For the first ten minutes, nobody knows what they're looking at. I think it's definitely true, but I also know that I have a reputation—and this comes from critics on down to studio people—that I am not America's Premier Storyteller. But who cares, really? Why does everything have to be the same?

BRESKIN: *Let's go back to the world of your childhood. I'm curious as to whether you think your character was almost fully shaped by the time you were five years old.*

BURTON: Number one, I really hate, more than almost anything— because it seems to be bubbling up—that fucking "child within" bullshit. Do you know what I mean? I don't know whether you've heard that shit. I've heard it related to me, where they say, "I've never lost that touch of the child." It's the remnant of some kind of yuppie bullshit, that whole "tapping into the child within you," and that it's important to make films that do that. And actually I find that a form of retardation. [Pause.] I am very interested in where you come from and what you are. What are you? That truly is a very interesting question. But not to the point where people perceive you as maintaining that "childish" quality. 'Cause I don't actually know any children, and I don't know what that's all about.

BRESKIN: *Well, in the past you've said that you were, in the films, working out or working from a lot of "childlike feelings" and that you felt you would move on from them.*

BURTON: Yeah, I find it very interesting, because I think it holds the key to everybody, that question of what you are. Children are not perverted, in a way. It has more to do with the culture. When children are drawing, everybody draws the same. Nobody draws better than everybody else. There's a certain amount of strength, there's a certain amount of passion, there's a certain amount of clarity. And then what happens is it gets beaten out of you. You're put into a cultural framework, which gets beaten into you. To punch through that framework you have to maintain a certain kind of strength and simplicity.

BRESKIN: *Do you think that when you were a kid there was an attempt to beat things out of you that you wanted to hold on to?*

BURTON: I think that in the atmosphere I grew up in, yes, there was a subtext of normalcy. I don't even know what the word means, but it's stuck in my brain. It's weird. I don't know if it's specifically American, or American in the time I grew up, but there's a very strong sense of categorization and conformity. I remember being forced to go to Sunday school, for a number of years, even though my parents were not religious. No one was really religious; it was just the framework. There was no *passion* for it. No passion for anything. Just a quiet, kind of floaty, kind of semi-oppressive, blank palette that you're living in.

BRESKIN: *How young were you when you felt that for the first time?*

BURTON: From very early on. As long as I can remember. My grandmother told me that before I could walk I always wanted to *leave*. I would just crawl away, I would crawl out the door. And then, when I was older, if anybody was going anywhere, I always wanted to go. I had that impulse. And I had the impulse for horror movies—that was a very strong thematic thing.

BRESKIN: *Young Vincent Malloy, in* Vincent, *is "possessed by the house and can never leave it again." That must have been your greatest fear.*
BURTON: Well, I think so. I think so. It's a funny thing, that. It has to do with this atmosphere. I don't think it even has to do so much with your parents. Just the kind of collective feeling. In some ways it's quite good. It's almost like dealing with a blank piece of paper. In some ways you had to create your own world.

BRESKIN: *You became quite private, and wanted to spend time alone.*
BURTON: Absolutely. Absolutely. To this day I'm happiest when I'm . . . I look forward to sleeping. And I did, even then, I liked sleep. And I love talking to people who like to sleep. There are a few things that just calm me down: when I hear about somebody making mashed potatoes, and when I hear about somebody sleeping, and liking to sleep. I get this sense of calm, and it's a wonderful feeling. And in Hollywood, nobody likes to sleep—they're losing out, they're not on top of it. There are a few people that enjoy sleep, and I love talking to them about it. People that like to sleep are able to talk about it in ways that are nice. There is something that's wonderful about it. I love to sleep.

BRESKIN: *But you don't remember your dreams.*
BURTON: No, I don't. I have like five dreams that I remember.

BRESKIN: *Do they repeat, consistently?*
BURTON: No, I only have one dream that's been recurring. It's a great dream. There was a little girl on my block, who I was in love with, and she moved away. Every ten years I'll have a dream about her, at the age we are now. We lost contact, but I have this very clear image of what she looks like and all that.

BRESKIN: *What are the other four dreams you remember?*
BURTON: I had a dream that—this is so weird, because it's like it actually happened. My parents went bowling, and there was this weird

place that they stuck the kids. I guess it was like a day-care center, but it was all Gothic, it was all rotted wood. And there were a few of us morose kids sitting there, and we saw this light—a skeleton was coming in with this candle. And the skeleton looks at me, and it opens a door, and I fall through a trapped door and I fall into my parents' bed. And I remember waking up in my parents' bed. Weird, huh? Whoa! [Manic laugh.]

I remember the ones that are so strong that I just couldn't forget them, and I remember each feeling, each detail. I remember one when I got into a Western axe fight with somebody. I remember every chop. I remember chopping off this person's face. None of us died, but we just went through this thing, in sort of a Western setting. There was another, where there was this horrible, [shudders] this horrible seaweed, like this tough purple rubberish sea plant, that was growing out of my mouth. And I kept tearing it away and it kept growing and growing and growing. That's all it was, a long dream about the feeling of that, and the wacky hijinks surrounding that.

BRESKIN: *But when you get deep into the middle of a film, nothing spills out of your unconscious about it?*
BURTON: No, my dreams then are the worst dreams in the world, which are dreams that I am actually awake and working. Nothing could be more nightmarish than that. The nightmare is that you're still working and you're still dealing with certain people. You wake up like you've just been through a day. Nothing is worse than that.

BRESKIN: *What was the kind of taste and smell of childhood for you?*
BURTON: This is funny, but I think I've always felt the same. I've never felt young, like I was a kid. I've never felt like I was a teenager. I never felt like I was an adult. I just have always felt the same. I guess if there was a flavor, I guess it was a kind of surreal, bright depression. I was never interested in what everybody else was interested in. I was very interiorized. I always felt kind of sad.

BRESKIN: *Were you lonely?*
BURTON: I never felt . . . yeah. Yeah. I've always likened it to that feeling, when you're a teenager, that grand feeling—which is why

I liked punk or some people like heavy metal or Gothic. You've
got to go through some kind of drama. I've always seen people who
are well adjusted, and actually, they are not that well adjusted.
Everybody is going to blow at some moment or other. In fact, the
ones that come across as the most well adjusted are like human
time bombs, waiting to go off. I just think that kind of dark catharsis,
that kind of dark, dramatic, depressed, sad, moody thing, was kind
of healthy.

BRESKIN: *When* Edward Scissorhands *came out, you said of your youth
that you were "perfectly happy" alone, in your own little world. When I read
that, I didn't really buy it.*
BURTON: I think my statement's a bit cavalier. I think that was a
broad-stroke statement. Lookit, nothing is ever one way or the other.
But I relate to that more than anything. Part of the problem when
I'm doing a movie is that I never see things simplistically. People ask
me if I'm happy. I never can answer that kind of question, because it's
always too mixed, in a way. Well, I'm never going to be happy, but
I feel absurdly lucky to be here.

BRESKIN: *Given this world, the fact that we're not starving makes
us extremely lucky, but nonetheless, within your world, you have certain
feelings.*
BURTON: Within an emotional world, nobody knows and nobody
cares what sort of torments somebody might go through to do something. Maybe it's good not to talk about it so much. Fact is, who
cares? Who cares? You can read about artists of the past, and you read
about their dark, horrific struggles . . .

BRESKIN: *The painter in the garret.*
BURTON: Nobody in Hollywood is cutting off their ears.

BRESKIN: *Well, they are cutting up their breasts and faces.*
BURTON: [Laughs.] Yes, but it's more for beautification reasons than
it is for dark, tormented reasons, although the result is pretty much
the same.

BRESKIN: *I think there's plenty of dark torment beneath the need to do it.*

BURTON: Oh boy, you bet! It all ends up the same.

BRESKIN: *I'm curious about your attraction to the horrific: monsters, ghouls, demons, and so on. One take might be that in the kind of nothingness of suburbia—the almost slyly attractive no-feeling nothingness of suburbia—which you can project anything onto, the kind of deep feeling of the ghouls and demons and monsters is compelling.*

BURTON: Exactly. I love it. Lookit, all monster movies are basically one story. It's *Beauty and the Beast.* Monster movies are my form of myth, of fairy tale. The purpose of folk tales for me is a kind of extreme, symbolic version of life, of what you're going through. In America, in suburbia, there is no sense of culture, there is no sense of passion. So I think those served that very specific purpose for me. And I linked those monsters, and those Edgar Allan Poe things, to direct feelings. I didn't read fairy tales, I watched them. I wasn't watching them because I liked to be scared. From day one, I never was afraid of them, ever.

BRESKIN: *Did you identify with the monster?*

BURTON: Completely! Every kid does. They were always taking the monster and kind of prodding him and poking him, especially the ones of the fifties. The way those movies were structured, the heroes were always these bland actors, who had no emotion. They were the suburbanites to me.

BRESKIN: *And you were the creature from the black split-level.*

BURTON: Sure! Of course. Grand drama. You've got to feel, you've got to go for the drama. Because if I didn't, I just felt I would *explode.* I always felt it was healthy—I enjoyed the drama of that. I just felt it was saving me. You deal with it, and you create, or, you become it.

BRESKIN: *Is the alienation that was present between you and your folks, and you and your brother, a lifelong thing, or is there any possibility for repair?*

BURTON: It's one of those issues . . . my parents are good people. They are not bad people. But, I feel it's much more of a cultural phenomenon. I'm not the warmest of people, when it comes to that.

BRESKIN: *Do you see any of yourself in them, or any of them in you?*

BURTON: Yeah, I think so. I don't think I was adopted, or hatched from an egg or something. There is some connection there.

BRESKIN: *You've said you grew up at the end of the nuclear family experiment, and that it didn't work. Did you mean yours, or the whole idea?*

BURTON: I think the whole thing. There was no sense of connection to emotions. In our culture, what you were taught about America in school is the way things should be—success and family, what they call traditional family values—and you know, things are not that simple. So when it's not working, rather than going, "This isn't working, this is fucked," people just feel like they are failures.

BRESKIN: *And the last twelve years in Washington, they've been shoving that "family values" idea down our throats.*

BURTON: And it's completely frightening, because they don't understand. The same thing about "America." It's just bizarre to try to maintain this feeling about America. And you see it most strongly in Los Angeles. America to me always seems like a country that's based on a movie. Here you've got presidents spouting lines from Clint Eastwood movies, and it's getting more and more that way. It's hard to find people to work with because nobody wants to be what they are. "Oh, I'm sorry, I'm not this, because I'm really *this.*" This level of success that's thrust upon you—you've got to be successful and you've got to be a certain way—nobody is what they are, because of this dream. And it's great to have a dream, and none of that should be taken away from people, because that's all people have, but not this materialistic dream. That's the problem, and everybody is fucked up from it.

BRESKIN: *Jim's dad in* Edward Scissorhands *being case number one.*

BURTON: [Manic laugh.] Absolutely, absolutely.

BRESKIN: *Do you remember when you first had the impulse to draw?*

BURTON: I think it started when it started for everyone. I'm just lucky that it wasn't beaten out of me. I was very lucky that I maintained a passion for it and didn't give a fuck what my third grade teacher thought of it.

BRESKIN: *And were your drawings stuck up on the fridge by your parents?*
BURTON: I got the normal parent routine. It's actually quite funny. You know, mom's reading a book, and you show her a drawing and she has X-ray vision through the book, where she can actually see your drawing without looking from her book. [Manic laugh.] That's the classic routine. I don't know what the whole deal was. My father was also a baseball player, in the minors, and he worked for the park and recreation district in Burbank, so there was a slight pushing in that direction. And my mother pushed me into the whole musical instrument routine. I think I played the clarinet, but I was never any good at it. So my drawing was always more *private*. I feel kind of lucky, because I think if they had supported it, I probably wouldn't have done it. Lookit, every kid is reacting against their parents. If the parents are radicals, the kid turns out to be a little accountant. It's not always the case, but that dynamic is pretty strong.

BRESKIN: *A couple of years ago you said you "freaked" because you didn't even know the most basic things about your parents, like where they were born. What caused you to freak about that?*
BURTON: I think it was that period of therapy, where I was trying to figure out what the fuck was going on. I felt a bit more depressed than usual. The fog got a little greyer. It's hard to see through it as it gets down a little bit closer to you. I was just not connecting to anybody. I was starting to feel a little too lonely and too isolated and too abstract and depressed. And it was around that time that it was pointed out to me that I didn't know anything about my parents. [Manic laugh.] It was kind of shocking.

BRESKIN: *Do you ever see them?*
BURTON: I see them occasionally. Not too much.

BRESKIN: *I know how important Vincent Price and his films were to you as a kid. You talk in terms of him getting things out of your system. What did he get out of your system that proved so helpful to you?*

BURTON: His movies probably spoke most directly to me. In fairy tales and myths, the symbolism is not so much intellectual as emotional. I could understand everything he was going through. Then, as I got older, I met the guy—and I still don't know him that well, and that's probably good in a way—and I realized that this connection made me feel good about my own intuition. Here you are, looking at a guy, and he's killing people and all this other stuff, but then you sense something else. It gave me a feeling, a human feeling, of intuition; and kind of a barometer of looking at people. There are very few moments like that that make you feel good. A little bit of a validating experience. A little bit of a reality check. A check on something that gets lost in the world.

BRESKIN: *Do you imagine depressed teenagers needing your work the way you needed his work?*
BURTON: I don't know. I've never really thought about that. You can't think about those things because it would be wrong. That's not the way things should happen. But if someone would say to me that that was the case, I would feel happy about it. I would feel an affinity for that, because of the way I felt, and feel.

BRESKIN: *How do you feel your background in animation shaped you as a director?*
BURTON: What I feel really good about, really happy about, is that I did *not* go to film school. I went to Cal Arts, and went through animation, where I got a very solid education. You learn design, you draw your own characters, you draw your own backgrounds, you draw your own scenes. You cut it, you shoot it. You learn the storyboarding process. It's everything, without the bullshit of film school. I can't even meet people from film school, because I feel like they've been in the industry for ten years. It's really frightening! Not to say that they are all that way, but I knew somebody who was at a studio and was going to look at a student's film, and then the student came in and said, "I'm not running this film, I need a *stereo* room!" The level of competition, of feeling like you're already in the industry, you don't get a chance to create.

BRESKIN: *But the torpor of being attached to the animator's desk was traumatic.*
BURTON: I couldn't handle it. At Disney, I almost went insane. I really did. I don't ever want to get that close to that certain kind of feeling that I had. Who knows what a nervous breakdown is? Or who knows what going off the edge is? I don't want to get that close again.

BRESKIN: *Was the monotony your biggest enemy?*
BURTON: Number one is, I was just not Disney material. I could just not draw cute foxes for the life of me. I couldn't do it. I *tried*. I tried, tried. The unholy alliance of animation is: you are called upon to be an artist—especially at Disney, where you are perceived as the artist, pure and simple, where your work flows from the artistic pencil to the paper, the total artist—but on the other hand, you are called upon to be a zombie factory worker. And for me, I could not integrate the two. I could not find that balance.

Also, at the time they were making kind of shitty movies. And it took them five or six years to make a movie. There's that cold, hard fact: do you want to spend six years of your life working on *The Fox and the Hound?* There's a soul-searching moment when the answer is pretty clear.

BRESKIN: *How do you react to the critical shorthand which suggests that your films are live-action cartoons?*
BURTON: You know what's weird? I never really liked animation. My attraction to it was: if I had the choice of being a court reporter or an animator, I would choose animation. [Laughs.]

BRESKIN: *That's right, your parents wanted you to be a court reporter.*
BURTON: There was a guy who lived near us, who was really creepy, who was a court reporter, and I remember I went to his office once to find out about it. It was creepy. So, beyond court reporting, I liked to draw—animation seemed good. But I'm not gung-ho about it.

BRESKIN: *So your connection to animation was really only that it was linked to drawing, which was something you did, and still do, obsessively and incessantly.*

BURTON: Well, sure. That's why the one thing I had to learn about live-action, which is still a struggle for me, is to *speak*. In animation, you would communicate through drawings, and I was perfectly happy to communicate that way, and not in any other way. So what you're saying is true: there was a direct link. You're able to maintain that privacy much more in that relationship, because there's nothing else happening, really.

BRESKIN: *Let's talk about the Disney work you did do. If you resist the connection between yourself and* Edward Scissorhands, *you can't really in good faith resist the connection between yourself and Vincent Malloy in* Vincent?
BURTON: No, I can't. It's probably the thing that is the most purely related to me, for sure.

BRESKIN: *And young Vince has some fairly aggressive fantasies: one of boiling his aunt in wax, and one of sending enough juice into his dog Abercrombie to turn him into a zombie.*
BURTON: Sure. All forms of experiments, yes.

BRESKIN: *So, did you have these kind of fantasies? And did you exorcise them by making the film?*
BURTON: I did both. But again, again, if you grow up in an environment that is not passionate, you have no choice but to have these dark fantasies. That's why I get so freaked out when I read about parents trying to stop their kids from listening to this or that music. It's like *Sesame Street*—I would never watch that. You got to understand, things are not perfect for children. There's a lot of darkness, there's a lot of abstraction. The only way to get through it is to explore it.

BRESKIN: *When you did all your drawing, did you do it to communicate with others, or just to pleasure yourself by doing it?*
BURTON: I pleased myself by doing it. I really did get enjoyment out of it, myself. I did these very big things. You know how kids would go out and play "army" or something like that—well, I would do it on paper. I would have these elaborate things where spaceships would attack, and so on, and by the end of it, it would turn into a gigantic

mess. It wasn't even a drawing by the end. It looked like a collection of obliterated figures. I enjoyed it. It wasn't for anybody else.

BRESKIN: *If Vincent Price had not cooperated with you on the film and done the voice-over narration, in hindsight, do you think your life would have been different?*

BURTON: That's an interesting question. I remember going through those feelings at the time, thinking, "God, will he like this?" It's hard to say what would have happened, but I know how I felt about the thing: it was one hundred percent pure. It could have been like one of those things that you see: [imitating jaded star] "Hey, kid, get away from me! Get out of here!" Everything is based on your first impulse, and I didn't do the thing for his approval. *Vincent* is probably the only thing that I can watch and not have to turn away.

BRESKIN: *Of all your work? Or just that early work?*

BURTON: Of anything. I can watch parts of things. Sometimes I'll turn on something, if it's on TV, and I'll just watch a little bit of something, just to see what my own reaction will be. I feel like everything I do is part of me, but it's very hard for me to watch things. I can't sit back and enjoy it. I feel an affinity for it, but I can't enjoy it. It takes me about five years before I can really see it at all. I don't know what that's about.

BRESKIN: *Do you watch your films with audiences? Do you go to test screenings?*

BURTON: I have to. Those things are really hard for me. There's such importance placed on test screenings, by studios, and unrightly so, because they're complete bullshit. The reality of the situation is—and I don't care what anybody says—that if you show the movie to a group of people, you'll get an idea of what's working and what's not working. That's really all you need to do. You don't need to have this lab animal experiment, where you dissect the audience and dissect the film. That's complete, one hundred percent bullshit! And they are completely locked into it. If you put the audience in a lab experiment scenario, they're gonna turn into critics and they are going to turn into lab animals. So I believe, in the broad-stroke, in looking at a movie with an audience—and you don't have to ask them, who is your most favorite character, and who is your least favorite character? You can tell what's working and what's not. That's all you should do. And that's why I constantly try to fight this *fucked* system. It's so horrible. It doesn't help the movie.

But after the movie opens, I don't go. I get too freaked out. I can't enjoy it. It makes me wonder why I do it. I don't enjoy this, I don't enjoy that. I wish that I could, because I feel like I'm cutting myself out of part of it that's maybe nice. I get too nervous.

BRESKIN: *With hindsight,* Frankenweenie *looks very much like a dress rehearsal for* Edward Scissorhands.
BURTON: Yeah. I was very lucky at Disney to do things that meant something to me: A, to be able to do a short film in any studio situation, and B, to be able to do some things that were personally meaningful to me—that's unheard of. And everything is thematically meaningful to me. Even *Pee-wee.* Whether it shows up to anybody else, I don't know.

BRESKIN: *When* Frankenweenie *got a PG rating instead of a G, Disney buried it in their vault, and from what I understand, they wouldn't even give you a personal copy of it.*
BURTON: That's absolutely true. They were very weird about it.

BRESKIN: *And yet, now that you are a famous director, they are releasing it on video, before* Batman Returns *comes out. It seems like Exhibit A of Hollywood cynicism.*
BURTON: Exactly! And you know what, though, I don't even get upset with this shit, because it's the way it is. I understand it. I'm cynical enough about things just to be happy that they are releasing it. I have plenty of other things to get upset about and paranoid about.

BRESKIN: *Victor Frankenstein, in reading about how to bring his dog Sparky back to life, has Elizabeth Kubler-Ross's* On Death and Dying *in*

his room. That's surely the only time that book has shown up in a Disney
fairy tale.
BURTON: [Manic laugh.] Yes. It's all heavy.

BRESKIN: *And a lovable little monster is Sparky, and a monster who*
survives, and prospers. The monster is supposed to die in a monster movie,
right, Tim?
BURTON: Yeah, but they never do! Even when they die, they don't
die. Even in *Creature from the Black Lagoon*, the creature dies, but he
comes back in *Revenge of the Creature* and *The Creature Walks Among Us*.
They never die. It's part of the mythology that they do. But they are
always coming back. They're always fighting. They fight through the
system, the system of bland B-actors.

BRESKIN: *After Disney, you had a couple of TV directing assignments:*
"Aladdin's Lamp," and "The Jar," for Alfred Hitchcock *Presents.*
BURTON: "Aladdin's Lamp" I guess was my first "directing" assignment. I did that right after *Frankenweenie*, for Shelley Duvall's *Faerie*
Tale Theater. It was a three-camera video thing and I didn't know what
the fuck I was doing. It came out looking like a Las Vegas show. "The
Jar" was my only other assignment, a case where it didn't work out
again. That's when I realized that nobody should treat me like a director, because I'm not. What we long for in the world is people doing
their own thing. I don't consider myself a director. I don't have the
capabilities. I can't use technique and proficiency, I can't hide behind
those things, because I don't have them. My shortcomings will quickly
come into play.

BRESKIN: *Do you still feel unaccomplished?*
BURTON: Well, I don't really care about that. I'm learning more
and more, but I'm relatively new to the whole thing. It's a mistake
for me, maybe, to try certain things.

BRESKIN: *You've admitted that your movies are "flawed" and that they*
could be shot full of holes.
BURTON: I think it stems from *story*. It makes me a little sad sometimes. People peg you. And they don't know what you go through with

studio people and executives, and they take their cue a lot from critics, and the feeling is that "Tim can't tell a story out of a paper bag." And when they peg you, then that's what they feed upon and that's their fight with you. And every time, when you're developing a script and you're talking to the studio and you have these stupid script meetings with them, I can say that if there is a problem with the movie it is *nothing* that you discussed. Nothing at all. So when you're fighting that, it does make you a little sad. And now, it's turning out to be a little boring. And *Beetlejuice* was kind of the one movie for me that gave me, again, that feeling of humanity, that *Fuck Everybody!* That made me feel very good, that the audience didn't need a certain kind of thing. Movies can be different things! Wouldn't it be great if the world allowed David Cronenberg to do his thing and people could tell the difference! And criticism would be on a whole other level! And the world would be on a whole other level!

BRESKIN: *But studios have the expectation that each film will be like one of those cookies coming off the cookie assembly line in* Scissorhands, *and that there are only three or four different shapes of cookies allowed.*
BURTON: Well, they're wrong! It's like with Warner Bros., because that's where my history has mainly been. I'm always amazed—movies that they fight tooth and nail, and are always the weirdest, those are the ones that end up making them all the money. All they have to do is look at their fucking slate of movies! The proof is there. Fuck! Fuck your system! Whoever's making the movie, give him a chance to make the movie, and you'll have a fifty percent chance of failing or succeeding, or working or not, and that's as good of a chance as you'll get on anything, and you're not going to do anything that's going to make it any better! So why not, if something is going to be flawed, why not have it be interestingly flawed, as opposed to boringly flawed? Why lower things? Why not let there be different things? Some people are better storytellers, some people are better at other things.

BRESKIN: *You don't feel that your "problem with narrative" is really a problem?*
BURTON: Well, I feel that less and less. Because now it's become redundant. And the fact is, I'm more interested in growing in ways I

don't even know about. Maybe I'll become better at it, maybe things will become more abstract.

BRESKIN: *Would you junk narrative if you could? Because you indicated once that if you were left to your own devices, "the result will always be very commercial because that's the way I think."*

BURTON: Well, I don't even know what that is. It's best for me not to say, "Everybody says I can't tell a story, maybe I should really *try* here." I don't think I will ever consciously try to do that. But what's important is to keep moving and to hone in and to keep exploring. I don't know whether the storytelling will get better, or *worse*, more abstract or clearer, or whether it will become its own form—because the thing that's always been very important to me is the visuals as story. The images, for me, *are* the story. It's not that it looks great or funny or cartoony. If I were to hone myself, it would be: how could I make images feel a certain way, so that what you're looking at is the *thing*? That's a desire, that's a goal.

BRESKIN: *You got closer to that in* Scissorhands, *where the feeling of the film is actually in the images themselves, rather than in the story.*

BURTON: I feel that way. And I feel like that's the thing for me to try to do. That's the thing I'm interested in. That energizes me.

BRESKIN: *It's a very abstract and pure enterprise, that attempt.*

BURTON: Yeah, it is. See, the problem with Hollywood is that you're always fighting the *same* thing. It doesn't change. They don't change their tune. And it gets really boring.

BRESKIN: *So why not just use the machinery of Hollywood, but do your work more independently, as Cronenberg does?*

BURTON: Well, that's interesting, and I think I'm certainly in that area now to find out. See, I've never talked to somebody like him, and perhaps I should. I think I'm getting there, I do. The odd thing for me is that I grew up in the studio system. And it's been odd to feel like I could do what I want, and have had the ability to do what I want, in a system that doesn't seem to allow that very much. I always felt like, if you're not getting it from these guys, you're getting it from some French guy or something. There's always going to be some problem. But now I'm getting to the point where maybe it's time to deal with somebody *else*, because it's getting too retarded and inbred among these people. I can't hear these same things from these same people anymore. I'd rather hear it from some French guy!

What they don't understand, no matter how anybody perceives me in Hollywood, is you're still trying to make something—film is still an art form. And you go through the same anguish as any artist does creating something. But this doesn't enter into their thinking. You can go along with it for a while, and laugh your way through it, but then you have to move along, because it gets redundant and you get angrier and angrier. Where I wouldn't get angry before, now I get angry and start to see red in a split second. I just fly off the handle now. It's anti-creative. It's not helping anything. It doesn't even help them get the movie made! I understand their goal, their goal is simple: take this movie, make it commercial, make it good, we want to make a lot of money on it! I understand that, that's fine. But I can't go through it anymore.

BRESKIN: *Forgetting the "they" for a while, I'm interested in what you feel the flaws or weaknesses of your films are.*

BURTON: It's funny, there's two levels to that. On an emotional level, I never feel bad about it. I don't have children, but to me it's like giving your child plastic surgery. I accept them, and on a very weird level I *love* them for their flaws. Now, there's a technical side of me that sees I could have cut this, or that could have been shorter; that's the boring, technical side. But on the emotional side, you accept them. What if you had a five-year-old with a whatever—would you give him plastic surgery? I wouldn't do that, because part of the joy in life is in the flaws. I feel a very strong emotional connection to everything, and treat them as a part of myself. The only movie I feel colder about is the first *Batman*. I feel close to parts of it, but it's not as emotional a connection as to everything else.

BRESKIN: *In that movie, Vicki Vale [Kim Basinger] asks Bruce Wayne [Michael Keaton] about his mansion, because she thinks it doesn't seem*

like him, and he says, "Some of it is very much me and some of it isn't."
And I felt that was Tim Burton talking there, about his movie.
BURTON: [Laughs.] Sure! Sure. That's why I decided to do another one.
Because I love the themes of it. I have to have those little links with it,
because that's the only thing that really keeps me going, otherwise I
couldn't do it. I don't have the technical talent to not have that.

BRESKIN: *Do you think you're disrespected by some people in the industry*
because you don't have that technical talent?
BURTON: I don't know. Nobody is perceived any one way. I'm in an
odd position. I'm looked at by independents as somebody in the studio
system. And I'm looked at in the system as somebody who's very lucky.
But I'm not in the system. I don't hang out with members of the
Academy, so to speak. I'm not entrenched in it. So I don't have many
friends in either world.

BRESKIN: *Do you feel any kind of simpatico vibration with silent film? It's*
not that dialogue doesn't matter in your work; it's that I can imagine your
films without it, and with their great scores.
BURTON: I think I know what you're saying. I actually don't like silent
films. I never got into them, and to this day I don't get into them. I find
them dated. I'm not into Charlie Chaplin. I guess though, the fact is, it
is true, that I find dialogue and speaking kind of meaningless unless
they're saying something. I think this has more to do with myself, my
own feelings of verbalization and communication and what words
mean to me. I am uncomfortable with dialogue. I do enjoy, when I'm
working, scenes where people are *not* talking. I do feel more comfortable with that.

BRESKIN: *But the type of melodramatic emotions of the silents, the kind of*
overweening dramatic elements, has a kind of resonance with your work—
BURTON: Yeah, but that maybe has more to do with the horror
films, in a way. Because they always had that feeling, the Edgar Allan
Poe thing. It doesn't come from silents, for me. They leave me cold.
I actually find them kind of cold and calculated. Whereas the grand
melodramatic emotion of horror movies was more of an attraction.
I like dialogue to some degree. It's just that, like in life, what you

say is not necessarily what you are *saying*. I just feel that too strongly to be able to do something where people are talking and it's being completely meaningful, because that's not the way I think and that's not my experience with people talking. God, all you've got to do is go to a studio executive meeting to understand that! [Manic laugh.]

BRESKIN: *Music is obviously hugely important to your work. The bond between your images and Danny Elfman's music is so tight that when I watch one of your movies I feel like I'm listening to them.*
BURTON: Well, exactly. Believe me, I feel I'm very lucky. I used to go see Oingo Boingo at clubs, when I was a student. It's like a dream come true to me to meet him, work with him. I'd sit there in the clubs and have this connection. There's nobody better for me. That's where a part of the idea of the silent film works—his music is part of the story. Every director will tell you, [as pretentious snob director:] "The sets and the music are part of the character of the film." It's bull-shit! Nobody knows how important music is to my things better than me, I guarantee. It is as important as some of the actors or anything, if not more important. Danny is an actor in the films.

BRESKIN: *His music really does seem like the fuel that powers your films.*
BURTON: Let me tell you: I will now only test my films once the score is in. It's too painful the other way. I remember testing *Beetlejuice* with no music and then with music. The difference was shocking! And it really has to do with the fact that when you're doing a movie where people don't know what the fuck is going on, the music is the guide-post, it's the tone and the context. Danny and I don't even have to talk about it. We don't even have to intellectualize—which is good for both of us, we're both similar that way. We're very lucky to connect. It's one of the most fun aspects of filmmaking. That's one of the things I look forward to: walking onto the stage with an orchestra and seeing live music being played to certain images. It's something that no one will see and is actually so exciting!

BRESKIN: *Let's talk about screenwriting. Do you think you'll ever write your own screenplay?*

BURTON: That's an uncharted thing for me. I don't know how writers really feel about me. I'm respectful, and I do enjoy working with people, but then I get on a set, and things change, and I really don't go by what anybody says or writes. I have great effect on what I do. And I don't know how people really feel about that. Most of my friends are writers, because I identify with what they go through. In terms of the artistic pain, they're in a bad place in Hollywood. I can relate to them. I feel closer to them. But I don't know how they really feel about me, really.

BRESKIN: *Why don't you do the writing yourself? Even on* Frankenweenie, *which was clearly your story, you had someone else write the screenplay, and also on* Scissorhands—*if ever there was a project where you would have been a natural choice to do it, that was it, and yet you didn't write it.*
BURTON: I may need somebody else as a balancing point for myself, no matter how much I change or push or whatever. That is one thing I've certainly thought about and I am thinking about it, and I think I need to try to write one, just to see where it is I am. It's like on *Beetlejuice*: everything I've done I feel has equal parts writer, director, and actors. I think if you read original scripts of everything I've done, and looked at the film, you'd see lots and lots and lots of changes.

BRESKIN: *And yet you, for some bizarre reason, have insisted that you're not an auteur. You said, "I know I'm not an auteur because I try to listen to people," as if that would disqualify you? The fact is, if you can put your stamp on all these films without actually writing them, that's more of a sign that you are an auteur.*
BURTON: I think what that comment says is that I don't really know what the fuck I'm talking about. I think that sums the whole thing up. [Manic laugh.] Lookit, I'm relatively new to all of this, and I have a very tough time with words. A lot of words don't have meaning to me, because I have no context with them. The words "normal" or "auteur"—there are probably several words that actually I don't really know what they mean. Part of that is just my inexperience and naiveté. I *do* believe that the director has to be the person whose movie it is. Whose else is it? If it's the actor's movie, then you don't need a director—let the actor direct it. It's got to be the director.

BRESKIN: *Since you do have such a strong take on things, perhaps paradoxically it's helpful for you to rub up against someone else's material.*
BURTON: Perhaps it is. There's always that whole argument about artistic suffering. I've wavered on that. At one point, where I was near suicidal, I didn't want to be completely suffering to create. That's completely negative. So then you work more positive aspects into your life, but it comes back to butting up against something. Maybe it's just always there. There's no such thing as anything being perfect, so maybe if you got that, you'd be a zombie by that point. [Laughs.] If things were perfect, you wouldn't want to do anything.

Whether or not it's your thing [the story and screenplay], you have to walk into a picture feeling like it's your thing. I walked into *Pee-wee's Big Adventure* and I felt one hundred percent connected to it. I understood it and it was mine, even though here was a character that was already created. I couldn't have done it—even with the chance of doing a first film—unless that feeling was one hundred percent there.

So the question is, should I or can I write, because I've got a bunch of ideas which I'd like to do. I think my biggest problem is focusing, because I get a little scatterbrained. What I'm curious about is finding out whether you go through more in working with other people than what I would have to go through in doing something myself. I'd like to go through as little torment as possible, because it's all tormenting.

BRESKIN: *You're known as someone who will cast an actor without first seeing their work. Is that true?*
BURTON: Casting is the one area that's really down to taste and choice. You can sit in a room with studio executives and casting people and blah blah blah, and argue who's right for a part and who's wrong for a part. There are probably cases where people are right or people are wrong, but there's a whole big area where it finally comes down to a guess. Once you make a decision, I prefer not to think about their other work.

One thing I realize now is that I don't want to work with actors who care about anything other than what they are doing. People who care about how they look—it's not interesting. You've got to work with people whose passion makes it exciting. They are trying to take something that is absurd, and not real, and in whatever way, invest it with some sort of life. I find that very exciting. So their attitude is very important. I also like to *like* people; it's really kind of psychotic. Part of the energy, with me, is working through things with people, and liking them. I don't want to work with people who have a different agenda.

BRESKIN: *There were a number of hours of discussion with Tom Cruise about him playing Edward Scissorhands. And part of the issue was his concern about the virility, or lack thereof, of the character.*

BURTON: [Manic laugh.] I thought that was a little odd. It kind of struck me from left field, because I certainly wasn't thinking about that. I didn't think it was worth writing a scene where Edward goes to a bar with a bunch of guys and ogles the babes! Or scores with the chicks! Or we see him watching a Raiders game! There comes a point where actors have too many fears—there's too much intellectualizing about the process. I understand him wanting to understand the character, wanting to understand me—you have to go through quite a lot to get that—but there comes a point where their fears are too great, and it makes you realize they shouldn't do it. You need to work with people who will go, "Well, fuck it! Let's do it!" That's exciting.

BRESKIN: *But are there situations when you will cast someone without having seen his or her work?*

BURTON: I *prefer* not to have seen it. I didn't know Michael Keaton's work at all before *Beetlejuice*. I actually liked that. Because I felt like I was getting to know somebody, for myself, freshly, and that excited me. And with Kim Basinger on *Batman*, if I had seen her work, I probably would have said, "Ugh! No!" We needed someone in a time frame in that case and I ended up really liking her, I *liked* her, when I met her. People talk—"this person is an asshole" or "that person is a monster"—there is so much categorization and I prefer not to go through that, and just have my own feeling about somebody, and not listen to what everybody says.

BRESKIN: *As you don't have any theatre or acting background yourself, I'd guess the level of discussion between you and your actors can get fairly abstract.*

BURTON: Yes. Part of the luck I've had is to be around actors who have been willing to go through that with me. That's what the process is all about. Part of the enjoyment is to watch these people dressed up in their funny costumes trying to bring something to life.

Session Two

BRESKIN: *I'd like to go through each of your five features, beginning with* Pee-wee's Big Adventure. *Although that was perceived as a children's picture, there was a lot of very adult stuff in it.*
BURTON: Well, I don't think of kids or adults. What's child? What's adult? Everybody is everything. It has more to do with a feeling. You don't get rid of who you are or where you come from, but the point is: everybody is trying to get back to a certain kind of purity anyway. Why are people looking for escape in movies or drugs or drinking or going to amusement parks? Or anything? Why does anybody read? Because it's a form of escape, or a form of recapturing not a "childish" impulse, but a way of looking at the world as if it were fresh and interesting. It has less to do with being a child than with keeping an open, wonderful, twisted view of the world.

BRESKIN: *Did it occur to you during the process of making that movie how phallic the story is?*
BURTON: [Laughing.] I mean the whole thing . . . you strip down any story or any fairy tale and you pretty much come down to the same thing, don't you?

BRESKIN: *Yeah, but that was fairly relentlessly phallic.*
BURTON: I find that if those things come out, then it's pretty much what it was about anyway. It's the unconscious. The time to worry is when you're consciously thinking about that stuff.

BRESKIN: *Well, you would have to have been in a stupor not to have been thinking about it during the filming. There are many, many lines of dialogue that are explicitly sexual, not to mention the basic story of a boy obsessed with his bike. You couldn't have been shooting that and not been conscious of the implications.*

BURTON: I grew up with a fascination for people that were dangerous. Why a fascination with clowns? Why do I like clowns so much? Why are they so powerful to children? Probably because they are dangerous. That kind of danger is really what it's all about. It's playing with that to a degree. It's that kind of stuff that I think gets you through life. Those are the only things worth expressing, in some ways: danger, and presenting subversive subject matter in a fun way. I link this stuff to the power of fairy tales. All roads lead to them, for me, because of what I think the purpose is of them.

BRESKIN: *What is the purpose and the function of fairy tales?*
BURTON: I think it does have to do with whatever that young impulse is—whatever you want to call that. Who are we? How are we created? What else is out there? What happens when you die? All that stuff is unknown. Life is unknown. Everything is under the umbrella of life and death and the unknown, and a mixture of good and bad, and funny and sad, and everything at once. It's weirdly complicated. And I find that fairy tales acknowledge that. They acknowledge the absurdity, they acknowledge the reality, but in a way that is beyond real. Therefore, I find *that* more real.

BRESKIN: *Does there need to be a moral, or something edifying, to make a fairy tale work?*
BURTON: Well, we're talking about the movie industry. There are things to be dealt with. I don't think it's necessary, personally. As a culture, and as an industry, people are looking for that, for sure. Especially the whole "happy ending" routine. They always like a happy ending.

BRESKIN: *Why do people seem to need that? You don't need it.*
BURTON: I don't need a happy ending. I feel much happier coming out of a movie like *Sid and Nancy* than I do . . . *Ghost* or something. I feel like: yes, I understand, and I love it and I get it, and because it acknowledges a certain way that I feel about life, I actually feel better. I see something like that and it makes me happy.

BRESKIN: *Because tragedy is what makes sense to you.*
BURTON: It does make sense. I think life ultimately is tragic, but in ultimately a very positive way. We all die. It is tragic. You go through

many tragic things in your life, but that's not necessarily bad. That's what I love about playing with tragedy in a fun way. [Laughs.] That's what I loved about *Pee-wee*. He was into something, in a passionate way, and it didn't matter what it was about. He was into it.

BRESKIN: *Pee-wee says to the girl who desires him, brushing her off: "There's lots of things about me you wouldn't understand, you couldn't understand, you shouldn't understand."*
BURTON: [Manic laugh.] So I didn't ask! Because I understood.

BRESKIN: *It's interesting, because we could say the same thing about all your protagonists: Beetlejuice, Bruce Wayne, Edward Scissorhands, they're all misunderstood.*
BURTON: It's very true, I think. Definitely. Who can pretend to know about themselves? It's too complicated, there are too many crossed signals, there are too many split sides and dynamics. Does anybody know who they are, really? Does anybody feel integrated? I mean, I don't know anybody who does. I don't certainly pretend to know myself. So for me, I find this dynamic to be realistic. And I enjoy it. It's often fun not to know things about people.

BRESKIN: *What about, in* Pee-wee, *the kind of sexual threat from women that hangs over the character during the whole odyssey he's on?*
BURTON: I guess the Pee-wee character is immature. It does go back to childish impulses, in a way. My take on what he's doing is that it's a perversion, there's no question about it. That's what's great about it. This weird, alternative character that's protecting, that's fighting off things in the world—and has mutated into something that's *separate*. I just see him as an outside character dealing with the world, in a heightened way. It had less to do with his bike than it did with just the idea of passion about something that nobody else cares about. I kind of feel that way about . . . *the movies!* [Laughs.] I make these things that are very hard to make—that are not pictures with a message, by most people's standards—so I identify with a character who is passionate about something that nobody else really cares about.

BRESKIN: *Edward Scissorhands is also an "outside character dealing with the world." But you brought a lot more baggage to him, since you'd had the idea first in high school, and had lived with it, and there were clear correspondences between Tim Burton and Edward Scissorhands.*

BURTON: Yeah, well, it was a different thing for me, and I tried, very hard, not to be too self-involved. See, I saw that character more thematically than personally. Again, I saw it as much more fucked up. I tried to make it—you know what I'm saying.

BRESKIN: *Yes, you said you tried not to make it too personal because you wanted it to be universal. But the more personal you make something, whether it be a poem or a song or whatever, if it's true, if it's pure, the more universal it is. So why the fear that the tighter the bond between you and Edward, the less universal the picture?*

BURTON: I guess because I don't know enough about myself. I'm not integrated enough yet. I don't know if that will ever happen. It just shows you how unintegrated I am, because the kind of characters that I enjoy are the kind of characters that aren't integrated. [Laughs.] So that's about as personal as it could get. Let's put it this way: I'm interested in the personal, because I take everything personally. I take Pee-wee, and Beetlejuice and Edward and Batman—I feel very close to those characters. I really do. I feel like they are mutated children. They mean a lot to me.

BRESKIN: *It's clearly where you find meaning in the movies.*

BURTON: Exactly. But there again, these characters are all fucked up. They are impurely pure. If Batman got therapy, he probably wouldn't be doing this, he wouldn't be putting on this bat suit and we wouldn't have this weird guy running around in a cape. So there is a form of things not being integrated that is quite appealing. So I don't know if I'm *stuck* or if I *enjoy* being stuck at that moment. Know what I mean? There is a charm about characters that know not what they do, but do it purely. Even Beetlejuice is that way. There's a charm in that which I enjoy.

BRESKIN: *Let me play Satan's helper here. Edward Scissorhands is a pathetic, beautiful, ridiculous but funny character, whose heart is always breaking—it's Tim Burton saying how sensitive he is, that he's the oversensitive artist, who as a child could not touch, could not communicate, without hurting. That's obvious. That's an obvious reading of the film.*

BURTON: [Laughs.] Sure. Right.

BRESKIN: *How does it make you feel when you get that reading?*

BURTON: Well, I guess it makes me feel that I wasn't one hundred percent successful. When you do a fairy tale, you are a little bit at odds with yourself. Because a fairy tale is a romantic version of certain things. Taking something real and heightening it. So what you have is an inherent balancing problem between the real and the unreal. I think that's where I run into trouble a lot of the time, because of the unwieldy nature of it. And then you've got Johnny Depp [playing Edward] who brings a certain thing to it himself. Actually, it turned into more my perception of him, in a way—what I saw in him, what he goes through, how he's perceived—than even of myself. It's unwieldy, it's unbalanced, and there's a constant desire on my part to find the right balance. And you know what? I'll take the hit, and miss with it, because it's the only thing that really makes it fun. So that thing probably does make me uncomfortable, but I did it.

BRESKIN: *Well, it was a harder shoot for you, emotionally, because of that.*

BURTON: I was very moody. I was very interiorized. And I don't think it had completely to do with being in Florida, though that helped. That's a weird place. It really had a lot to do with how I felt about having the background that I did. It *was* personal. But whatever worked or didn't work is part of the nature of it.

BRESKIN: *Kim [Winona Ryder] at the beginning, as the old woman, says of Edward, "The man was left by himself, incomplete and all alone."*

BURTON: Well, there again, it's that tragic thing. There is that tragic element of fairy tales. Everybody can look at it and go, "Aww!" If that is the case, then I have not been successful in what I was trying to do. See, I'm interested in the grandeur of tragedy. And I didn't want people to look at that and go, "Aww! Poor character!" I see it as just like life: you're up against a lot. I see the ending not as, "Oh gee, the poor character doesn't get what he wants," I saw it more as, "This is the way things are. You get some good things and you get some bad things." It's not a happy ending, it's not a sad ending to me—it's more a symbolic ending. Some things work out and some things don't.

BRESKIN: *Why was it necessary to kill Kim's evil boyfriend, Jim? That shocked a lot of people—because the tone of the movie changed.*

BURTON: See, that's again how people misperceive fairy tales. I'm not interested in softening what that's all about. Yeah, I think it was completely necessary. And I think it's belittling the idea of a fairy tale—I think it's a mutation of our culture. People's idea of a fairy tale is that it's all white. Why don't they read one of them!

BRESKIN: *It's some of the nastiest stuff in the world.*

BURTON: Exactly. It's about as disturbing as it gets, for anything. And the point is, it has more to with the homogenization of our culture, and that needs to be fought, on all counts and by everybody.

BRESKIN: *The first words of a movie are usually important. Here, they are Kim saying, "Snuggle in, sweetie, it's cold out there." To me, that could almost be the epitaph to the entire film—and not because it's snowing.*

BURTON: Yeah. Everybody goes through it every day. It's not the most sensitive place. [Pause.] Lookit, if you analyze what you go through in a day, in your job, when is anything completely one way? And you know what, you can drive yourself crazy thinking about it. Good and bad. Positive and negative. Funny and sad. Every second is a flip-flop of some feeling. And ultimately, that's what it's all about. It's unbelievably complicated. *I don't get it, but I get it:* that, to me, is about as real as it gets. That's why I hate most movies. They kind of simplistically tell you what they are all about. They don't capture what life is about in any way. What am I talking about? I have no idea.

People are weird. And I think we forget, because we're so intelligent, that we are all basically animals. Animal instincts take over all the time, under the surface of things. People say to me, "Oh, you must be really happy!" Well, there's no sense of happiness, there's no connection to anybody, people aren't being nice to you because they really want to be, a lot of the time. You know who your friends are—people you like and respond to—and you know when it is complete bullshit. And most of the time it is bullshit. It's not like anybody acting real to you. Because there's no real context anymore. Especially, here, where it's all *business*, even the social. And America is founded on that principle—that's why everybody is over here to begin with. That's the whole point. It's frightening.

BRESKIN: *If these characters are the repositories of meaning for you, I'd like to talk about each of them. We've talked about Pee-wee already. What does Edward Scissorhands mean to you?*

BURTON: I loved the idea—and this did go with an impulse that I felt, and still feel, and I think a lot of people feel—of feeling misperceived, the feeling of being sensitive, and overly sensitive, and wanting things you can't get. I remember going through a very strong feeling, a very teenage feeling, of not being able to touch or communicate. I had that, very strongly. I've never been a very physical person. I didn't grow up in a way that was very physical. And I always resisted that. So there are simplistic things like that—which I would call the melodramatic teenage impulses. And then the subtext of presenting yourself in such a way that is not the way you are meaning. For me, I saw that character as all of that. He is a way that you feel: what you say is not coming across, what you want is misperceived. Just a way of seeing the world. I often feel, I look at things and see them in a way, and wonder if anybody else is seeing them that way. It's really just about each person feeling very individual. And just on a humorous level, I love a character that is open and sensitive to everything. There is something very funny and tragic about that. I've known people like that, that are overly sensitive, and you know what? It's *sad.* I've known five people in my life who are overly sensitive, and the pain and the torture they go through—it's almost funny.

BRESKIN: *You wouldn't include yourself in that group?*

BURTON: Again, I don't analyze myself. [Pause.] I have that tendency, yes.

BRESKIN: *Do you feel there's been some movement in you, away from that adolescent angst?*

BURTON: Do I feel like I've changed in that way? I think that you exorcise that, but I don't think you ever completely know if it's exorcised. I think it moves along a little bit.

BRESKIN: *Let's talk about some of the small, quirky things you put in Edward Scissorhands. The striped, canvas house that's in a couple of early frames. Are they supposed to be fumigating it?*

BURTON: That's just a little pest control.

BRESKIN: *It looks like a circus tent.*

BURTON: Yes. I have a lot of little things that nobody ever gets, but are there just for myself, like that. That was just the interlinking of the idea of a circus-like atmosphere, and the theme of getting rid of pests.

BRESKIN: *As they are going to want to get rid of Edward. There's also a soundtrack foreshadow, about a third of the way through. When the boys are up in the treehouse, listening to the baseball game on the radio, and Edward is below them, starting to cut his first hedges. The announcer describes a home run, and he says, "It's gone . . . it's out of here . . . it's history!" Now, I'm sure the first time through, nobody really gets that, but the second time through, it just leaps out: what's "out of there" and what's going to be "history" is him, Edward.*

BURTON: That's another theme that I love. I love the links between things. You take something that is a baseball game, that is in this world, and you make a direct link. Again, since we have no culture, it's just so interesting to explore things that way. It's too big to understand, but it is fun to see these links. Sometimes these things are planned, sometimes they are not. For me, they are the things that make me think it's great, that it's fun and it's worth doing. It makes you think that you're on some course.

BRESKIN: *What about Edward's "V" cap that he wears during and after the robbery that will be his downfall?*

BURTON: [Laughs silently.] We just had a couple of hats, and there was something about the image of that, something about that clicked. It was kind of like a weird, scissory peace sign. Something about that image, which has been used so many times before.

BRESKIN: *For "Victory," which this is not going to be!*

BURTON: Exactly. And it kind of points down to him. It was more of a feeling, in a way.

BRESKIN: *Many, many years ago you did a drawing of a gardener, without shears but with two long, sharp fingers on each hand, and he seems like a nascent Edward if there ever was one.*

BURTON: Yeah, yeah, yeah. It's an impulse from a long time ago, for sure.

BRESKIN: *What about the repeated offers to help Edward, in the film?*
Three different people tell him they know doctors who could help him, but
nothing ever comes of it.
BURTON: That's one of my favorite things. I've always loved that.
That's Hollywood, isn't it? "Yeah, yeah, we'll do your script." Or, "Yeah,
yeah, we'll do this or that." Again, is it the culture? They might as well
be saying "Have a nice day!"

BRESKIN: *How do you say "Fuck you" to someone in Hollywood? "Trust me."*
BURTON: Yeah, exactly. The meaning of things, to me, has gone out of
things. It's all like guilt—no one has any real intention of doing anything,
but it's actually just a cultural thing. It's unfortunate, because it makes
you not believe anything. And that's not a good place ever to get to.

BRESKIN: *In the script, or in the shooting, was there more between Edward*
and his inventor [Vincent Price] than there was in the finished film?
BURTON: No, not really. I just wanted to keep it what it was. I didn't
want to get into too literal a thing. It would have opened up a whole
can of worms, basically. I just tried to treat it as an idea of what was
going on. In some ways, the vagueness of all of that, or the blankness . . .
I didn't want to go into that. It's tough with these kind of characters.
Vagueness is a tough thing to get at, 'cause people don't quite know
what to make of it.

BRESKIN: *Well, that's the second great criticism of your work. One is that*
you can't storytell your way out of a paper bag, and two is that your charac-
ters, while they are fascinating, tend to stay emblematic—
BURTON: They're symbolic.

BRESKIN: *They tend not to grow, or push through, or develop in such a way*
that we come to understand them differently at the end of the movie than we
did upon introduction.
BURTON: Yeah. That may have a lot to do with my own problems. I
may not be integrated enough to get at that yet. Take the *Beetlejuice*
characters, for example, the ghosts [Alec Baldwin and Geena Davis]. I
loved those characters, but they were perceived as the *bland* characters.
I never saw them like that. The point is, they're stuck. They can only go

so far, and that's part of their problem—in life and in death. It's all in this limited framework. And I thought that was part of the theme. But again, it gets lost.

BRESKIN: *They can't have children and their name is "Mait-land."*
BURTON: Things get misperceived in the broad-stroke of the visuals. [Resigned.] Sometime, maybe things will all work out. I'll just keep trying.

BRESKIN: *Where's the meaning for you in the Beetlejuice character?*
BURTON: He's a classic character, a true fantasy character, the good side of that. The good side of being labeled, and misperceived, and put in a box, is that even though that is being done to you, you also have, in some ways, a complete freedom.

BRESKIN: *You're not responsible to anybody's idea of you.*
BURTON: Yes. You can dress how you want. You can act however you want. You can be however you want. "Well, that's just Tim." The freedom that comes with that is a sad kind of freedom—there's a freakish quality to all of that—but, it's got its benefits. And I think Beetlejuice shows the complete positive side of being misperceived, and being categorized as something different. He can do whatever he wants! He's horrible and everybody knows it, so he's a complete fantasy of all of that. That's part of the lure of movies, in a simplistic way—just the freedom. People respond to it. And then you put him up against the other characters, which are really about repression.

BRESKIN: *About the tyranny of their desires.*
BURTON: Yeah, they've got their house, they've got their world. I just love the dynamic between them. It's just very much like life.

BRESKIN: *During the filming of* Beetlejuice, *you apparently took a lot of flak from the studio about the "realism" of it. What were they talking about?*
BURTON: I don't know. I have problems, to this day, understanding. I go through these meetings, and you know what? It's just so tiring, because on anything that I've ever done, there's nothing that they can ever say or have ever said that is meaningful to the outcome of the picture. They say their normal things—"The third act needs work," or "It's

too dark"—they have a list of ten things in the Studio Executive List of Comments. None of it has any bearing on how the fucking thing turns out! So, on *Beetlejuice*, I was sitting there, thinking, realism? What do you mean, realism? The whole thing is fucking ridiculous. What are we talking about here? They often treat films as if they are radio shows. Unless every line says something, there are problems—almost as if they are doing a radio program. "You don't have to film it, we just can hear it!" So I had to fight that a lot.

BRESKIN: *I can't imagine anyone criticizing that movie for too much realism.*
BURTON: You'd be surprised. I went through a twenty-four-hour script meeting with them, over a two-day period, line by line, asking about this and that. Luckily, I bullshit my way through the whole thing. It's a big waste of time.

BRESKIN: *You said once that the things in your films which you really have to fight for turn out to be their shining moments. Like what?*
BURTON: Well, in *Beetlejuice*, little things that they would think were disturbing, like eating a cockroach. Anytime there was any kind of thing that was strong, in any way, shape, or form. Really, the movie industry, in my experience, rarely gets excited—they mainly approach things from a fearful point of view. That's why so many boring, bland things get made; they read ten scripts on a weekend, it's a good read, it's an easy read, you put the right elements in it, it's a great thing. The things that disturb them are things that jump out. It's almost why you get audited by the IRS! Things that jump out—whoa!—get you in trouble. The guy eats a cockroach? His head spins around? What's that coming out of Danny De Vito's mouth in *Batman Returns*? It's stuff that's based on fear. It's stuff that jumps out at 'em, really. And you know, it has a better chance of working if it's potentially risky than if it's not. Especially nowadays. It's proven itself.

BRESKIN: *Did you spend a lot of time when you were doing* Beetlejuice *thinking about what death might be like?*
BURTON: Sure! It's a classic. It occupies a little time, sure.

BRESKIN: *How much did your visual representation of the afterlife parallel what you actually think might go on?*

BURTON: What I'm reacting against is that people expect to be taken care of when they die. Which I find like giving up on life. I react very much against that impulse—these people that use religious belief as a way of disassociating themselves from their lives, and their responsibility for their lives. My feeling, in *Beetlejuice,* is a reaction against people doing that. I saw the Maitlands as those sort of people. I liked them, but they almost expected not to have to really deal with things because they'd be taken care of in the hereafter. And what I think is that basically you should never expect your problems to be taken care of, because they won't be. It's not necessarily bad, but it's an alternative universe where it's pretty much the same.

BRESKIN: *Hell is the continuation of life by other means.*
BURTON: [Laughs.] It's not necessarily hell. But they are experiencing hell, because they are expecting something nice and perhaps wonderful. That's the philosophy that I was most interested in, and that's what I enjoyed about it: they didn't get what they expected. If anything, why should the afterlife be any real different from *this*?

BRESKIN: *Let's turn to* Batman, *the first one. Now there were, Tim, some rough narrative spots. There were periods on that shoot where the script was being changed every day and you didn't have time to reflect upon the changes—*
BURTON: Yeah, it was bad.

BRESKIN: *—And you were, in your own words, "near death."*
BURTON: I was probably as sick as I've ever been, on a movie, all the time. I was out of it. I was sick. See, the problem is, it was my first big movie. There's all these people around. There's a different energy. There's no way to prepare. No way to prepare. More money. More tension. More fear. Everything: more, more, more. More. And I just let something happen which I'll try to never let happen again, which is to let the script unravel.

See, lookit, people in Hollywood, it's like territorialism, it's like animals peeing on little patches of ground. Unless somebody can do that, they don't think they're being creative. Hollywood is not *real*, it's not founded on reality, so there's a lot of subconscious paranoia. There's a lot of deep-down fear, people thinking: what's my worth? Am I necessary to this process? It's filled with that. And what happened on *Batman*, and I let it happen, is that the script unraveled. Here we started out with a script that everybody said—again, it's classic Hollywood—everybody goes, "Oh, it's a great script, it's a great script." But at the end of the day, they basically *shred* it. So it went from being the greatest script in the world to completely unraveling. And once it unravels, it unravels. You're there, you do it. I remember Jack Nicholson going, "Why am I going up the stairs?" I was like, "I don't know Jack, I'll tell you when you get up there." [Laughs.] And a lot of it had to do with dealing with the energies of the studio and the producers and everybody just being there and doing it. There was no one thing—it was a big animal.

BRESKIN: *What was the original ending, before you had to substitute the big deal in the tower?*
BURTON: God, I have no fucking idea. I have not a clue.

BRESKIN: *Well, a lot of those problems don't show up in the movie, or they show up, but we don't care about them, because we're swept forward by other things. But the one thing that everybody did care about is that the tension leading up to Vicki Vale finding out that Bruce Wayne is Batman is completely unresolved. She just walks into the Batcave and—*
BURTON: And obviously, that was one thing I got killed for. It was rough. I'll tell you exactly what the impulse was. The initial impulse, for me, and again, this is where I can go . . . 'cause I . . . I . . . my problem is, I can be a little belligerent. I can respond to things, like maybe when you read about those little kings in England or Egypt who go, when they're really young, [as petulant, spoiled child] "I don't care!" My impulse was, I said to myself, "Fuck this bullshit!" This is comic-book material. I thought, you know, who cares? Who really cares? But it was a mistake. It went too far.

BRESKIN: *We expect, at least, Bruce Wayne to play off of the fact that he is discovered there, by her, for the first time. But he doesn't. So the audience is left wondering, did he already know that she knew who he was? Did we miss something? And we don't know. So we're sort of thrust out of the narrative.*
BURTON: This is the trouble I have. This is where sometimes there will be big gaps in something that I do. I try very hard to create your own

environment. And so far it's worked out. But sometimes there will be a leap that people don't buy, they don't buy, they don't buy. They go, "Whoa!" and it takes them out of it. I don't want to take people out of something. I spend a large time trying not to have that happen.

BRESKIN: *Because the rule you are playing by, until then, is that you do want the audience involved in her quest to figure out who Bruce Wayne is and who Batman is.*

BURTON: Yes. Yes. Part of the problem with that movie is that there are two things I made mistakes on. I think it has to do with the nature of a big, big movie. Number one, I said, on the effects, "Let's do the effects like on *Beetlejuice*, where they're just kind of fun and all." Well, that did not work at all! Because it's perceived as a big movie with cheesy effects, as opposed to a movie like *Beetlejuice*, which is a small movie, and cheesy, and so it fits. Mistake! Same thing with the structure. The original script was laid out like a grand kind of thing. And also, because the push was in that direction, I was playing into strengths I don't have. I think that's why I wanted to do another one: so I could look at *Batman Returns*, and whether or not it worked out, I could feel about it as I did about other things. I do feel differently about the first *Batman* movie.

BRESKIN: *One of the interesting things about that movie is that the action sequences are not nearly as interesting as the rest of the movie.*

BURTON: There's a zillion great action directors and I'm not one of them. Yet this is the genre. On this new thing, I feel better about the action. It's not James Cameron. There are a few people that can jack things up to that kind of level, and why try? I feel like, in the second one, I tried something a bit more representative of myself. I do feel better about it than I did about the first. The action feels more like a part of the movie, as opposed to: here's the movie, and here comes some action, and I've seen better action in my day.

BRESKIN: *The other thing in the first one that felt horribly intrusive was the Prince music. We're in this Tim Burton world, and all of a sudden, like him or not, in rides Prince.*

BURTON: Yeah, it's true. It's the unholy alliance of me and . . .

BRESKIN: *Warner Bros. marketing, pure and simple?*

BURTON: This is what happened. You learn something new every day. Now, here is a guy, Prince, who was one of my favorites. I had just gone to see two of his concerts in London and I felt they were like the best concerts I'd ever seen. Okay. So. They're saying to me, these record guys, it needs this and that, and they give you this whole thing about it's an expensive movie so you need it. And what happens is, you get engaged in this world, and then there's no way out. There's too much money. There's this guy you respect and is good and has got this thing going. It got to a point where there was no turning back. And I don't want to get into that situation again.

BRESKIN: *It had to be painful for you to put that music into that movie.*

BURTON: It was . . . it was . . . it completely lost me. And it tainted a lot. It tainted something that I don't want to taint, which is how you feel about an artist. So it tainted a lot for me. And actually, I liked his album. I wish I could listen to it without the feel of what had happened. And you know what? To tell you the truth, I understand the marketing side of it. I think it would be cleaner if you created cross-marketing, where you don't have that taint, but you can still do things. The idea of somebody looking at a movie and getting ideas about it and doing a musical interpretation of it is a potentially wonderful idea. But it needs big thinking, and it needs truly interesting, creative business people to do that, and it's not at that level. It would be great to cross-over movies and opera and records and dance.

BRESKIN: *What's* Batman *about to you? Bruce Wayne's depression?*

BURTON: It's about depression and it's about lack of integration. It's about a character. Unfortunately, I always see it being about those things, not about some kind of hero who is saving the city from blah blah blah. If you asked me the plot of *Batman,* I couldn't tell you. It's about duality, it's about flip-sides, it's about a person who's completely fucked and doesn't know what he's doing. He's got good impulses, but he's not integrated. And it's about depression. It's about going through life, thinking you're doing something, trying very hard. And the Joker represents somebody who gets to act however he wants.

BRESKIN: *He's playing the Beetlejuice character.*

BURTON: Yeah. There are two kinds of people, even with double personalities. The ones that are fucked and they're still trying to muddle through life, and then the ones that are fucked and get to be completely free, and scary. And they're basically two fantasies. There are two sides.

BRESKIN: *Which one are you closer to?*

BURTON: Well, I'm probably closer to the Bruce Wayne character, but I much prefer the fantasy of the other. That's much more the liberating side of it.

BRESKIN: *It's curious that Bruce Wayne/Batman is actually the only character in the movie who's not a cartoon character, but a human being.*

BURTON: I get the most gravity out of him. That's why I like Michael Keaton in it. He's got that—all you got to do is look at him, and he looks fucked up. So, for me, the context is immediately there. He's an unintegrated, kind of goofy, sad, passionate, strong, misguided, in some ways quite clear and in some ways completely out-to-lunch-type character.

BRESKIN: *Why didn't you explore that more in the movie?*

BURTON: Because, again, I always found that the deeper you went, the more of an intrusion it was. Maybe there's a way to do it which I haven't figured out yet. I always felt trying to figure him out more would be too intrusive.

BRESKIN: *You don't want to demystify?*

BURTON: Yeah, there's something about not knowing which I like. That was always the impulse.

BRESKIN: *I assume there was a challenge for you in directing the sequel. Because you said a number of times that sequels don't interest you, unless there is a challenge—something for you to discover which you know nothing about.*

BURTON: New characters. New characters. New characters. New characters. I like them very much. Catwoman, Penguin, and the Christopher Walken character, I like him too. It's a smaller cast. It's much more . . . uh . . .

BRESKIN: *Interpersonal?*

BURTON: Yeah! I don't know what it is, but there's a different energy about it. I didn't analyze it except to say, I don't feel about *Batman* the way I do about my other movies. It has to do with an energy and finding another field. And I feel good about that. I don't know what it means. It could be bad for the movie, I don't know. But I was much more interested in it. And I find these other characters very compelling.

BRESKIN: *Is it more open to interpretation? When you did* Scissorhands, *you said it was nice to finally make a movie that was a little bit more open to interpretation than your first three pictures.*

BURTON: I guess if people get it, no. And if they don't, yeah. I don't know. It's hard for me to predict. It could be a big, giant mistake. I have not a clue. Part of the good thing is not knowing what worked on the first one. I certainly know what didn't work.

BRESKIN: *This one feels more personal to you?*

BURTON: Well, I feel like there's more effect. I feel like I learned some-thing. I feel better about this one. It sounds abstract, but it's really the only feeling I have about it. Lookit, it's an expensive movie, and they don't want you to say this kind of stuff, because it's like, "We're letting somebody do this, and he feels like *that?* Jesus!" Then they get more afraid, and it'll be harder the next movie.

BRESKIN: *I want to go back to talking about your filmmaking process. Do you draw everything first?*

BURTON: No, I don't get to the point where I draw every frame. I think the process is ongoing. I start by doing fairly naive sketches of characters, just for feeling, and then as it gets going, they get updated. It's more doodling. Sitting, talking on the phone, I do it. It's not that they are that elaborate, or that I say, [in deep, pretentious voice:] "I'm going to create this character." It's really a way for me to get my thought process out. It's really a way of thinking. I never used to even speak. That was the way I would speak. And I don't push it on people. It's really just a process I have.

BRESKIN: *You have such a strong visual sense that your production design and art direction people, whoever they are, have to be locked into that, otherwise—*

BURTON: It's meaningful, it's the one area that I feel, I guess, quite confident in. And I like working with people who are good, because they give you something. Most of the people who I've worked with have been very talented, and give you a lot. I prefer that, but I could do without.

BRESKIN: *Do you storyboard?*

BURTON: I used to, but I don't as much anymore. In fact, I'm getting anti-storyboard. I pretty much stopped on *Beetlejuice.* You storyboard things that need effects. I still do it to some degree. But certainly after the first *Batman,* I really stopped. And now, I can't even come up with— I'm getting very twisted about the whole thing. There's something about being spontaneous and working shots out. And when you work with these kind of actors—if they're good, you're just not going to give them a storyboard, and say, "Here." There's an energy and there's a working through things with people.

BRESKIN: *You're more comfortable with improvisation now?*

BURTON: Yeah. I've started to learn it. The most fun day I think I've ever had was on *Pee-wee's Big Adventure*, in the scene at the Alamo, with Jan Hooks, who played the guide. That was *all* improv, and it was so much fun. So I learned it on that, and that was Paul Reubens's background. And I realized that I loved it. And working with Michael Keaton and Catherine O'Hara on *Beetlejuice*—it was exciting, and it was a lot of fun! You get good stuff, sometimes. I think that kind of turned me into anti-storyboarding.

BRESKIN: *Are you a "first take" director?*

BURTON: No. It depends on the actors. I think my average is about seven to nine takes. There's always something technical fucked up and it depends on actors.

BRESKIN: *What's your favorite part of the process?*

BURTON: It's very private and it's very quiet. It's really the hardest part. It's the creation of being on the set and shooting. Right then and there. You're dealing with people that you like, and you're taking some weird idea and trying to make it work. You get that, with the layer of seeing stuff that people don't see, and the light, the way it hits the water, and a guy is sitting up there reading a cheesy magazine with this beautiful light behind him. And the people working on the movie are the greatest. Because they're the ones *working* on it. You're cutting through the bullshit of other things. That's the best thing about it. Those are the only people I can stand to be around.

BRESKIN: *I get the feeling that editing is fingernails-on-blackboards for you.*
BURTON: When I look at rushes I sometimes get chills because it reminds me of shooting, but editing? What can I tell you? I don't slap 'em together, but I'm not going to win any editing awards. It's okay. It's fine.

BRESKIN: *What about your camera? Do you feel it's as clunky as you used to?*
BURTON: Well, it's kind of moving around a little bit more. Things are happening. I'm getting a little more confident. I'm knowing about more things. But again, I never think about it too much. I'm getting much more now into looking at it, and trying to respond to it in the moment. Which gets me into trouble, with no storyboards . . .

BRESKIN: *Because it makes things technically more difficult.*
BURTON: It takes a little longer. I make up my mind very quickly, but I've got to do it when the time is right. Maybe I'm less professional. This is all stuff that worries people. Less professional, maybe more moody.

BRESKIN: *Do you go out to the movies?*
BURTON: I think because of living here—this sounds like a stupid cop-out but I don't have any other explanation, to tell you the truth—it just feels redundant. It's such a one-industry town. I grew up here, I live here, you go out and it's all movies. It just feels redundant.

BRESKIN: *So how do you see work you want to see? Go to screenings? Rent cassettes?*
BURTON: I guess, right now, I'm feeling kind of bad about it. For the past few years, I just don't go out and see movies very much. I rent things on videos, but not new stuff. I haven't seen much new stuff.

Somehow, when I'm in a video store, I go to the *lowest* common denominator. When I walk into a video store, I'm not going for the latest Martin Scorsese, I'm looking for the latest *Chainsaw Massacre Babe-o-rama Fest*. I can't help it! There's something about video where you seek the level of the medium.

BRESKIN: *Is there anybody's work out there that you feel connected to, or are interested in?*
BURTON: Well, I don't have a good answer. My answer is bullshit in a way. I mean, I know who I'm *for*. I mean, I do like David Cronenberg. He's great. Basically, you got to like anybody who's doing their thing, don't you?

BRESKIN: *You and David Lynch sometimes get put together in the same sentence.*
BURTON: But, don't you think that's because of categorization?

BRESKIN: *Maybe comparison and not categorization. You both have strong visual arts backgrounds, you both really struggle with the language, you both have an interesting take on—*
BURTON: But I'm sure that's true with lots of people. I grew up with reading critics bemoaning the state of movies, right? Everything is a conglomerate, everything's a cookie-cutter, and blah blah blah, and in fact, doesn't the categorization and lumping people further support that? When I was working Disney, I got the same thing, and this is why I have such a twisted interpretation of it. People would come into my office and say, "Oh, your drawings look like Charlie Brown." And then somebody else would say they look like something completely different. What's the point? The point is people are trying to categorize. Is it positive or is it negative?

BRESKIN: *It depends which side of the binoculars you're looking through. If you're looking through the wrong end of the binoculars, it makes everything smaller. If you're looking through the right end of the binoculars, by comparing and contrasting two bodies of work, it enlightens: it makes both richer, deeper.*
BURTON: But *you* know that, and I know that, but I guess my point is that in the context of the culture, a context of where things are headed

in terms of the arts, you know, it's *scary*. It's bad news. It's headed in a negative direction. And my point being (and I know what you're saying and there probably are a small group of people that would look at it in the positive way that you might look at it but) I'm afraid it does everybody a disservice. I was like tortured at Disney. I was treated like a king and tortured at the same time. It was like a farce. You are allowed to be in a room and do your own stuff, but then someone would go, "Oh, that looks like such and such." It's the way I took it. It was like Chinese water torture. Jesus Christ!

BRESKIN: *On the day of our first session, you changed agents. You left William Morris and joined CAA. How come?*
BURTON: Things happen. I guess it has its evil connotations. Everybody has a perception of CAA, and I'm not sure it's altogether untrue. But on a very personal level, things made sense. I've been very lucky, dealing with Hollywood, but nobody really knows . . . I just am very moody and I have my own agenda, and I don't even know what that is. But I know it's to fight a certain thing; it doesn't have to do with money, it doesn't have to do with position in the industry. Except that, in America, the better position you have, the more freedom you have— which I know now is not true completely. So that's why I'm always one hundred percent interested in finding out how to deal with this system. I don't want to get *hot* scripts. I don't like meeting actors. I'm not interested in any of that stuff. That's what Hollywood is all about, and I guess you could look at CAA and say they're the pinnacle of all that. But that's not the conversations with them I had. I had conversations where nothing was said literally, like "We're going to get you this, Tim"—I was just spoken to in a way I'd never been spoken to: as a person.

BRESKIN: *Not as an "artist"?*
BURTON: As a *person*. I wasn't out to change agencies, I love my agent. What mattered was, things were presented to me and I was spoken to in a way, it was almost uncanny. I've been trying to figure out how to deal with all this stuff, and to be in this industry. All I'm interested in is in punching through and trying to do interesting things. That's all.

BRESKIN: *You are interested in doing some theme-park attractions.*

BURTON: This is what I'm interested in: I'm not interested in anything literal. I'm interested in, if an idea comes up—and it could be painting a mural on a building, it could be doing an underwater Bob Hope special, it could be *anything*. See, what I'm tired of, to give you the clearest example, is that whole idea of marketing. Things are changing, and these people are not interesting thinkers, for the most part. They are not going to look at me and they are not going to look at you, and say, "Wouldn't you like to do interesting things? Wouldn't you like to *try* something?" See, I don't consider myself like a film director. I'm interested in openness, I'm interested in trying to create an environment for myself. I mean, I've gotten offers for things that are more money than anything. But I won't do it. No one understands. They think once you're hooked into the movie industry that you'll kind of do *whatever.*

BRESKIN: *"We've already established what you are, now we're just negotiating price." The famous punchline to the joke about the prostitute.*

BURTON: [Laughs.] It's that whole thing about what project is next. You know when you get there. And that's the only thing that will allow you to do it. You've got to have one hundred percent passion for it. See, part of my problem is, I'm a guy who is very discombobulated. I cannot, I realized fairly recently, deal with things the way other people do. Especially when people perceive you as something. For instance, I hate talking on the phone. You spend all day on the phone, and all that bullshit. People get upset with you if you don't return calls. In one week, you could end up having most of Hollywood angry at you, if you didn't return their calls. Now, I never returned my calls two, three years ago, but all of a sudden, it's a problem. I will *destroy* myself if I get into it.

BRESKIN: *What do you do when you're not working?*

BURTON: I'm never bored but I can't account for my time. What do I like to do? Fuck knows. I'm not a loiterer necessarily. I don't go down to 7-Eleven and hang out in the parking lot. I do my drawing and fool around with painting, I do enjoy that. But, I don't know. I'm not sitting there drooling and staring out of a window. I can't account for my time. Maybe that's why I was audited by the IRS. [Pause, laughs.] Maybe I *do* hang out at 7-Eleven parking lots.

BRESKIN: *You're not preparing for fatherhood, are you, Tim?*
BURTON: No, not yet. You can't prepare for that sort of thing.

BRESKIN: *Well, you can take steps to prevent it.*
BURTON: Well, those steps are being taken. We sleep in separate bedrooms, much like the Hayes Code. When we kiss, we both have one foot on the ground at all times.

BRESKIN: *You wear full-body condoms?*
BURTON: Yes, we wear full protective gear. And one foot on the floor at all times.

BRESKIN: *Because I know at one point you said that the idea of family for you was an impossibility.*
BURTON: Well, you know, it's a problem when you see too much. It usually happens with the firstborn. It's like a fucking lab experiment.

BRESKIN: *The first waffle gets burned, and tossed.*
BURTON: Exactly! How many firstborns do you know that are completely fucked up? And once the parents get through that, it's better. I'm just too *sensitive* for it, right now. I'm overly sensitive about it. I think I'd end up throwing little lizards on the child's bed to see what he'd do. Treating it much like the experiment that it is. It's an *experiment.* Let's throw water on it and see what it does!

BRESKIN: *Why bother making another movie, Tim? You hate putting them out.*
BURTON: It's like some sort of drug or virus, that takes over your body. The desire to do it is there.

BRESKIN: *What terrifies you so much about putting them out?*
BURTON: It's funny, I question it. It's a split. Obviously, I do this stuff. I'm talking to you. I'm not holing up in my castle in Switzerland, away from anybody, but I have a strong fear of letting this stuff out, for some reason.

BRESKIN: *What do you think you're afraid of?*
BURTON: I think because I don't know who I am. I think I haven't figured myself out. It's personal. The movie is my *baby*, and I'm putting it out there into the cruel world. It's scary, that's all. Just really scary.

BRESKIN: *What's the worst thing that could happen to it?*
BURTON: See, the worst thing that could happen, would be something you could understand. I wish they would tear down the screen, if they didn't like it. That would be the worst "good" thing that could happen. The worst "bad" thing would be . . . I don't know. It's fear of the unknown. Is anybody going to like this? It's judgment. Being categorized, and judged. I have a very strong aversion to that. I don't know where that comes from, but there it is. I'm in my little world, trying to do this film, then boom, it's out there. The film may have its unreality but the people that watch it are one hundred percent real people. And they always look angry. Everytime I go to these fucking screenings, the audience always looks angry to me. They look very scary. Its just fear.

BRESKIN: *You're not afraid of failing, are you?*
BURTON: It's funny, in some ways I'm not, and in some ways I guess I am. I will not base my decisions on what to do based on the thought of "success." So in some ways, I'm not afraid of that—I'll do what I want to do, and hope for the best. The fear just has to do with that aspect of *showing* it to people. I don't know if that's failure, or just the fear of coming out into the open.

BRESKIN: *You really kind of want to be in a cave, hanging upside down, with your drawing.*
BURTON: Yeah, but then again, I've been through that. At Disney, I was in my own little cave, and I was not getting out, and that's no good. Definitely, you want to get out and you want feedback. I think I am just afraid of it. I think that my impulse is to hide in the cave. Again, it's the split, it's Batman. It's classic, really, it's classic.

Dark Knight Director

MARC SHAPIRO/1992

Reality and fantasy tend to blur for Tim Burton when he's directing. Making *Batman Returns*, however, turned out to be a blur-and-a-half.

"When I was on the set, doing it every day, that movie became my total reality. Going outside the studio became the biggest fantasy. In fact, picking up my laundry was probably the most mind-blowing experience the whole time we were making this movie."

Picking up his shorts and socks has now become less terrifying for him, since *Batman Returns* wrapped up principal photography (and is due for release this month). Burton—whose speedy response to questions often takes side-trips into the eclectic—now feels at ease enough to discourse on the Dark Knight's further adventures while editing the film on what he calls "a nightmare schedule."

Helming *Batman Returns* ended the director's four-year-old promise that he would *not* be involved in any follow-ups to his 1989 megahit. "I wasn't blowing smoke to get a better deal," he says now.

"For a long time, 'No' was *exactly* the way I felt. The studio wanted to make a sequel the moment they knew the first film was successful, which was right after the opening weekend. I was in no way, shape, or form to do it at that point. So, I went away and did *Edward Scissorhands*. But, even after that, I still wasn't prepared to do it."

Part of Burton's reluctance stemmed from his own perfectionist nature that, upon subsequent viewings of *Batman*, brought to him the reality that he hadn't done a *perfect* job.

From *Starlog Magazine*, 180 (July 1992), 40–45, 75. Reprinted by permission.

"I would just keep looking at it and think it could have been better. I saw the first movie as being flawed. I didn't like the tone—what I did with the elements of darkness and mood, and the character relationships. I felt like I hadn't done 100 percent of what I *wanted* to do with that picture, and part of me felt that I wanted another chance at it."

Burton's indecision was fed early on by a *Batman* follow-up script by Sam Hamm that—while introducing Catwoman and the Penguin—ultimately didn't captivate the director.

"The earlier things happened, the less intrigued I was with the idea of doing another *Batman*. But I hoped something would happen to get me excited about doing it again. There was a feeling I had hoped to get by doing the first *Batman* that I didn't get. I wanted another chance at capturing [that feeling]."

However, the filmmaker's interest was piqued when Dan (*Heathers*) Waters came aboard and began a creative give-and-take with him. Five script drafts and a year later, Wesley (*Cape Fear*) Strick joined the endeavor as co-writer (although the script's actual credits are, at presstime, in arbitration).

"Dan's a very interesting writer with a funny point-of-view," relates Burton, "and he proved to be just the person I needed. The ideas were flying back and forth. We were attempting to piece together a story based on characters and a world that had no basis in reality. So, with both Dan, and later Wesley, it was a matter of going through ideas to try and get a perspective, and to figure out what the hell this *Batman Returns* thing was all about."

What Burton and the writers quickly discovered was that *Batman Returns* would ultimately live or die by establishing the characters of Catwoman and the Penguin as interesting, formidable foes for the Dark Knight.

"There was no rhyme or reason to include these particular villains," Burton explains. "Including them just seemed the logical thing to do. I didn't feel having two villains was absolutely necessary, but it added some variety by helping us avoid doing the same kind of explanation things we did with the *one* villain in the first film.

"I always felt that Catwoman was a strong character, but the Penguin presented a bit of a problem. For my money, he was the *least* interesting character in the comic books, and I could never figure out what the character was all about. But it seemed like a real challenge to take a character I basically didn't care for and make something out of him, which, as the script developed, we did."

Burton points out that villains, in general, tend to play a more integral part in Batman's world. "Unlike Superman, Batman isn't simply a good-vs.-evil thing. You get a lot of grey areas with Batman, and that was a major consideration in the script's development. I wanted the villains to be these weird but interesting characters who could fill in those grey areas in Batman's life."

According to Burton, fine-tuning Batman, and thus Bruce Wayne, was a classic example of less being more.

"We chose not to try and uncover any more skeletons about this guy. Batman has always been a tricky character because, by his nature, he wants to remain in the shadows. He's a tough character because he's so internalized.

"I got ragged on for the first movie because Jack [Nicholson] was so out there and Michael [Keaton] was laidback, but I didn't see any other way of doing it and keeping true to the character.

"Character-wise, we're not trying to up the ante with this film. We're not trying to make Batman too cynical or too dark. We didn't want to make him too dangerous or too aware, and Michael has been very clear on that. It took him a while to find that in his character in the first film, but he came in with it right away on *Batman Returns*. He's just this character dealing with other characters, so he's pretty close to where he was in *Batman*."

Burton recalls that the casting process, a pregnant Annette Bening's succession by Michelle Pfeiffer aside, "went pretty easy. It wasn't the typical casting situation; everybody knew they would be spending much of their time in costumes and makeup. In that sense, the whole casting process came down to choice. We knew who we wanted and hoped they would be interested. We were very lucky in that we got exactly who we went after."

Choosing to shoot *Batman Returns* in Los Angeles rather than take advantage of the remaining *Batman* Gotham City sets in England came as a surprise to many fans. Reports circulated that making the second *Batman* movie on Burton's home turf would put less pressure on the filmmaker.

"The movie *wasn't* shot in Los Angeles in an attempt to put less pressure on me," Burton responds. "It was just one of those corporate, logistical decisions. In many ways, I would have preferred doing it in England. I prefer to be away from Hollywood when I make my movies, because there's a lot of unnecessary stuff that goes on in this town that gets in the way of making the movie.

"In this case, it made sense to do it in LA or England because it was a big movie. We needed to be close to the things we would need, and doing it in Mexico—like it had been suggested at one point [at Churubusco Studios, where *Total Recall* filmed]—definitely would *not* have put us close to the things we would need," he chuckles.

What Burton probably needed that first day on the *Batman Returns* set was a tranquilizer. "That first day, I had what I would consider my normal case of nerves. I'm always kind of nervous and hyper. The first day is *never* a breeze. But I do remember that it was great, after all the preparation, to *finally* get to that point. Once the actual filmmaking process began, *Batman* became the normal thing; everything outside of that movie became frightening and ridiculous.

"We didn't film anything in the way of real deep character scenes, but there's more going on in this movie, on all levels, than in the first movie. I don't know if that's bad or good, but on a technical level, it did seem much more difficult.

"The action sequences were like several trips to the dentist," Burton quips. "We were faking everything, so it wasn't like everything could happen quickly. The action process was very specific, so it went a little slower than I would have liked. Trying to create big action on a limited soundstage can be a drag."

How painstaking it can become was evident during the filming of the rooftop battles between Batman and Catwoman.

"In that scene, we were dealing with complete fabrication. There was a lot going on and we were shooting things real tight. If we had moved the camera 1/16th of an inch up, you would have seen the studio ceiling. If we had moved it 1/16th of an inch down, you would have seen the floor. That was just the surface stuff. Now, imagine Catwoman in four-inch high heels trying to kick the *#$%¢ out of Batman while fighting on an upward-curving roof.

"But, I've got to hand it to Michelle. She took it upon herself to do all the weird stuff I had her do. In terms of selling the action scenes, she was so good, she was *better* than the stunt people."

The director turns inward at the suggestion that he describe his state of mind during the making of *Batman Returns*.

"If you had been a fly on the wall, you would have seen a morose, depressed person," says a semi-serious Burton. "I was moodier than I usually am on a movie, and I think part of that came from the fact that I was afraid doing a second *Batman* movie was going to weigh on my mind. I tried to think about it just often enough to where I wasn't damaging the kind of feeling I was trying to get across with this film."

Between Bat-outings, Burton combined fantasy and reality in the acclaimed *Edward Scissorhands*. "It was less of a logistical nightmare than the *Batman* movies have been," he notes, "but in a creative sense, it was probably just as taxing."

"I wanted to project something sweet and tender in that film, but, at the same time, keep reminding audiences that there was a sense of reality that had to be dealt with. Blending the two sides, knowing when to pull back on one to favor the other and how the whole thing would cut together, was an ongoing challenge."

After collecting dust on the Disney Studio shelves, two very early efforts from Burton's career, *Frankenweenie* and *Vincent*, are being released on video. "I feel good. I sort of distanced myself from both of those films for a long time. I kept hearing things were going to happen that never did, so I lost interest in keeping on top of them. But I'm glad that people will *finally* get a chance to see them."

Burton will face new challenges after *Batman Returns*. His projects include the animated *The Nightmare Before Christmas*, a movie musical version of the Japanese comic *Mai the Psychic Girl*, *Sweeney Todd* and, possibly, *Beetlejuice in Love*. The director claims "it's too early to talk about *The Nightmare Before Christmas*," and the other projects.

"It's really hard for me to figure out what I'm going to do *next*. I treat every movie like it's my next-and-last. I've gone through that melodrama with everything I've done. There was a lot of pressure to get me to do *Batman Returns*, but I couldn't say yes until something inside me got real excited about it. I don't go by money or anything else. Why I say yes to things is something I can't intellectualize. I just need the clarity and excitement in myself. When I have that, then I'll know what I'll do next."

Burton's "clarity and excitement" kicked in on *Batman Returns* when he was able to mentally remove the first film's excess baggage.

"Part of me will always think *Batman* was a big hit because it was a wonderful movie," he says. "But the reality is that *Batman* was a success because it was a cultural phenomena, which had less to do with the movie than with something else that I can't begin to put a finger on. I didn't see a second *Batman* movie falling victim to the same thing that happened with the first, so I felt free to just go in and make the best *Batman* movie I could.

"But, because I have that attitude, I sometimes find myself at odds with the studio people. This movie was harder to make because there had been a previous film, and that worries studio people. You can't just tell them that *Batman Returns* isn't a sequel, that it's just another movie. So, even though my attitude has been that it *wasn't* a sequel and that we're making a separate movie, I'm having to fight that out with other people, and even, occasionally, myself."

Fielding the inevitable question of whether he would return to do a third *Batman* film, Burton replies, "*Batman* movies are a perverse kind of business. Making them is unlike making any other kind of movie. That's kind of the long way around to saying that even if *Batman Returns* drops dead, I think there will be a *Batman 3*. There's *no way* I can think about doing it right now. Right now I would definitely say no—like I did the last time."

Burton's emotional roller-coaster ride on *Batman Returns* doesn't seem that far removed from the tortured/confused character he has now twice directed. Could it be that he keeps returning because he sees something of himself in the hero?

"I don't know if I would go so far as to say that Batman is my alter-ego," he concludes, "but I certainly do respond to his split personality and obsessions in wanting things done a certain way. He's just a weird guy who does strange things." Laughing, Tim Burton adds, "I wonder what that makes *me*?"

Ghoul World

MIMI AVINS / 1993

The naked woman stood immobile under the fluorescent lights until, in a brief stolen moment, she stretched, a flicker of relief crossing her previously expressionless face. Most of the group gathered for the life drawing class at the Burbank Adult School that evening were indigenous blue-haired ladies satisfying a long-dormant lust for creativity. A few guys, barely into their twenties, stood near the back of the room, including a rangy, towheaded artist intent on his sketch pad. These nude models, Henry Selick thought. They're always more what you'd call interesting than beautiful. The things you gotta do to keep your drawing skills up.

Unlike the model, the figure Selick's pencil described was a fully clothed male, wearing loose khaki pants, a rumpled short-sleeved shirt, and the kind of big Converse gym shoes that had been part of the unofficial uniform at Burbank High in the late '70s. With his anarchic black hair and long, slender fingers, Tim Burton seemed a far more compelling subject than the fleshy mannequin struggling to hold her pose. Selick finished his portrait of Burton and scrawled a caption: "Typical Disney geek."

Actually, of the young artists who flocked to Disney in the early '80s, eager to draw adorable little animals, few were less typical than Burton and Selick. Burton conjured up stories of ghoul-obsessed boys, and Selick found experimental German animation as inspirational as Mickey Mouse. Although they were both too weirdly gifted to stay at the studio for

From *Premiere*, November 1993: 102+. Reprinted with permission of *Premiere* magazine. Copyright 1993 Hachette Filipacchi Media U.S., Inc.

long, the fact that they have now, respectively, produced and directed a Disney feature is in itself a tale of the Revenge of the Art Nerds.

The movie is *Tim Burton's The Nightmare Before Christmas*, a twisted holiday fable that takes place on a night when the sky is so dark and the moon shines so bright and a million small children pretending to slumber nearly don't have a Christmas at all to remember. Although it is an animated musical, it is as different from recent Disney toons as Dr. Seuss is from Dr. Ruth. Sure, *Aladdin* was hip, but it still has a conventional hero, a hissable villain, and tunes that wouldn't be out of place in an old-fashioned Broadway musical. *Nightmare* features less melodic, narrative songs by Danny Elfman, the rock star—film score composer who put calypso in *Beetlejuice* and added musical menace to *Batman* and its sequel. A manic-depressive skeleton serves as the movie's confused antihero, and what he's up against is more a bad situation than a clearly identifiable bad guy.

And *Nightmare* isn't a cartoon. It uses an animation technique called stop motion that dates back to the silent era but has rarely been employed for a full-length feature. In the same way that drawn (or cel) animation projects 24 static, two-dimensional images per second to give the illusion of movement, in stop motion, three-dimensional puppets or objects appear animate because their positions are slightly altered in each frame of film.

The idea for *Nightmare* came to Burton a long time ago, longer now than it seems, in a place he had seen in his most favorite dreams. "I was born in Burbank, right down the street from the Disney studio," Burton says, "and like a lot of people who grew up liking to draw, I thought Disney would be a great place to do it. But the turnaround period from dream to nightmare was about as quick as it could get."

The early '80s were the Dark Ages at Disney animation, when charmless movies were worked on endlessly with scant enthusiasm. Burton was hopelessly miscast, set to drawing a fox named Vixey in *The Fox and the Hound* that matched Sandy Duncan's voice. "I felt they were saying, 'Okay, this is Disney—this is supposed to be the most incredible gathering of artists in the world.' At the same time they were saying, 'Just do it this way; shut up and become like a zombie factory worker.' After a while I was thinking, Is my restaurant job still available? I realized I'd rather be dead than work for five years on this movie."

While he was suffering from massive Disney disillusionment, Burton found allies—other misfits—such as Rick Heinrichs, a sculptor, and Selick, a former art prodigy from New Jersey who had already scored a grant to make a short animated film combining cel and stop-motion animation. They appreciated Burton's brilliant doodles—skeletons with pumpkins for heads, an odd Burbankite observed on the street, a canine Frankenstein—all rendered in his spidery drawing style. "I thought that people, especially kids, would love his work in the way they loved Charles Addams," says Selick. "But nobody recognized that at Disney. They thought, Oh, this is just too weird."

Times change. Studio heads' heads roll, and new management teams take power, bringing with them fresh philosophies. Fast-forward to 1989. After the critical and financial success of his first three features—*Peewee's Big Adventure, Beetlejuice,* and *Batman*—Burton was now Hollywood's great white hope (although he had taken to dressing only in black) and was savvy enough to know he had the clout to make a movie based on his dental records. Jeffrey Katzenberg was chairman of the Walt Disney Studios and a passionate supporter of its animation division, recognizing it as the studio's valuable birthright. Burton, flexing his new muscles, tried to rescue the children's story he conceived seven years before from the black hole it had fallen into at Disney.

The story, *Nightmare Before Christmas,* was written as a poem and described the parallel worlds of Halloweentown and Christmastown, where the holidays are made ready for presentation in the Real World (think Burbank). Jack, the Pumpkin King and chief architect of Halloween, is a misguided, albeit benevolent, Grinch who wreaks havoc when he kidnaps Santa and tries to take over Christmas. Burton initially drew three characters: Jack Skellington, a skeleton as delicate as a dragonfly; Zero, his ghost dog, complete with Rudolph-like lightbulb nose; and a big hill of a Santa Claus, with a paramecium-shaped, fringed beard and a circle for a face. The seminal color sketches appeared to be either clever, visionary, or the work of someone who is seriously disturbed.

Burton had a personal affection for the holidays that encompassed an appreciation of their distinctive palettes and iconography. To even his childish artist's eye, Burbank looked bland. But dress it in Christmas lights or decorate it with Halloween symbols and it became a place touched by magic. No stranger to alienation, he felt a kinship to Jack Skellington, tortured by his own soul-sickness. Since the visual imagery, story, and characters of *Nightmare Before Christmas* were close to his heart, Burton had felt particularly frustrated when Disney and all the TV networks to whom he and Heinrichs originally brought the project rejected the idea of making it as a half-hour television special. Burton thought of *Nightmare* often as the years passed and it slumbered, like Sleeping Beauty, in Disney's development dormitory. And though he wasn't sure what form the prince's quickening kiss would take, he always believed his beloved story would somehow be awakened.

Since Burton had been a Disney employee when the notion of a stop-motion movie based on the holidays came to him, the studio had sole rights to pucker up to *Nightmare*. "You signed your soul away in blood when you worked there. They owned your firstborn," Burton explains. "I kind of gently said, 'Could I just have it back?' "

Could the Indians just have Manhattan back? "When it comes to animation, we believe in and enjoy the notion of a monopoly," Katzenberg has proclaimed. But Disney wanted its prodigal son to return. David Hoberman, president of Walt Disney Pictures and Touchstone, was smarting from criticism that the company's formulaic comedies were mind candy full of empty calories. It became his personal mission to persuade Burton to make *Nightmare* for Disney. "We were looking to do something completely unique," Hoberman says. "This was an opportunity for us to be in business with Tim Burton and to say, 'We can think outside the envelope. We can do different and unusual things.' "

"Disney understood from the beginning that it was a really personal project for Tim," says Denise Di Novi, Burton's coproducer. With the contractual promise of creative autonomy, a deal was struck to make *Nightmare Before Christmas* as Disney's first stop-motion animated feature.

Skellington Productions moved into a warehouse in San Francisco's South of Market district in July 1991, and production on *Nightmare Before Christmas* began the following October. Since then, in this place north of L.A., just a bit far away, all the goblins and ghosts go to work every day.

It is winter's end, 1993, and *Nightmare* won't be finished till late in the summer. Most of the crew of 110 men and women have been toiling in virtual isolation here for so long that members of the group have experienced everything that occurs on an extended submarine voyage: feuds, love affairs, marriages, births, illness. The process of stop-motion animation is agonizingly slow. If observing a typical movie being shot is usually as exciting as watching paint dry, then stop-motion filming would compare to the thrill-a-minute spectacle of a mountain eroding.

Headway is measured in seconds of film completed per week; the weekly goal is 70. Animators work on twenty stages at once, manipulating puppets on any one of 230 exquisitely detailed sets built for the movie. Black curtains function as dividers in the ground floor area where the makeshift stages are, creating an atmosphere like that of a fun house rigged by children in an abandoned building.

The puppet shop fills two rooms on the second floor. Puppets in various stages of undress litter wooden worktables, boxes of their snap-on facial features looking like so many Mr. Potato Head parts. No one thought puppet maintenance would become such a constant chore. (No one had worked on a stop-motion movie for more than a year at a time.) Stop motion has traditionally been used as a special effect in short experimental films, commercials, and in children's television. Gumby is a stop-motion character, as were the 1933 King Kong and, in some scenes, RoboCop. The dancing California Raisins are Claymation, a stop-motion technique in which clay is sculpted and resculpted between shots.

A number of special effects and commercial production houses with stop-motion expertise, including Industrial Light & Magic, are located near San Francisco. The Bay Area offered psychic and real distance from the studio, but the veteran talent pool available was the paramount factor in locating the production there. It also happened to be where Henry Selick lived. If Selick wasn't born for the job of directing this movie, he does seem to have spent the last twenty years in training for it. After he left Disney, he worked in special effects, designing, storyboarding, and executing elaborate stop-motion sequences before landing his dream job, creating a series of station IDs for MTV. Selick became sought after as a director of stop-motion commercials and did 30 featuring the Pillsbury Doughboy.

Tacked on walls throughout the warehouse is Selick's schedule for the day; he inevitably misplaces any copy handed to him. But it would be a mistake to label him the absentminded artist. "Henry thinks in animation frames," Heinrichs says. He has been known to take note of a distinctively lit scene in dailies, identify another scene 25 minutes earlier in the film in which the identical effect was created, and suggest an alternative lighting scheme to avoid repetition. As much as Selick has insisted on elevating the movie's production values—lighting the scenes as beautifully as if he were working with vain movie stars, attempting sophisticated camera movements like those used in big-budget live-action films—he is admired for his restraint and sense of pace. Technological bells and whistles can dazzle an audience, he knows, or exhaust them.

Burton journeys to the warehouse every few months, but the daily crafting of the movie is overseen by Selick. Shuttling between two editing machines, he suggests a puppet be repositioned within a frame, decides a different camera angle would intensify the emotional content of a shot, then rises from his chair to act out the body moves he'd like to see a singing Wolfman mimic. He reassures, praises, challenges, never forgetting the common, Gepetto-like goal of willing puppets to life. "What the animators do is as hard as neurosurgery," Selick says. "They have to almost bleed their energy into the puppet."

It was always understood that *Nightmare* would, in every way, be a Tim Burton movie. But what is that? It is a film, his critics would say, in which details of the extraordinary production design are given more attention than the story. (The script is the work of Caroline Thompson, who also wrote Burton's *Edward Scissorhands*.)

In *Nightmare Before Christmas* design always ruled, even if serving Burton's vision meant discarding long-held conventions. "The first rule of animation is to give your characters expressive eyes," Burton says. "We designed these characters that are pretty weird. The lead character doesn't have any eyeballs." Even the film's palette proved problematic. A puppet needs to stand out against the background, but in Halloweentown almost everything and everyone is black and gray.

Burton's carefully cross-hatched illustration style, reminiscent of Ronald Searle and Edward Gorey, has been faithfully maintained. Selick describes the movie as having the look of a pop-up book, and at times it appears as if the characters are moving around in a fantastic drawing that's spookily bathed in light and shadow.

Background characters created for the movie had to be appropriately Burtonesque. A particular favorite is the corpse kid, who, with his little eyes sewn shut, is, as Heinrich puts it, "just the right combination of cute and ghastly." The corpse kid, like the other denizens of Halloween-town, is blissfully un-self-conscious, and such transparent vulnerability illustrates several themes that recur in Burton's films: It's okay to be different, it's okay to screw up, and it's okay to be miserable. Jack, the tortured artist, is bored with his life and plagued by an inner emptiness even success has not mollified.

Whether children will relate to such midlife angst remains to be seen. But frequent Burton collaborator Danny Elfman does. Elfman, who temporarily walked away from his rock band, Oingo Boingo, to find fulfillment as a film composer, found writing *Nightmare's* ten songs one of the easiest jobs he's ever had. "I have a lot in common with Jack," he says. "I made demos of all the songs, but I felt with Jack's character I had nailed it, and no one else would be able to do a better job than I had." Elfman convinced Burton to let him be Jack's singing voice. (Chris Sarandon provided Jack's speaking voice, and Catherine O'Hara is Sally, Jack's rag doll love interest.)

Questions remain at the end of the day. Will children go for the ghouls, or will they be scared away? Will Evil Scientist dolls with heads that open to reveal their gooky brains be a hot Christmas item for children with a finely tuned taste for the macabre? "I hope it goes out and makes a fortune," says Hoberman. "If it does—great. If it doesn't, that doesn't negate the validity of the process." The budget of *Nightmare* was considerably less than that of a Disney animated blockbuster, so it won't have to earn *Aladdin*-size grosses to satisfy the studio.

Burton is already satisfied: "People will look at the movie and go, 'Oh, this is really great,' and a lot of stop motion will be done, and some of it will be really great. Some will be really bad. Too much will be done, and then we'll put a pillow over it and smother it for another 30 years, and then it will come up again. Cycle of life, you know?"

A Meeting of Minds: Tim Burton's *Ed Wood*

LAWRENCE FRENCH/1994

"Greetings, my friend. You are interested in the unknown, the mysterious, the unexplainable . . . that is why you are here. So now, for the first time, we are giving you all the evidence, based only on the secret testimony of the miserable souls who survived this terrifying ordeal. Can your hearts stand the shocking facts of the true story of Edward D. Wood Jr.?"

So intones famed psychic to the stars, Criswell, in the opening prologue of Tim Burton's *Ed Wood*, a rigorously faithful adaptation of five tumultuous years in the life of the film director whose name has become synonymous with lack of talent. Touchstone Pictures is due to open director Tim Burton's quirky ode to Wood in October.

Poughkeepsie, New York, was the birthplace of Ed Wood, and the place where Burton decided to turn Ed Wood's life into a movie. Screenwriters Larry Karaszewski and Scott Alexander had written a treatment that, at first Burton thought he would produce, but not direct. "I was staying at a farmhouse out near Poughkeepsie," remembered Burton, "and I started to read *Nightmare of Ecstasy* [the Ed Wood biography]. Then I found that Ed was from Poughkeepsie and I started to get into it thematically. There were a lot of things happening that I could relate to. I was thinking about doing the movie, after hanging out in Poughkeepsie a little bit and reading about Ed.

"I wanted to do it, but we didn't have a script. Scott and Larry wrote the script in the quickest amount of time I've ever seen. They must have had it in their heads already, because they wrote it in about a

From *Cinefantastique* 25:5 (1994) 32–34. Reprinted by permission.

month. I read the script and liked what they had written very much. Then I really wanted to direct it. I like it when things go real fast. They wrote it very quickly and sometimes when you do that, there's not a lot of hashing it over. It just is, what it is."

"It's got a strange edge to it," said Martin Landau, a two-time Academy Award nominee, who was Burton's first and only choice to play the pivotal role of Bela Lugosi. "Tim has an empathy for these underdogs," continued Landau. "He admired the fact that in the face of all this adversity, Ed Wood remained loyal to his troupe of players and was able to get these movies made, which were so abysmal. Yet, there's something about the movies that is fun to watch. They're so bizarrely awful that it's great.

"*Glen or Glenda* is a picture that doesn't know what it is. You're watching it and it suddenly becomes an informational film on cross-dressing! *Plan 9 from Outer Space* is classically awful! *Bride of the Monster* is actually the only one that makes some kind of sense, in that there's a beginning, a middle and an end. It's great to get a bottle of beer, a couple of friends and some popcorn and sit down and watch them."

Burton decided to make *Ed Wood* before he started filming *Mary Reilly*, a retelling of the Jekyll and Hyde story, which he was scheduled to direct for Sony Pictures. "I had been thinking about *Mary Reilly* and working on it for awhile," said Burton. "In some ways I was pushed out of that, because the studio wanted to get it done. It was a high priority for them. I'm sure that now they're getting what they want with it." The movie recently began filming in London, with John Malkovich as Dr. Jekyll and Julia Roberts as his sexy young chambermaid.

After doing a big production like *Batman Returns*, Burton saw *Ed Wood* as a chance to do something more personal and on a smaller scale. "Tim has the choice to do whatever he wants to," said *Ed Wood*'s cinematographer Stefan Czapsky. "I think by picking something small to work on, it will show that he can be creative with the most simple and basic things."

Although the budget of *Ed Wood* is considered small, at $18 million, it is about 200 times more than Ed Wood had on any of his pictures. When asked if he was trying to work with less money in an attempt to emulate Wood, Burton laughed and said, "It's just impossible to do that in Hollywood, these days. You could be doing a movie on the scale of

Batman, or on the scale of an Ed Wood movie, and you know what? It's pretty much the same problems. When things don't work, it doesn't matter if you have $1 million or $50 million. If the car doesn't start, it doesn't start.

"No matter which way you go it pretty much shakes down to the same thing. The problems of making a movie is really such a goofy thing. It's not an exact science and so many things can go wrong. Somebody was telling me that run through a computer, filmmaking is an impossibility. Too many things can go wrong. That's great, because that's what makes it kind of fun."

Working on a smaller film that is more character oriented, and lacking in special effects has allowed Burton more freedom with his shooting style. "I've gotten more away from storyboards," admitted Burton. "Obviously on a effects picture you board a lot more. On a picture like this I find you don't need to storyboard. You're working mainly with actors, and there's no effects going on, so it's best to be more spontaneous. We did this one a little more on the spot. The approach I took was to start with the concept. Who the characters are and so forth, then just sort of do it. It's got an episodic, matter-of-fact approach. We didn't want to impose too much of a style on it. Let the people be the focus and the style will come out of that. Both Stefan and I looked at the Ed Wood movies, but we both kind of prefer to have a strong idea and then see what happens with it. We didn't try to emulate something, or have any direct references. We just chose to do it relatively matter-of-fact."

At the present time, Burton has no idea how the film will be received, but finds the characters are what makes it so endearing to him. "This group of people are so special and tragic," said Burton. "You have Tor Johnson, Vampira, Bunny Breckinridge, Ed Wood and Bela Lugosi. They're like faded royalty. There are times in history, like Paris in the '20s, when groups of artists happen to get together at the same time. I think of this as kind of the bad version of that [the surrealist movement in Paris, which included filmmaker Luis Bunuel, Salvador Dali and Andre Breton]. There's something very compelling about seeing Dracula at this stage of his life. It's a very strange feeling. It's like a weird Andy Hardy movie."

To bring this assorted cast of down-on-their-luck characters to life, Burton was quite pleased with the performances he got from a cast that

included Landau, Johnny Depp and Bill Murray. "It was a fun gr‹
work with," said Burton. "We had an ensemble of characters, wh
of float in and out. Martin has done so much, he's bringing all this
experience to it. We'd be talking and Martin would say, 'Hitch did this,'
and I'd think, 'Who's Hitch?' Then I'd realize, 'Oh, Alfred Hitchcock.'
It's mind-blowing when people have such a body of work.

"Martin has done great movies. He's done weird cheesy horror
movies. He's done it all. Actors and directors and everybody go through
these periods of peaks and valleys. Martin was able to bring a knowl-
edge of all sides of the character in playing Bela Lugosi. Bela was very
theatrical and Martin had done all those kinds of things.

"Johnny was bringing something else to it, and it was great to be
working with Johnny again. I had worked with him before [on *Edward
Scissorhands*], but it was fun working with a lot of new people, who I
hadn't worked with before. It was a very interesting mix of people. The
actors were all so good. I think we found the right spirit for the characters. The humor and the off-kilterness of them all."

Although Burton wanted to be very accurate in recreating scenes
from Ed Wood's movies, he didn't want to overload the movie with
them. "It's just little snippets," said Burton. "You see behind the scenes
things, as they're making the movies. There isn't a lot of direct recre-
ations from his movies. There's only one Ed Wood. I may be bad, but
I'm bad in my own way. You can't be Ed Wood."

In contrast to the pains-taking effort that has gone into duplicating
scenes from Wood's movies, Burton noted he's glad he didn't adhere
strictly to the known facts of Wood's life. "We didn't try to delve into
the history of these people," explained Burton, "because there wasn't a
lot you could delve into. I felt lucky that we didn't have to treat it as a
realistic bio picture."

Actor Vincent D'Onofrio appears as Orson Welles towards the end of
Ed Wood, and there is a sequence in a carnival funhouse which might
bear traces of influence from the funhouse ending in Welles's *The Lady
from Shanghai*. Does Burton admire Welles's work? "I never really saw
Citizen Kane," claimed Burton. "The Welles's films sort of passed me by.
I haven't seen *The Lady from Shanghai*. I have seen *The Third Man*, and I
guess I must have seen *Citizen Kane*. Yes, I'm sure I've seen *Citizen Kane*.
That scene with Orson Welles was more a device of the writers. Ed was

obsessed with Orson, and fancied himself as a writer-producer-director, as was Orson. The scene is just a sort of inspirational moment for Ed, when he's a little low. It had to do more with Ed Wood's connection with Orson than with mine."

Burton was still a few months away from finishing *Ed Wood* and claimed to have lost all objectivity about his work. "I have no conception of what is cheesy, and what isn't," admitted Burton. "The lines to me are now completely blurred. I have no idea between good and bad anymore. That will be for others to decide."

Did that mean that Burton would be willing to take advice or give up some control of the editing to Disney honchos, such as Touchstone Pictures president David Hoberman? "Sure, I'll take suggestions from them," exclaimed Burton. "There's always that vibe of us against them, but I'll take any suggestion if it's good. If my plumber had an idea of how to make it better, I'd listen to him. It doesn't matter. You take any suggestion that is good and you feel works. If I don't agree with it, we might have a little problem. They haven't seen it yet. Right now I just have the pleasure of working on it. It's a hard thing to juggle around, because you're dealing with something that's funny and sad, and you don't know what the ultimate outcome will be. It's always shocking to see what works. You never really know, but that's part of the ethereal nature of making movies."

When Burton completes *Ed Wood* he hasn't decided what he'll tackle next, but admits to a desire to work on a Gothic horror film, like *Frankenstein* or *Dr. Jekyll and Mr. Hyde*, which are currently undergoing big budget remakes. Though Burton didn't mention it, *Variety* speculated that his next project might be *House of Usher*, as he awaits the completion of a script for the *Catwoman* movie at Warner Bros.

"I'd love to do one," enthused Burton about a gothic horror project. "They're doing them all again now. It's a kind of regeneration, which is Hollywood's tendency to find a trend and do it to death, until nobody wants to see it anymore. Then they move on to another genre they smother to death. I don't know, because I'm at a place now where I want to try to keep being interesting, and find the right thing to do. I don't want to jump on the bandwagon that everyone else wants to jump on, whatever it is."

When asked about the possibility of remaking a Hammer horror film, several of which director Richard Donner recently brought the rights for, Burton was more hesitant. "What's the point of it?" asked Burton. "I love all those films and I grew up with them, but I think the point has to be, what are you bringing to it. If it was a bad movie that had a good idea, maybe that's a good reason to do something over. Maybe somebody can bring something new to it, but why not do something different?"

One project Burton hoped to finish soon is his documentary on Vincent Price. "It's pretty loose," said Burton. "It's the last footage of Vincent and I've got a little bit more to do on it. It's just a conversation with him in his art gallery, at East L.A. College. It's nice to see him, because he's just incredible. Vincent was really the first person I worked with from Hollywood and he turned out to be a wonderful person. He gave me a lot of hope and was a great inspiration to me. He really shaped my life when I was starting out. *House of Usher* and *The Pit and the Pendulum* are just beautiful movies. I hope to be finished with it soon. Maybe in the Fall."

Tim Burton Attacks!

BILL WARREN/1997

Making a movie based on bubble gum cards would be a strange undertaking for almost any director, but for Tim Burton, somehow it seems entirely appropriate. "I grew up with this kind of movie," Burton says. "They're in my blood, as they are with many people. I remember when I saw the cards briefly, to the point where I didn't know . . ." he breaks off in the middle of the sentence, something he does frequently. "You ever see something that kind of disappears, and then you wonder if it was a dream, or something that was real? Was it just something you thought up yourself? When I saw the cards years later, I just loved the way they looked. I love the naive quality of the original cards, and the style of the painting is beautiful, just the color and the way they look." For Burton, this fully explains why he decided to direct a star-laden, big-budget motion picture based on those cards: *Mars Attacks!*

In the colorful North Beach section of San Francisco, right where the Italian part of the city intersects with its famous Chinatown, there's an odd building several stories high, shaped like a slice of cake. Atop the building is a blue dome, with the largest offices at the narrow end contained in a column-like structure. This building was once owned by the folk group the Kingston Trio—it's even on the cover of one of their albums—and now it houses Francis Ford Coppola's American Zoetrope production company. From time to time, other productions rent out space in the building; this time it's the turn of the *Mars Attacks!* team, and director Burton has one of those offices in the narrow tip of this

From *Starlog Magazine*, 234 (January 1997), 50–54. Reprinted by permission.

handsome old building. Working here puts him in close proximity to ILM, across the Bay to the north.

Somehow, the eccentric building is exactly right for Burton, one of the most imaginative and unusual directors ever to helm a big-budget movie like *Mars Attacks!* He's considered strange by many, and the building is unquestionably peculiar—but both are marvelous curiosities, not nearly so strange as they might seem, and they're both inviting and friendly, the director much more so than his reputation might suggest.

His famous unruly black hair is shorter now, and he's wearing dark glasses that look like long, narrow capital "D"s. His clothing is dark too, but his spirit is light. As his movies reveal, Burton doesn't think like everyone else; in fact, he talks more like how we all imagine a true artist would than anyone that this *Starlog* interviewer has ever met, in show business or out.

Burton rarely gives straight-ahead, obvious answers; sometimes his replies sound as though he didn't hear the question asked, but instead is answering an entirely different question. He laughs a lot, and giggles even more. He frequently breaks off in the middle of a sentence, or even a word, and starts over with a new but related thought. There's nothing about this that suggests a disorganized mind, but rather a busy, complicated one. Some people, when interviewed, can reply in a flow of words so fluid that it's as if they don't just have a writer in their head, but an editor, too. Tim Burton's mind is like an exploding fireworks factory: vivid, exciting, colorful, surprising and all over the place.

The very idea of basing a movie on trading cards makes Burton chortle and dash off onto what other things movies are based on. "Comic books—from novels to comic books, and you end up with *Bazooka Joe, the Movie*, based on a fortune cookie!" He first came up with the idea for a movie based on the *Mars Attacks!* cards "a few years ago," he says. "When you get the opportunity to make something, this is more like it. I love the old Ray Harryhausen movies, so a lot of this draws inspiration from those, even though he never did anything like this, except *First Men in the Moon*. We're using a different technique, but still trying to capture the feeling that those movies created."

Burton originally planned to have the movie's Martians rendered in stop-motion animation; in fact, a lot of Martian footage—none of which is still in the movie—was shot employing that technique.

"I'm definitely a fan," Burton asserts, "and love stop-motion. My first film [*Vincent*] was done in that medium, and then later *Nightmare Before Christmas*. Growing up with Harryhausen, like many people, I love that stuff.

"I think what finally made me switch over [to computer graphics] in this case was a few technical elements. One was being able to shoot anamorphic [film format], which was more difficult with stop-motion. If you read anything about what Ray Harryhausen went through in *First Men in the Moon* . . . ! I realized what it finally comes down to is not so much technique any more, it's just finding good animators. Stop-motion will always have something that *only* stop-motion has, but with this [CGI], I'm amazed. We were able to create something that's not truly three-dimensional, but *seems* three-dimensional, and has the feeling of that old stop-motion. I feel really excited and amazed by it. It has gotten to the point where you can capture the feeling of stop-motion, and get that same kind of visceral response that you felt when you first saw it."

Like Steven Spielberg, George Lucas, and some other filmmakers who often work in the fantasy field, Burton thinks that perhaps there has been too much explanation about how special FX are done. "When we were growing up," he says, "and saw a Ray Harryhausen movie, we were interested in how it was done. But thank God we got to go through the magic of seeing it *before* we knew how it was done. That's why I somewhat try to resist these behind-the-scenes things, or talking too much. When I saw those movies, *Jason and the Argonauts* or whatever, I was blown away, and would have killed to have seen how they did it—but after the fact. You were able to get this beautiful, pure, visceral response to something without knowing too much about it. I feel lucky to have gone through the period in life when you could see things and they were magical."

In *Mars Attacks!* there are these Martians, see, and they attack. Of course, the movie is full of well-known actors, from Jack Nicholson, through Jack Nicholson (in two roles), Rod Steiger, Paul Winfield, Glenn Close, Pierce Brosnan, Annette Bening, Michael J. Fox, Danny DeVito, Sarah Jessica Parker, Lukas Haas, Jim Brown, Pam Grier, Barbet Schroeder (a director turned actor for Burton), Sylvia Sidney, and Tom Jones as Tom Jones. Martians land on Earth and start blowing away

cities and people with giddy abandon. Many famous stars meet spectacular demises. The leaders of Earth are helpless; it's up to the little people
to save the day.

The question arises, naturally, as to just why the Martians (who've
been hiding in craters) are attacking in the first place. "We know not of
their ways," Burton giggles. "That's part of the thing I liked about it.
Everybody categorizes everything, everybody thinks they know so
much. There are so many experts, but what does anybody *really* know?
Not too much. That's what I like about the Martians—they do things
you kind of recognize, but they're a different culture. I like the idea of
meeting a culture you don't know anything about, and you think you
know, but you're wrong. It's kind of the way that I, anyway, feel about
life, which is that you think you know but you really don't, you kind of
see things another way. It's a little bit abstract, it's like a force of nature,
it's not something you can easily identify and understand."

Burton cast Brosnan as Professor Donald Kessler, one of Earth's fore-
most scientific experts. "There are always those guys in the movies who
expound endlessly on their theories. I remember when I first saw
Psycho, and that guy at the end [Simon Oakland as the psychiatrist]. I
kept looking at my watch, thinking how long is this guy gonna . . . But
it's great, though, that there are always these guys in the movies, often
it's Richard Carlson. The monster is in the movie for 10 minutes, then
there's some guy explaining for the rest of the hour-and-a-half. I always
loved that, and Brosnan was great at it. He's a great guy, I really loved
him," Burton raves.

As screenwriter Jonathan Gems told *Starlog* Burton decided to base
the structure of *Mars Attacks!* on those old, star-laden disaster movies,
like *Earthquake, The Swarm, The Towering Inferno*, and *When Time Ran
Out*. The director's reasons were very simple: "*Mars Attacks!* is like those
old movies; this is just that kind of genre that has been around for a
while and seems to fit with it. The cards indicate that—they're little
snippets, so it pretty much follows the structure of that type of movie."

He asked Gems to write the film because they had worked together
before. "I wanted to do something where we just wrote it, and tried to
capture the kind of naive spirit of those cards. I pick writers because I
like them, or because they're friends or whatever," Burton says with a
laugh. "I couldn't tell you a good script if it hit me in the face. Part of

the key [to making movies] is finding people you can speak to without speaking; to get people who like the same stuff you do, who get into it, get energized by the same things. They're out there," he says, laughing again.

Burton's personal approach to movie making permeates everything he does; when he talks about his collaborators, actors, writers, and the like, it generally relates to what they're like as people. For example, in discussing production designer Wynn Thomas, Burton says, "I met him, I liked him. I don't really look over portfolios in depth, or read scripts. Maybe I should. When it comes to other people, a lot of it is, 'Well, can I get along with them?' Obviously, I've got to like their work, but any time you work with anybody you haven't worked with before, you're trying something. So, I always just take that approach, and most of the time, as in this case with Wynn, it's great.

"It takes so long to get a movie going. You work with many people, friends that you worked with before, but sometimes they're working on other movies. It's also fun to mix it up a little, and kind of work with the old and new. There was a good healthy mix of that in this movie."

Burton took the same eclectic, genial approach to casting the film, which may account for the fact that Nicholson appears as both U.S. President James Dale and Las Vegas real estate dealer Art Land. "I knew Jack Nicholson was working on something, so I thought he might not want to do it. I was in the airport, and talked to him. He said he read the script, and I asked which part he wanted to play—whatever you want. He said, 'How about both of them?'

"Jack really energized the project. He's perfect to go up against the Martians. If anybody was the human counterculture to the Martians, it would be him. He's so fun, he's so smart, and he's just a great actor. On the first *Batman*, he was so supportive of me, so helpful, and it was the same on this. He's a guy I really love. He's really generous to me, and a pleasure to watch. Here's a guy who has been in so many great movies, and done so many things. I loved him way back, like in *The Terror*, seeing Jack as a French officer. Gimme a break! He's the greatest! Every take he does, it's a different thing; you wish you could print all of the takes to see a real artist at work. It adds something to the crew, and it's really fascinating to watch. It's a real energy boost, you know? You've been on sets, you wait, it's not quick and moving, and then you see somebody really working, and it's a real boost to everybody.

"I'm so lucky to work with actors who aren't heavy Method, who can act to nothing, which is basically what you're doing in movies like this one. You're acting like you did when you were a kid—let's pretend. So, we have all these great actors . . . pretending!"

Many people associated with *Mars Attacks!* have marveled at how much fun it was to make the movie, and Burton is no exception. "I really loved it. I laughed every day on this movie, and got a real joy out of seeing these fine actors just pretending. I almost thought of releasing the movie with no Martians so you could see what these people were reacting to—nothing—because that's true acting. I'll tell you that right now. It's fab!"

That bit of '60s slang, which is so natural to Burton that he doesn't seem to notice he said it, is typical of this man, who's very comfortable with his imagination. From the fascinating world inside his head, he makes reports to us in the form of movies. His ideas come from his intuition, his heart and soul, not from any overt desire to impress the audience. He hopes they *will* be impressed, and is very concerned that his investors get their money back, but he's not driven by the market-place, by fads or fancies, or by anything other than his own restless, naive/sophisticated imagination. He makes a particular movie, he says, when it feels right to make it.

In discussing the possible future project of *House of Usher* (another Gems script, a comedy based on Edgar Allan Poe, set in suburbia), Burton admits that it's one of the things he wants to do. "I've got a few things like this that I'll feel when it's right. I can see me making it, I have this image of making it a little bit later, but I'm not sure when that is, if it's months from now or a year. I don't know how I'm going to feel. Even though the movies are fairly abstract in how they're presented, they have to have some sort of . . . some sort of thing for me. One of the reasons I got into *Mars Attacks!* is the idea that you don't understand the Martians, though you're trying to. They're this green force." Which connects with his giddy explanation as to *why* it's an appropriate movie for Christmas: "Green death rays from a red planet. Christmas colors!"

Warner Bros. has acquired rights to "The Architects of Fear." The classic *Outer Limits* episode, scripted by Meyer Dolinsky, chronicled the efforts of a group of idealistic scientists who transform one of their number (Robert Culp) via painful surgery into an alien monster. The idea is he'll "invade" and save the world by uniting a fearful Earth against him. The property is intended for Burton, though he hasn't committed to the movie version currently being scripted by Jeff Welch.

Another promising Burton project is *Catwoman*, which may yet be filmed. "We are actually working on a script that I feel good about. I'm writing it with Laeta Kalogridis. I love Batman, he's my favorite comic book character. He has the best villains, the best everything, and Catwoman is great. She's a real icon, like Batman."

His involvement with the third *Batman* movie, directed by Joel Schumacher, was only in the form of advice, when it was sought. He liked Val Kilmer in the movie, but also thinks it's perfectly fine that Batman will be played by George Clooney in the fourth one, that perhaps a different actor should play Batman in each successive movie. However, as much as he loves the character, it's clear that Burton is content not to be the permanent director of the Batman series. "It became a franchise thing for the studio, and once that has hooked in, you've got to have meetings with McDonald's six months before the movie's even started, to say what it's going to be like. Reality seems to take a back seat to everything.

"I'm happy to be who I am; [Warners has] been good to me, we're one big happy dysfunctional family. And I also know the truth—that they're happy I didn't do another *Batman* movie, because I put them through a lot. I didn't mean to; I felt a lot of pressure on the second one. A friend of mine had just died, and I felt really bad; I was going through some personal things. My primary concern was to make a good movie, the same goal they had. But they were happy I left."

On the other hand, Warners is reportedly quite happy with *Mars Attacks!* possibly due to its obvious similarities to the big hit of summer 1996, *Independence Day*—which, at the time of this interview, Burton had yet to see. "I'm probably the only person who *hasn't* seen it," he admits a little ruefully. "This is the kind of movie I grew up watching. I'm sure it's great, but I don't go to many movies, especially when I'm working on one. People have told me that there are some similarities in terms of basics, but I'm putting all my energies into what I'm doing. It's a genre; there are a lot of them in that genre, including lesser ones like *Target Earth*, that we all love."

So far, all of Burton's movies have been on the strange side; when the film itself is relatively conventional, such as *Ed Wood*, the characters are weird. At other times, as with *Beetlejuice* and *Edward Scissorhands*, the movies are pretty weird conceptually. Burton knows this, obviously, and wonders at times what it would be like to make an absolutely straight movie in the classic Hollywood style. He suspects "it would probably be really terrible, because I take everything seriously, but I always have a thing in there where I . . . it stems from when you're a kid, and people tell you stuff, and you say to yourself, 'Are you serious? Is this real?' People are always saying you're weird, and you're looking at everything else, and you're going, 'This is completely surreal. How can they tell me I'm weird when everything else is so abstract?' "

"I have an internal thing about that; I don't know if I can ever get away from it enough [to do a straight movie]. I love to think about it, but I have this thing inside my head that says it would be a really bad movie."

Burton admits that his fondness for strangeness comes from being something of an outsider when he was growing up. "When you don't have many friends, and you don't have a social life, you're kind of left looking at things, not doing things. There's a weird freedom in not being the school president, and not having people treat you like you're part of society, or where you have to fulfill social relationships. You're at a distance from the rest of society; you feel like you're kind of looking out a window," he says with a laugh.

On the other hand, he's cautious about being labeled as an artist (though that's clearly what he is). Instead, he surprisingly talks for a moment almost like a businessman. "Movies obviously cost a lot, even if you're doing a low-budget movie, and I try to keep that in mind all the time and not be somebody who's thinking, 'I'm an *artiste*! Leave me alone!' I try to be responsible, because that's a lot of money they're giving me. But at the same time, I don't have real trouble having to do something I didn't want to do.

"It takes longer and longer to get a movie going, and less and less time to make them. We're basically jamming, which is OK in some ways, but I'm always hesitant to say whether it's a drama or a comedy or whatever. You can only take your own feelings into something when you're doing it. I always appreciated movies and things that had *everything*, because that's the way I feel about life. There's nothing that's just funny, just dramatic or just scary. It's all mixed together. I've always felt, and still feel probably even more, that life is an incredible jumble of being funny and sad and dramatic and melodramatic and goofy and everything.

"I never know how people will react to what I do," concludes Tim Burton. "I only go into it hoping that anybody gets the same enjoyment out of it that I get. Really, that's all you can do. I see shots coming through as they're edited, and I wonder, 'Oh man, will anybody feel about this, get into it like I'm getting into it?' That's all you can do."

Men Are from Mars, Women Are from Venus

CHRISTINE SPINES/1997

His nose is firmly planted in that warm, safe area where shoulder meets neck. Just above this cozy love zone rests the delicate face of Lisa Marie, the alien in question and his girlfriend of four years. She's sporting a beehive that would make any astronaut's wife jealous—a masterpiece of Aqua Net engineering. Her gown, a floor-length web of red spirals, is an alluring combination of Madonna-meets-Morticia-meets-the-B-52's.

Amid a spread of coffee urns, cheese logs, Wheat Thins, and a big pile of doughnuts, the two engage in an intimate public display of affection sidled up against the craft-services table. They haven't said a word to each other for nearly ten minutes. They're just holding hands, gazing into each other's eyes, rubbing noses. No one dares go near them. It is one of the few breaks Burton takes during a long day of shooting *Mars Attacks!*, his wacko Martians-invade-Earth comedy adapted from the ultraviolent 1960s trading cards of the same name. No *Independence Day* this; Burton's movie is a patently low-concept, low-tech story of what happens when an army of little green men fly their saucers to Vegas, the White House, and Grandma's house, aiming their ray guns at everything that moves.

Lisa Marie has the honor of being the only flesh-and-blood Martian in the movie. Her towering coif is more than a fetching retro tribute to '60s cheesecake—it's hiding her hideous, big-brained Martian skull. In a

Tim Burton movie, the alien, monster, outsider, or freak is always the plum role.

If Burton took his mind off Mars for a nanosecond, he might notice it's Oscar day in Hollywood. The day the phones stop ringing after 4 o'clock, the streets empty, and an almost religious silence descends upon the city. It's like Jerusalem on a Friday. But here on the Warner Bros. lot, a pleasant lack of concern for the whole affair has shrouded the set. Only the teamsters seem to be aware that they're missing out on a big-money night.

"Cheese!" yells Martin Short from across the cavernous soundstage. "I need more *cheese*." The word in its adjectival form is used frequently by cast and crew to describe *Mars Attacks!: cheesy* as in good cheesy, like the old Vegas casinos they have yet to demolish, like lava lamps, like Tom Jones—basically, all the elements that compose this film.

The next scene is ready to be shot. The set is all you'd expect from Burton: the Kennedy Room, an imagined secret love pad in the White House where the president and friends can conveniently conduct their domestic affairs. It is a lavish, otherworldly spectacle of naughty and nice: a round, womblike space lined in ladyfinger couches with a circular bed sunk into the middle of the room like a Jacuzzi. If the Trump Taj Mahal has a honeymoon suite, this is what it must look like.

His seven minutes in heaven are up, and Burton and Lisa Marie disengage. Burton clomps across the soundstage with an uncanny forward motion. His long, spindly legs and combat boots propel him instead of weigh him down. For all the cool style in his movies, Burton himself is endearingly passé. He would fit right in at a New Jersey mall food court circa 1988: black jeans, untucked black oxford, his face sweet with innocence, his large hair a Medusa-like tangle of black curls. If he looks like he still listens to the Cure, he does.

The scene he's about to shoot is one in which Short, who's playing a lusty presidential press secretary cut from the Dick Morris mold, invites Lisa Marie's mysterious, mute bombshell into the president's love lounge for a little hanky-panky, unknowingly giving a Martian access into the executive suite.

Burton has his face pressed up to a giant tropical fish tank that makes up one wall of the set. The idea is to get alternating shots of Short and Lisa Marie looking at each other through the aquarium, as if their heads were actually inside. But the fish aren't cooperating. Each time the cameras roll, Short says his line ("Pretty nifty, huh?") and they mysteriously vanish into the bottom of the tank.

A crew of fish wranglers, bearing long poles with nets at the end, try to coax these Greta Garbo extras out of hiding by stirring up the bottom of the aquarium. The fish reluctantly start swimming, Burton yells action, Short says his line, and the fish disappear. Again. And again. And again. This quick-and-easy scene is suddenly taking an inordinate amount of time. Lisa Marie has gone off-stage to hang out with two set visitors—her yoga teacher, who is wearing a big turban on her head, and a person called Cherry Vanilla. Somehow, Burton keeps smiling.

Between takes, Short whistles "Disco Baby" and dances around the set. Burton is forever giggling. If he's feeling any pressure at the moment, he isn't letting on. It seems odd that the guy responsible for this $80 million sci-fi extravaganza with a galaxy full of stars—Jack Nicholson, Annette Bening, Danny DeVito, Glenn Close, Pierce Brosnan—is sporting a Teflon demeanor as the meter tick, tick, ticks with take after take of one line. It's getting late. Dinner is ordered.

Meanwhile, a small group of people has given in to Oscar day, gathering around a TV offstage to watch the awards. Theme music blares as Susan Sarandon accepts her Best Actress trophy for *Dead Man Walking*. She's crying. The camera keeps cutting to Tim Robbins. He's so proud of her! Lisa Marie and her hairdresser mosey up to the TV. Sarandon thanks a nun. Burton wanders up and watches for a moment and slyly wonders aloud, "Hey, guys, what's on?"

The gifted and oblivious wunderkind—it's a role Burton has down pat. To studio executives searching for that elusive hit-movie X factor, Burton is a creative genius who makes weird flicks they don't understand, but the kids just love 'em. Ever since his 1985 feature debut, *Pee-wee's Big Adventure*, turned into a runaway box office success, Burton has managed to give his quirky and bizarre sensibility a phenomenally commercial spin, making hits out of *Beetlejuice* and *Edward Scissorhands* and a mega-megafranchise out of the *Batman* movies. It's an enviable record, but one that gives Burton the artist the unwelcome responsibility of also being Burton the hit machine.

During the production of *Batman Returns*, the burden of that responsibility started to get to Burton. Though the movie ended up grossing

$163 million in the U.S., many were put off by its grim tone, and it was widely seen as a disappointment, costing much more than the original and making much less. Burton started to question whether he should remain in Hollywood. He sank into a deep depression and became ever more aloof and noncommunicative, alienating many friends and colleagues. "Tim was nice and great while he needed you," says his college chum director Henry Selick. "And then he would just stop calling."

Mars Attacks! marks a significant leap of faith for Burton. He has made a concerted effort to mend fences and, after a four-year absence, make up with a fickle old friend: big-budget movies. Most people close to Burton say that falling in love with Lisa Marie is what pulled him out of the abyss. In the carnival of the absurd that is Hollywood, Lisa Marie seems to have given him a grounded focus outside his job—or, at the very least, a warm neck to retreat to from the pressure-packed world of aliens, cheese, and prima-donna fish.

When screenwriter Jonathan Gems stepped into a Melrose junk shop and picked up two packs of trading cards—one featuring incredibly gory images of suburbia being torn to shreds by dinosaurs, and another depicting a troop of crafty Martians firing their ray guns at scantily clad blonds—he immediately knew their kitschy, anarchic sensibility would appeal to Burton. Initially, Burton loved the idea of making a dinosaurs-stomping-on-tract-homes epic, but he was concerned about its similarity to Spielberg's *Jurassic Park*, and as for the Mars Attacks! cards, he wasn't sure whether anyone still cared about invaders from outer space.

What ultimately won him over was the idea of making an Irwin Allen–style disaster movie with aliens, a cast of thousands, and a groovy, subversive message. "It was during the Gulf War," says Burton, "when the media seemed to have taken it to another level—wars having titles and theme music—and I found it kind of disturbing. I felt like these characters were just a good cathartic shakeup of that kind of thing. There are things you recognize about these Martians, but at the same time you can't understand them."

Gems envisioned the story as a satire of American culture. "There's a certain kind of joy in the way that the Martians just come and smash everything up," says Gems. "I was a punk in London and we always used to do pranks. So here you get the Martians taking the piss out of society."

Which is classic Burton. "I just thought it would be fun to see big stars getting blown away," he says. "It's like all those movies that they used to make where you never know who's going to make it. I remember seeing Robert Wagner on fire in *The Towering Inferno*. I didn't expect Robert Wagner to be on fire. It's kind of cathartic in a way."

Cathartic, perhaps, but a bit of a handicap when it comes to casting. "Agents didn't want to see their star clients play loser roles, and a lot of big actors passed on the project," says Gems. "At one point we actually thought we were going to have to cancel the film. The guy who saved our butt was Jack Nicholson."

Burton had cut his teeth on big-budget movies working with Nicholson on *Batman*. But when Burton sent Nicholson the *Mars Attacks!* script, Nicholson one-upped him in out-there sensibility. "I was location scouting," recalls Burton, "and I phoned Jack from the plane and asked him, 'Which part would you want to do?' He answered, 'How about *all* of them?' He was joking, but it was perfect." Burton cast him as both president of the United States and a sleazy Vegas land developer.

Pumping up the movie's star wattage was tricky, but creating its walking, talking, five-foot-tall, giant-brained Martians was like triple-bypass surgery. Unlike the aliens in *Independence Day*, the Martians in *Mars Attacks!* go *mano a mano* with the film's characters. They run, they fight, they drink martinis, they speak to Congress. Burton wanted these brothers from another planet to resemble the elegant, hobbling stop-motion-animated skeletons that special-effects wiz Ray Harry-hausen created for *Jason and the Argonauts*.

At first he approached Selick, a stop-motion guru and the director of *Tim Burton's A Nightmare Before Christmas*. But Selick was still in the throes of directing his own stop-motion feature, *James and the Giant Peach*, and didn't have time to create what Burton needed. Though *Mars Attacks!* had yet to be green-lighted, Burton imported an international troupe of about 70 animators headed up by Barry Purvis, whose English stop-motion art films caught Burton's eye.

"The success of the film depended on the Martians' acting," says Purvis, "so I kept renting *Sunset Boulevard*, because I thought Norma Desmond with her big eyes and wild movements was an absolutely perfect role model." Unfortunately, even though both Burton and the studio adored what Purvis's crew was coming up with, the arduous stop-motion process was taking longer and costing more than Burton had anticipated. "The movie was being budgeted at a little over $100 million, and Warner's wanted to do it for under $70 million," says producer Larry Franco, who tried to persuade Burton to use computer animation.

Burton, ever the purist, had said no to computers twice before, but the advantages were increasingly compelling: Computer-generated imagery is cheaper and faster than stop motion and provides options at the flick of a finger. As Purvis and crew toiled away, Franco, fresh off of the CGI-laden *Jumanji*, went to Industrial Light & Magic and requested a test reel. The results looked enough like the stop-motion footage to convince Burton, and the animators were history.

"We were green British people working without contracts," says Purvis. "The same day big knobs at the studio had been applauding our rushes, they came in two hours later, while I had my hand up a Martian, and said, 'Sorry, folks.'" Without severance or official credit, Purvis's entire crew was sent packing (and as they exited the studio lot, they were searched). "I was there for eight months," laments Purvis. "And now it's as though we've been swept under the carpet."

While all this creature discomfort was being ironed out, the rest of the production was left in limbo. "There was a period, maybe about five weeks, we had to lay off our crews because of script changes and budget things we couldn't carry—like a construction crew, our decorator—and then we started back up again," says art director James Hegedus.

Missteps in preproduction—and the consequent bitterness—are par for the big-budget course. But it's a credit to Burton's unlikely finesse with executives that throughout it all, he was still able to get his unique vision through the bottom-line studio brass. "Tim's amazing because he really does protect the film, and he really does have a strong vision of the film and how it should be," says Gems. "But he does it in a way that's extremely subtle, so that he outwits the studio some of the time. He doesn't confront. He doesn't do it by yelling and screaming. He does it by diplomacy. Tactical diplomacy."

Burton also put himself on the line to cast lesser-knowns in heroic roles and give a second shot to people whose careers were on ice. "He went against everything and said, 'I want you,'" says Jim Brown, the ex-football legend and one-time blaxploitation star. Burton cast him as an ex-boxer cum Vegas greeter, the film's only true martyr. "There weren't any screen tests," says Brown. "He was interested in my mind, in the things I thought."

Which the big stars appreciate as well. "Tim laughs harder than anybody else when you're doing something," says Bening, who plays a UFO-obsessed ex-stripper whom she modeled after Ann-Margret in *Viva Las Vegas*. "He's a wonderful audience, which is a terrific quality in a director."

"He assumes you're going to do what he wants—you never feel intimidated by him," says Sarah Jessica Parker, who worked with Burton in *Ed Wood* and plays a talk-show host in *Mars Attacks!* "You want to make him happy. If he asked you to stand on your head and shoot flames out of your heels, you would just do it, and you wouldn't even ask why."

While Burton's distanced, easygoing personality keeps the cast happy, it can also make a crew person's hair fall out. "You can sit in meetings [with Tim] for months and not get anything," says Hegedus. "The communication isn't there for you to understand what the parameters are. Somebody would want a decision and he wouldn't give a decision—repeatedly. But I think when you realize what Tim brings to the table, you leave him alone."

A small, black portable telephone is ringing, and it's causing Burton great pain. He looks around helplessly with each successive ring. He is sitting on the back porch of his Mission-style retreat in the mountains an hour north of Los Angeles. The decorations from his 38th birthday party still adorn the otherwise barren yard: An Indian-style harem tent with giant, red-and-gold batik throw pillows sits beside his kidney-shaped pool.

"I *hate* the phone," he says, absentmindedly getting up and going over to some bushes with the phone in hand, as if to chuck it into the shrubs. Then he reconsiders, turns around, and brings it back to the table. "Every time it rings, I feel like I'm about to have a heart attack."

It's Friday the 13th, and Burton looks stricken and pained when asked to describe the look of his not-yet-completed movie. Still, he's doing his best to communicate, which he does with images and feelings. His hands are in a constant state of motion, as if he were speaking in sign language.

The reindeer from *Edward Scissorhands* sits atop a green mound at the center of a circular driveway in front of the house. Just beyond is a large crop of six-foot-tall sunflowers just past their bloom. Their heads slump downward atop their emaciated bodies, like Jack Skellington from *The Nightmare Before Christmas*. Filled with random objects that seem loaded with sentimental value—an upright piano, some Indian antiques, a few leopard-skin chairs—the decor is a cross between a Luis Buñuel and a *Brady Bunch* dream sequence.

Indeed, Burton frequently brings up dreams in reference to the things that make him feel safe and good in an otherwise hostile world. "Seeing *Invaders from Mars* when you were young," he says, explaining the origins of his B-movie fetish, "you never knew if you really saw the movie or you dreamt it. It had that stylized symbolic power."

When Burton was growing up in Burbank, monster movies and sci-fi creep shows provided a necessary injection of passion into his stifled suburban boyhood. He spent countless hours devouring Godzilla movies, Ray Harryhausen sci-fi, and anything starring or narrated by Vincent Price. Both making and watching movies have been Burton's ways of dealing with the alienation he's always felt. "A lot of why you make movies is 'cause you couldn't get dates in high school," says Burton matter-of-factly. "A lot of emotion gets welled up and you put it into this."

As a child, Burton spent his time hanging out in the cemetery down the street from his parents' home. His room was a dizzying splash of '60s bad taste ("bright red shag carpet and this black-and-white psychedelic-pattern quilt—where the hell I got that, I don't know") and it was his refuge from the world. At twelve, he decided not to live with his parents—Mom owned a cat-accessory store; Dad was a former minor-league baseball player—and moved in with his grandmother. He doesn't much like to talk about this period of his life, except as it applies to his movies and artwork. "By the time some kids are, like, ten years old, they think they can't draw or something," he says. "But you go through school and people get it beaten out of them."

In high school, Burton had an art teacher who saw something in him and encouraged him to keep drawing his strange, quirky sketches. "She let you kind of do what you wanted to do," he says. "She got you excited about doing something, as opposed to saying 'No, no, you draw houses exactly like so.'" But in college, at the prestigious California Institute of the Arts animation program, he still felt a lot of pressure to conform and draw by numbers. "I remember sketching in Farmer's Market in L.A.," he recalls, "and I had this—I never had this happen before—mind-blowing experience. My mind felt as if some weird drug was kicking in. I went, 'I can't draw, and I'm just going to draw how I want to draw.' And then I was able to draw. Maybe not great, maybe not the way anybody else liked, but it really did something to me. I can still feel that feeling."

When Burton left CalArts to become an animator at Disney, he was lucky enough to find some executives who understood his talent, principally Julie Hickson, who set him up with the means to make his short film, *Frankenweenie*, a sweetly macabre *Frankenstein*-meets–*Leave It to Beaver* story about a kid who revives his dead dog. "I remember a test screening for *Frankenweenie* where kids started crying," says Burton. "Parents forget that for some kids, being scared isn't a bad thing. It's actually helpful in your life."

Not surprisingly, some of Burton's best work has arisen from terror. "Without the struggle, Tim's movies wouldn't turn out as good," says Selick, who has often seen Burton trying to convince the studios that people will "get" his movies. "If he had unlimited budget and free rein . . . who knows?"

With nearly every film he's made, Burton has had to fight against a lack of confidence in his work. But he's been on the side of the majority almost every time. Paul Reubens hired him to direct *Pee-wee's* after seeing *Frankenweenie*, and the critics, for the most part, trashed it. On *Beetlejuice*, Warner's fought with Burton over the low test-screening results, but then the film surprised everyone with its mass appeal. (He does have the studio to thank, however, for nixing his desire to cast Sammy Davis, Jr., in the title role.)

The immense popularity of *Batman* gave him more freedom to make *Batman Returns* in the manner he pleased. He decided to make this one reflect his sensibility—tormented, conflicted, filled with psychosexual energy and dreamlike violence—and was devastated by its negative reception by critics and the industry. "It made me realize that I shouldn't do sequels," says Burton, insisting that he still feels the film is funnier and closer to his heart than the original. "It was hard. I was going through a lot of stuff that affected me more than I realized. I think, even though I blamed it on the pressure, it was much more what was going on with me personally."

His aloofness at that time struck people as inconsiderate, and they were wounded by it. "What makes it so difficult with Tim is that he's not like Pablo Picasso, who was just a genuinely talented asshole," says Selick. "Tim is so charming and childlike that people end up falling in love with him."

Then came some bad press. *Vanity Fair* ran a venomous piece cataloging Burton's sins—he'd fired assistants and alienated collaborators—and implying that Burton's not returning calls was a contributing factor to *Batman* production designer Anton Furst's suicide.

Everything seemed to be crumbling under Burton's feet. The sudden shift from public acclaim to criticism was devastating; his marriage, to German painter Lena Gieseke, was breaking up, and he was still reeling from Furst's death. "After *Batman Returns*," recalls Gems, "he was very depressed about the possibility of making films in Hollywood. I remember him saying that he wanted to give it up. He wanted to just be a painter."

It was during this dark period, on Christmas of 1992, that Gems introduced Burton to an old friend, a former Calvin Klein model named Lisa Marie. The three of them went out with a group of friends to a yuppie-friendly New York go-go bar. Burton and Lisa Marie were left at a small table talking long after the others had left. "Tim wasn't looking for a girlfriend at the time," says Gems, "but they just fell for each other the first time they met. I think she saved his life."

As Lisa Marie tells it, the lifesaving was mutual. This was a girl who left her New Jersey home at the age of sixteen and headed for Manhattan, did some modeling, and basically made a profession out of hanging out with cool people. Then she got serious about acting and her life hit the skids. "I was really a blue girl," she recalls. "Things were not happening for me at that time."

From the beginning, holidays have been very significant in their relationship, as they are in Burton's movies. They fell in love on New Year's Eve, but they didn't consummate until Valentine's Day.

"An old-fashioned courting thing," says Lisa Marie. "Tim was really glad he waited. At the beginning he wasn't, but he realized it later."

Others were realizing that all of a sudden Burton was a lot more focused, well adjusted, and easier to deal with. "Tim was very successful very young, and he was surrounded by gold diggers who would betray and lie a lot," says Gems. "He just lost his faith in people. Then Lisa Marie comes along and she's like a child—very loving and generous and giving. And gradually, over the past few years he has healed up to the point where he has lost his distrust of people."

Burton's friends agree that love has changed him. "Tim has started to make a big effort to make amends for mistakes he's made in the past," says Selick. "I think Lisa Marie has had a huge impact on his life. I've seen him eating vegetarian, he dresses better, and his personal hygiene has definitely seen a dramatic improvement."

Before Lisa Marie met Burton, she says his friends told her that "he wouldn't be able to hold on a conversation, he would hide in his hair and he could barely speak. But what he is today was always there. When you have love, you gain confidence. I don't think anyone ever loved Tim—really loved him—in his life."

So the misfit redeems himself with love, makes up with his old friends, charms the pants off the studio again, and rides off into the sunset. Close, but not quite. The real Burton is no fairy tale. He describes *Mars Attacks!* in sarcastic sound bites—"On the depth chart, it's like a *Love Boat* episode"— and then sloughs off a probe for specifics: "Just make it up, it's more interesting that way."

More interesting or less threatening? "Up until a few years ago, I never spoke very much," he says, a vague sense of tranquility settling over his distant and distracted eyes. "You always feel like you're on borrowed time to some degree, but you just keep on truckin'. I'm just having some fun watching great actors acting to imaginary Martians. It's just so beautiful and funny, and I laugh at it every day." Burton's face lights up as a blanket of gray storm clouds descends upon the canyon where his house sits. It's a welcome break from the persistent sunny glare.

A Head of Its Time

CHRISTOPHER NASHAWATY/1998

"Hey, can I get some blood over here!"

As Tim Burton hollers for fresh gore to smear on Johnny Depp, he rocks back and forth in his director's chair like a giddy teenager hopped up on sugar. A demented grin spreads across his face, and a thought occurs: Is it some kind of career goal for Burton to make Depp look as ugly as humanly possible?

In *Edward Scissorhands*, Burton turned the teen idol into a hideously scarred and pasty-faced outcast with razor-sharp shears for hands. In *Ed Wood*, he transformed Depp into a dentally challenged hack filmmaker with a weakness for tight angora sweaters and dainty pumps. And now, with *Sleepy Hollow*—Burton's adaptation of Washington Irving's gothic 19th-century fairy tale about Ichabod Crane and the Headless Horseman—all he can think about is smearing his leading man's million-dollar mug with so much blood that Depp looks like a guy who just made love to a box of jelly doughnuts.

Even Depp, an actor who *welcomes* ways to drab down his looks, who attacks his roles with the rabid gusto of a rottweiler, appears to be wondering about Burton's sanity as the director flings crimson syrup at his face as if it were a Jackson Pollock canvas. "C'mon, let me just give you a fresh basting," says Burton. He dips a tiny paintbrush into the tub of red goo, then again, and again—until Depp can't hold back any longer . . .

"Tim, what kind of sick movie is this?"

From *Entertainment Weekly*, (November 1999) 39+. © 1999 ENTERTAINMENT WEEKLY INC. Reprinted by permission.

Good question. The moment you step inside Soundstage H at Shepperton Studios—an hour north of London—you're immediately transported to a haunted Hudson River forest, circa 1799. A thick curtain of fog hangs in the air, along with a heavy, death-like stillness. Blood-dappled autumn leaves cover the moist mossy ground. And the trees . . . well, they're *Tim Burton* trees. Twisting branches reach out like agonizingly arthritic arms, and one, the so-called Tree of the Dead, rises 50 horrifically misshapen feet. It's through this gnarled gateway that Depp's Ichabod Crane—a skittish New York City constable sent to investigate a series of bizarre murders in the superstitious hamlet of Sleepy Hollow—will find the lair of the Headless Horseman and his grisly stash of evidence.

It's also here that we find the source of all that fake blood. The black-clad Depp—looking more Colonial undertaker than constable—is hacking away at the Tree of the Dead's base with a hatchet, each blow bringing a new squirt of red stuff to his face. Twenty-five feet away, Burton gazes into a monitor and smacks his lips with eerie delight. And as Depp peels back a strip of bark, revealing a cache of human heads, Burton literally rubs his hands together with fiendish glee. "*Ooooh*," whispers the director. "It's like a giant piñata of heads."

That was Christmas of 1998. It's now two days before Halloween 1999, in Manhattan, where midtown shops are decorated with holiday cutouts of ghosts and black cats. Outside delis, stacked pumpkins wait patiently for the sharp knife that will be taken to their throats. It's the time of year when a guy like Tim Burton should be a pretty happy fella.

And yet, the 41-year-old director's in a state of white-knuckled panic. Tonight is the first press screening of *Sleepy Hollow*, and he's lurking around an editing suite seven floors above Broadway, making harried last-minute trims and fixes. Burton's pre-curtain jitters are understandable. First, there are the box office concerns: At just under $80 million, *Sleepy Hollow* isn't way over budget, but it *is* Paramount's best hope for a holiday hit. Then, there are the stars: Johnny Depp may be one of the finest actors of his generation, but his drawing power remains uncertain—and indie darling Christina Ricci (*The Opposite of Sex*), as Depp's love interest, isn't exactly a proven audience magnet either. And finally, there's *Mars Attacks!*: Burton's last film was a big-budget flop—rare for the man behind *Batman, Pee-wee's Big Adventure, Beetlejuice,* and *The Nightmare Before Christmas.*

On the other hand, it doesn't hurt that *Sleepy Hollow's* script—credited to Andrew Kevin Walker (*Seven*)—received a stealthy stem-to-stern overhaul from *Shakespeare in Love's* Oscar-winning screenwriter Tom Stoppard. Or, for that matter, that Burton's not-even-100-percent-finished version of the film is as hauntingly gorgeous as anything he (or anyone else) has ever directed. "I don't even know anymore," says an exasperated, deadline-sweating Burton. "You spend so much time on something that when you get to this stage, your nerve endings don't allow you to let it go. If I had three more months I could keep playing with it, but sometimes it's good to just pull the plug." Dressed in his signature all-black Goth uniform and hiding behind an enormous pair of blue-tinted wraparound shades, Burton adds, "If you have too much time to think, you can dig yourself into an emotional hole."

And Burton knows from emotional holes. Before producer Scott Rudin approached Burton about directing *Sleepy Hollow*, the director was stuck in a deep one. It wasn't the fate of *Mars Attacks!*, which seemed to come and go overnight. "That kind of thing doesn't stay with you too deeply because you really can't control it," says Burton. "I'm equally surprised if a movie does well or badly."

No, the director was heartbroken over his experience with Warner Bros. on *Superman Lives.* After he'd worked on the project for a year (with Nicolas Cage set to star), the studio yanked the film away from Burton, citing script problems and a steep budget. "That was extremely painful," he says. "I had locations scouted and I had meeting after meeting. I don't think those people realize how much of your heart and soul you pour into something." Burton slumps in his chair. "I was pretty shell-shocked by the whole situation. And I didn't want to make any old piece of crap just to move on—I didn't want to be like, 'Okay, I'll do *Police Academy 8* because I need the work.' So when *Sleepy Hollow* was presented to me, it was like 'This is the script. Do you want to do it?' Who knows, maybe it was because of my previous year that I related to a character with no head."

Before Burton came on board, the idea of a film about Ichabod Crane and the Headless Horseman had been kicking around for years. Well, not so much kicking around as sitting on a shelf in Rudin's office. After reading Walker's screenplay for *Seven*, Rudin bought the scribe's *Sleepy Hollow*. He then held on to it for six years, until Paramount chairman Sherry Lansing got it rolling in 1998.

Rudin says the failure of *Mars Attacks!* never crossed his mind when considering Burton. "Sometimes I think it's good to get someone whose last film didn't do well, because they're a little hungrier for a hit," he says. "Although *Sleepy Hollow* is a big film, it doesn't need to be *Batman* or *Superman* . . . no one's life is going to be made or destroyed based on how well it does, which can be creatively freeing."

But Burton was also drawn to the Headless Horseman for very personal reasons. As a kid growing up in Burbank, he'd while away the hours in darkened theaters, watching mind-warping triple bills of *Scream Blacula Scream, Dr. Jekyll and Sister Hyde,* and *Jason and the Argonauts. Sleepy Hollow* was a throwback to those flicks, the kind that made him want to be a filmmaker in the first place. "I always remember how grateful I was to see them because they let you work through things," says Burton. "They were a catharsis."

Listening to him riff on the therapeutic powers of *Scream Blacula Scream,* it's hard *not* to wonder: When a kid finds catharsis, redemption, even his basic sense of well-being watching schlock horror, what kind of freakish misfit does he grow up to be? "I don't consider myself strange at all. Ask my girlfriend," he says, referring to actress Lisa Marie, who plays Ichabod's dead mother in *Sleepy Hollow.* "*I'm not*! . . . In fact, early on in my career that made me quite sad, and that was the inspiration for *Edward Scissorhands.* I'd always wonder why people are treating the monster badly—from King Kong all the way up. They treat it badly because they see it as different."

If anyone seems suited to see things from Burton's misunderstood-monster point of view, it's Christina Ricci, star of two *Addams Family* movies and no stranger to oddball labeling by the press and movie industry. Come to think of it, the oddest thing about her is that she hasn't been in a Burton movie before now. "Something I thought was kind of impressive about Tim is he didn't see me like other people," says the 19-year-old, who plays Katrina Van Tassel, the strong-willed, porcelain-doll daughter of Sleepy Hollow's richest resident (Michael Gambon) and a no-good stepmother (Miranda Richardson). "He cast me in the part of a completely angelic, sweet, and naive young thing. And I thought, Wow, he must not have seen any of my other movies."

It's now two days after Burton's jittery last-minute rush, and Halloween has finally descended upon New York City. High above Park Avenue, in a swank Regency Hotel penthouse suite, the only signs that Johnny Depp has changed his appearance for the holiday are two blinding gold-capped teeth. Depp says he got them to play a Gypsy in his next film, *The Man Who Cried*. "A lot of the Gypsies I was hanging out with had them, so I went to the dentist," says Depp of the gilded choppers, which actually make him look more like a Bond villain from *Moonraker*. "Taking them off I'm going to be in big trouble. Apparently, it's a pretty violent process."

A less apparent but no less shocking change for the onetime tabloid bad boy is fatherhood: Depp and French pop-star girl-friend Vanessa Paradis recently had a baby girl, Lily-Rose Melody Depp. "I feel like there was a fog in front of my eyes for 36 years, and the second she was born, that fog just lifted and everything became totally clear and focused. To say it's the greatest thing that's ever happened to me is the understatement of the century." Then Depp—a guy who in his younger, wilder days savaged fancy hotel rooms like this one—catches himself and laughs, "Look at me, I've become a cliché."

While "Depp the father" may be a cliché, "Depp the actor" has carved a career out of very emphatically *not* following the ABCs of stardom. He hasn't saved the world from giant meteorites; he hasn't partnered with Jackie Chan to play a pair of wacky cops. And as a result, he's never had the kind of Happy Meal tie-in blockbuster that makes an actor an A-list star. "Maybe I'm a dummy," says Depp, who seems more interested in hand-rolling his cigarette than in pondering this dilemma. "But I don't worry that a lot of my films haven't had big results at the box office, because I'm not a businessman. Believe me, I would love for one of my movies to be accepted by a wide audience, but I'm not going to do a film just because it's going to do that."

That's fine with Burton. "Johnny isn't going to be the same in every movie. Plus, there's a freedom with someone who's not concerned about how they look in a movie. . . . Actually, if it were up to him, he'd look *a lot* worse."

Depp initially wanted to play Ichabod Crane with a long prosthetic snipe nose, huge ears, and elongated fingers. Not surprisingly, those suggestions were shot down. But after he read Stoppard's rewrite of the script—which amped up not only Depp's romance with Ricci but also the bunglingly comic aspects of his character—the actor was inspired to take the character even further. "I always thought of Ichabod as a very delicate, fragile person who was maybe a little *too* in touch with his feminine side, like a frightened little girl," says Depp. "It's true," says Burton. "We may have the first male action-adventure hero who acts like a 13-year-old girl."

In truth, Depp's Crane comes off more nervous dandy than prepubescent girlyman. But that doesn't mean there weren't moments of concern over his unique interpretation. "At the very beginning of the shoot, Johnny told me that his inspiration for the part was going to be Angela Lansbury in *Death on the Nile*," says Rudin, whose initial horror disappeared as soon as he saw the dailies (at which point he started referring to Depp as "Ichabod Crane: Girl Detective" on set). "For his birthday I got him a signed photo of Angela Lansbury that read 'From one sleuth to another,' and he absolutely *flipped*."

Wait, let's get this straight: A blood-soaked Johnny Depp is channeling *Angela Lansbury* while hacking away at a tree full of human heads? Sort of makes you wonder . . .

What kind of sick movie is this?

Head Trip

STEPHEN PIZZELLO/1999

With his keen pictorial instincts and his affection for all things fantastic, Tim Burton is a lightning rod for eccentric, stylized images—which may explain his distinctly unruly coiffure.

Raised in Burbank, California, Burton grew up on a steady diet of classic horror films, and spent much of his youth drawing outlandish cartoons and illustrations (including an anti-littering poster that embellished local garbage trucks for an entire year). He attended the Cal Arts Institute on a Disney fellowship, and later joined Walt Disney Studios as an animator, lending his talents to such projects as *The Fox and the Hound* and *The Black Cauldron*.

While toiling at Disney, Burton made his directorial debut with the stop-motion short *Vincent*, which told the autobiographical story of a young boy who wants to emulate his hero, horror icon Vincent Price. The film won a number of awards, including two from the Chicago Film Festival, and marked Burton as a talent worth tracking.

His next project for Disney, *Frankenweenie*, was an amusing black-and-white effort about a young boy who uses mad-scientist methods to revive his dead dog. After this initial foray into live-action film-making, Burton left Disney to pursue his own path. His first full-length feature, the surreal comedy *Pee-Wee's Big Adventure*, was a hit at the box office, and paved the way for a succession of imaginative efforts: *Beetlejuice*,

From *American Cinematographer*, December 1999: 54+. Reprinted with permission of *American Cinematographer* and the American Society of Cinematographers. Copyright 1999, 2004.

*Batman, Edward Scissorhands, Batman Returns, The Nightmare Before
Christmas, Ed Wood,* and *Mars Attacks!*

Burton's latest picture, *Sleepy Hollow,* is based on Washington Irving's
classic 1819 short story *The Legend of Sleepy Hollow,* but inventively retools
the legend of Ichabod Crane and the Headless Horseman. Inspired by
his affection for classic horror films, the director sought to imbue the
production with a look and feel that recalled the spirit of England's
Hammer Studios. He took a break from his busy postproduction schedule to speak with *AC* about his creative strategy on the project, as well
as his collaboration with director of photography Emmanuel Lubezki,
ASC, AMC.

AMERICAN CINEMATOGRAPHER: *You reacted very enthusiastically to
the script for* Sleepy Hollow *[which was adapted by Andrew Kevin Walker
and Kevin Yagher, and polished by Tom Stoppard]. What excited you most
about the material? Was it the story itself, or the inherent visual
possibilities?*

TIM BURTON: Both, really. I was familiar with the original story
because I'd seen the [1958] Disney cartoon *The Legend of Sleepy
Hollow*—I didn't actually read the source novel until after I'd seen the
script. Most kids in America have never read the book either, but
somehow they all seem to know about the Headless Horseman.

A big reason that I liked the script was that it reminded of one of
those old Hammer horror films. It had a fresh take, but it also respected
the source material, which has a very Germanic tone. I always like a
good fairy tale, or any story that has symbolic meaning. This script had
a good, strong folktale vibe that I liked very much. I was particularly
drawn to the idea that Ichabod Crane is this guy who lives inside his
own head, while his nemesis has no head at all! That juxtaposition was
interesting to me; it really worked on a symbolic, almost subconscious
level.

AC: *When you're reading a script, do you immediately begin seeing the
story in pictorial form?*

BURTON: I think more visually than not, so I'd have to say yes to that
question. I don't rely completely on that process for my eventual
approach to a movie, because a lot of other things come into play later

on when you start casting people, building sets, and so forth. But this script did get my mind going in a very visual direction. That type of strong visual response happens more often when a story really speaks to you personally.

AC: *You mentioned on the set that you were partially inspired by the look of Mario Bava's 1960 horror film* Black Sunday *[a.k.a.* La Maschera del demonio*]. What specifically do you like about that film?*

BURTON: I love the imagery. I saw *Black Sunday* at one of those horror-film festivals that last a whole weekend. The people who stay through all of the continuous showings start to drift in and out of consciousness a bit [laughs], and certain films really have an impact when you're in that state of mind! Out of all the films they showed that particular weekend, *Black Sunday* really stood out for me, because it had very lurid, vivid, and stark images, which is what you want from a good horror movie. Some of the old Mexican horror films have that quality as well. They're so strange and strong that they become almost like a dreamscape when you're watching them. The best movies in the horror genre have a good mix of imagery and subject matter, and they just dive right into your subconscious.

AC: *Did you have any other visual inspirations, such as paintings or sculptures? Did you discuss your various influences at length with cameraman Emmanuel ["Chivo"] Lubezki?*

BURTON: I try not to draw too heavily on those types of influences, because then you're just trying to emulate something as opposed to creating something new. For example, the influence of the Hammer films didn't result in a rigid visual scheme; it was more the *idea* of those films that inspired us. One of the things I like about Chivo is that he *gets* that—he understands that when we're talking about a potential influence, it's not literal. I might like to draw a certain feeling or flavor out of an older movie, but I'm not trying to make a Xerox copy of it. In actual fact, the idea of what Hammer was is quite different than the reality. Those films weren't necessarily technically superior, but people love them anyway. They're often more intense in your memory than they are when you actually watch them again.

AC: *What inspired you to hire Lubezki as your director of photography?*
Were you familiar with his previous work?
BURTON: To be honest, I wasn't overly familiar with Chivo's
previous films, but I knew a few people who had worked with him.
I don't analyze or look too deeply into a cameraman's body of work,
but I certainly was aware that he was good. I don't necessarily base
my decisions entirely upon a person's resumé; it really comes down
to whether or not I click with him or her. When you're working on a
film and standing right next to someone every day, you want to
make sure you're both on the same general wavelength. Chivo is a
great guy, and I felt a real connection with him. He also works
very fast; I never had to wait for him. The collaboration was a real
pleasure, because Chivo is a very thoughtful person who is able to
understand and enjoy the constantly evolving aspects of a film
project.

AC: *How did the two of you break down the responsibilities on the set? Did*
you get very involved with the camera and lighting issues?
BURTON: I was more involved on the conceptual level, but Chivo and
I would certainly talk about those issues. Part of the charm of filmmaking is that it's not an exact science—I find it to be a very organic
process. There were a lot of technical issues on this film, so it wasn't
like we just went out there and shot things casually. Every shot
involved a certain amount of "manufacturing," but someone like
Chivo makes that process fun, which is the way it should be. When
we were addressing a specific shot, we'd talk about the various elements
we needed, and then change things as necessary. That's why it's nice to
feel comfortable with your key collaborators; if you're on the same
wavelength to begin with, you know that everything will turn out
fine, even if you're whipping something together on the spot. We sort
of felt as if we were making the world's biggest Mexican horror film.
[Laughs.]

AC: *How much of the film was planned out in storyboard form?*
BURTON: We did do some storyboarding, but I've found that over the
years I'm using them less and less. Storyboards can sometimes confuse

people instead of helping them. Generally, the people who want to see the storyboards tend to get too rigid in their adherence to them; they focus entirely on the boards and they lose sight of the big picture. On *Sleepy Hollow*, we had to do storyboards for certain sequences, but we tried to simply use them as guidelines without relying upon them too heavily.

AC: *Chivo said that you considered shooting the film on location in upstate New York, but later decided to go for a more stylized look that combined sets constructed in soundstages and at locations outside London. What was the impetus for that decision?*

BURTON: Listen, I'd never have bet a million dollars that I'd ever be doing a movie where the people were dressed like George Washington! I mean, Dutch Colonialism is not what you'd call the most dynamic lifestyle in the world—it's not coming back into fashion any time soon, you know? [Laughs.] In order to bring the story back to its folktale roots, we wanted to have a strong, controlled visual environment. We didn't want the movie to fall into this naturalistic rut where you'd have a bunch of people dipping candles and watching them dry. That's not the most exciting thing to see at the movies.

Working at Leavesden Studios was a decision based mainly on cost. The facilities had the amount of space we needed, but the stage heights were very low. I've worked in England before [on *Batman*], and the film industry there offers everything you need, including great crew people and artisans. To me, if you're doing a heavily designed movie, the only two places where you can really do it right are Los Angeles and London. Even New York doesn't have the same level of resources that those two cities offer.

AC: *How fine a line were you trying to tread in terms of creating a pictorial but slightly artificial look? Lubezki said the use of smoke factored heavily in the equation.*

BURTON: We were trying to create our own reality for the film—a fantasy feel that would still seem *real*. I think that's important in a movie like this, because you don't want it to feel completely phony. I feel very good about what we achieved. I hate using smoke, but on this film we used it in almost every shot, because it really helped us to hide the

stage ceilings and create some atmosphere. That was our biggest nightmare, because smoke can be hard to control and it's very unpleasant
to have to breathe it in all the time.

AC: *How would you compare working on the stages with your location-
based sets? Which situation did you prefer?*
BURTON: Any time you're in one of those places for enough time, you
start to long for the other one. When you're stuck in stages for awhile,
you say to yourself, "God, I can't wait to get outside," but once you get
outside you think, "I'm freezing my ass off, I can't wait to go inside
again." [Laughs.]

One of our biggest challenges on this show, which Chivo and I discussed quite a bit, was making the setbound scenes match with the
location stuff. In those old Hammer films, you could *really* tell when
they were on a stage, and when they were on location. We did our best
to kind of bridge that gap and blend the sets and locations into a seamless whole. Quite often, sets can feel very claustrophobic, and when
you're shooting "exteriors" inside, it's very difficult to make it seem as if
you're someplace other than a soundstage. In this film, though, there
are many shots set in the forest that have a sense of sky that feels real,
which is amazing to me. The scenes breathe, and they have an openness that's quite effective. Chivo did a great job on that.

AC: *You also shot some complex action scenes, including horsebound
chases, within the soundstages at Leavesden. That must have been a
challenge.*
BURTON: In a way, it really helped to have standing sets at Leavesden,
because we didn't have to strike them immediately. That allowed us to
build upon those sequences if we had to. We were editing during production, so we could look at our action footage to see what we'd gotten.
If we needed any other shots, we could just go back into the sets and
grab them.

The chase scenes were definitely a bit of a challenge, though. We
used a flight shed at Leavesden that was long and narrow, but it still
didn't give us much of a run. When you've got to time horses with
stunts and everything else, you're lucky if you can get three seconds of
usable footage in one go. For those scenes, we used a Jeep-like [Barbour

All-Terrain Tracking truck], which we nicknamed the "Batmobile." It had a Libra 3 remote head mounted on its hydraulic lift to help us control any jitter. The Batmobile came in quite handy, because we could get it up to speed really quickly and maximize our runs.

AC: *What made you choose to use Deluxe's CCE process over some of the other special lab processes?*
BURTON: We just felt right about it. Using that type of process is like picking out the right colors for the set, the right costumes, or the right music. You just treat everything as if it's part of the fabric of the film. Chivo and I both agree that you don't ever want to do something as a gimmick, you just want to feel that it's right. You may do something in one movie that you'd never do in another; you just have to deal with each project on its own.

AC: *Chivo mentioned that you generally worked in a lens range between 21 mm and 40 mm. Did you simply feel that a wider perspective was right for this project?*
BURTON: I usually gravitate toward wide lenses, but I'm not sure why. Maybe it has something to do with my background in animation—I just like to *see* things. We also wanted to make *Sleepy Hollow* like an old-fashioned movie, so that range seemed right. We didn't necessarily plan specifically to stay within that range, we just wound up doing it. We did use a couple of longer lenses here and there, but the range you mentioned seemed to fit what we were doing.

We shot in 1.85:1 for the same reason. I do love widescreen, but until they start showing films more completely on television or on video, it's too painful for me to watch only half of my film on the screen.

AC: *Apparently, you used Steadicam quite sparingly.*
BURTON: That's true, but Chivo and I agreed that we should only use that technique when it was appropriate. Often when you see that kind of stuff in a movie, it's a bit showy and it takes you out of the narrative. We only did it when it felt right for the story. The Steadicam work in *The Shining* was great, but it was perfect for that particular story.

AC: *What type of balance did you strike between digital effects and more traditional special effects?*

BURTON: We've tried to do as much of the effects work live as possible. We wanted to keep the digital stuff to a minimum, which is one of the reasons we built so many sets, and pumped so much smoke into the rafters. As amazing as digital technology is, you can still feel it on the screen while you're watching a movie—there's a certain *thinness* to it. To my mind, when you know that anything is possible technically, it tends to diminish a film somehow. Digital technology is very interesting and certainly has its place in film-making, but when you're watching a movie like *Black Sunday* you really feel as if you're *there*. When you combine the stagebound sets with the actors, their costumes, and everything else, you really feel as if you're within that particular world, because it has a more human quality. There might be a certain shot looking down on a town that's done with a cheesy miniature model, but it still somehow feels real in the context of the film. In other words, even though it's unreal, you still feel the reality of it. That's the vibe we were trying to capture on *Sleepy Hollow*.

Gorillas Just Want to Have Fun

MARK SALISBURY/2001

Therapists, students of psychology, and those who earn a living deciphering the alpha-wave patterns of human beings, make of the following what you will: Last night Mark Wahlberg had a dream. Nothing unusual in that, perhaps. Surely, movie stars dream as we do, even if their nocturnal adventures inevitably involve bigger toys, better locations, and more photogenic partners. But Wahlberg's dream was about chimps. "It wasn't anything sexual," the star of *Boogie Nights* and *The Perfect Storm* says quickly. "I always have these recurring nightmares. Actually, it wasn't a nightmare last night, because the chimps were nice to me. I was driving in a car, and I pulled up to a hotel, and these chimps and orangutans were the valets."

Since Wahlberg has just spent four months playing a beleaguered human in Tim Burton's action-packed reimagining of the 1968 sci-fi classic *Planet of the Apes*, his vision of primate parking attendants could easily be interpreted as well-justified turnabout. "I can live with that," he says of this cut-rate analysis. "Of course," he adds, "I got into trouble and went to a prison, where I saw friends of mine."

Interesting . . . but let's save that for our next session, shall we? On a cavernous Hollywood soundstage in January, a *Planet of the Apes* unlike any you've seen before has taken shape. The central premise of the story remains the same—an astronaut crash-lands on an upside-down world where talking apes are the dominant species and humans are slaves—but under Burton's direction, the apes are more like *apes*.

From *Premiere*, July 2001: 54+. Reprinted with permission of *Premiere* magazine. Copyright 2001 Hachette Filipacchi Media U.S., Inc.

They fly through trees, climb walls, swing out of windows. They go apeshit when angry. And they tear along the ground on all fours—a technique the production calls "loping"—at speeds of up to 30 miles per hour, during a climactic battle sequence unparalleled in the original series. "The point is not to make it the same," says Burton, who has previously reinvented the worlds of *Batman* and *Sleepy Hollow*. "There was room for other explorations, bringing in more ape mannerisms, interesting behavior patterns, having more fun with that. But you need it to be serious to some degree, because it's somewhat absurd anyway, talking apes and all of that."

Ape City, a mountain kingdom in a rain forest, has been created from nearly 2 million cubic feet of raw space by production designer Rick Heinrichs, who bagged an Oscar for his work on *Sleepy Hollow*. Its influences include the ancient Aztec, Mayan, and Incan civilizations. Twisted trees soar to the rafters; vines creep across jagged rocks on which strange markings have been carved. A thin veil of mist hangs in the air. Even the atmosphere seems chilled. Dwellings—some mere caves with bamboo shutters on the windows, others elaborate exercises in ape interior design—have been hewn out of the mountainside. Thirty-foot stone ape idols gaze down impassively. Rough steps lead to enclaves like the processing area, where slaves, including astronaut Leo Davidson (Wahlberg) and the native rebels played by Kris Kristofferson and Estella Warren, arrive in human-drawn carts and are deposited in cages belonging to an oily orangutan named Limbo (Paul Giamatti). To one side of a central rock plaza, there's a fenced-in garden terrace, lit by flickering torches, on which an ape dinner party (sample course: kabobs of banana squash, black radish, and bitter melon) is under way.

The scene as written is simple enough, yet it hints at the social and political concerns prevalent in this topsy-turvy society, as well as the division that exists between the liberal chimp Ari (Helena Bonham Carter), who calls for man's release from subjugation, and Thade (Tim Roth), general of the ape army, who's all for wiping them out. Over the course of three days, Burton will shoot dozens of takes and angles of this scene, which climaxes with Thade knocking Leo, who is working as a domestic in Ari's household, to the ground, prying his mouth apart, and peering inside. "Is there a soul in there?" he snarls before tossing Leo aside and calling for a towel on which to wipe his hairy hands.

("I love that," Burton says after one particularly vibrant take. "It's really creepy.")

As the hours tick by, cast members periodically slip off their ape feet and leave them lying like sleeping animals beneath the table. "The things you hear on the set, like 'Where are my hands?' or 'Have you got her teeth?'" laughs Bonham Carter, sipping a soda through a straw. The apes, she says, have set up a kind of support group to discuss "the psychological effects of being up all night and under [the make-up]." The dentures that push their mouths out are making them lisp, and though some of the dialogue will be rerecorded in postproduction, for now everyone is struggling to make sense of one another and not sound like a kid with a retainer. "It feels like you're underwater," says Lisa Marie, Burton's longtime love (previously featured in *Ed Wood*, *Mars Attacks!*, and *Sleepy Hollow*), cast here as a chimp trophy bride of an orangutan senator. When Roth can't hear David Warner (*Titanic*), who plays Ari's father and who's sitting next to Roth, the only solution is to drill a hole in the side of Roth's ape head.

Wahlberg, unhampered by prosthetics, has his own difficulties with the scene. During one take, Cary-Hiroyuki Tagawa (*Pearl Harbor*), who plays Krull, a silverback gorilla and protector of Ari, whacks him with a wooden spatula, and Wahlberg can't stop laughing. Take two, and he's still fighting the giggles. "Did I make it?" he asks. "Almost," says Burton, shaking his head. "There were a number of times where I just lost it," Wahlberg reflects later. "Seeing Tim Burton get a little frustrated helped me gain control of myself."

"Dinner parties are hard," Burton says. "They drive you crazy because everybody feels like an extra. And they are!" He cackles. "Mark's been bussing tables for three days." Says Bonham Carter, "He's bored stiff. Mind you, he's being paid, and he doesn't wear the makeup. He's very aware he can't afford to be late, 'cause he's got a load of cranky chimps around."

Upon its release in 1968, *Planet of the Apes* became an international phenomenon, spawning four sequels, two TV series (one of them animated), and a banana-boat-load of merchandise. So, naturally, the idea of reviving the franchise had been bouncing around Twentieth Century Fox for some time. Producers Don Murphy and Jane Hamsher (*Natural Born Killers*) took a stab at it in 1993, roping in Terry Hayes

(*Dead Calm*) to script and Oliver Stone to produce alongside them. Director Chris Columbus was later attached, and even James Cameron expressed interest, but the project languished in development until Tom Rothman, then president of Fox Film Group, brought in screen-writer William Broyles Jr. (*Cast Away*) to start afresh. Armed with Broyles's script, Rothman approached Burton, who had just come off of *Sleepy Hollow*. "To reenergize a familiar idea, you need a uniquely iconoclastic film-maker," the executive says. "Tim has that uncanny ability to walk the line between making very commercial films and yet very individualistic and distinctive films." Burton was a fan of the *Apes* series but was uncertain about doing a remake. Fox, however, insisted that this was neither a remake nor a sequel, but something else entirely. (For one thing, it's not even the same planet, so don't expect an Earth-shattering twist at the end.) "Knowing that was helpful," Burton says. "I don't think about [the comparisons] because that'll just be a nightmare." Instead, he focused on the dichotomies inherent in the story. "What I liked about this is, it's just reversals," he says. "There's a human outsider; there's also an ape outsider. You see reversals on different levels, double juxtapositions. I don't know how much of that will come through, but it's interesting to play with. Watching the chimp channel all those years influenced it as well," he adds with a laugh.

The project was fast-tracked by Fox when Burton signed on in early 2000. But while Broyles's script was enough to get the director to com-mit, it wasn't exactly ready to go. The reason? "Too big. It would have cost 300 million whatever . . . rupees," Burton says. Explains Richard D. Zanuck, who was head of production at Fox when the first *Apes* movie was released and is producing this new version, "To get the picture green-lighted was a very, very difficult task because the studio wanted to make it at a price that made sense. [Tim] was dragged into all kinds of budgetary problems." Burton says this is standard: "To me, that kind of stuff helps to bring it back down so it's a little more basic, more about character." Although a source puts the final figure at $100 million–plus, Rothman will say only that the budget was "more than *X-Men*, less than *Titanic*."

After working first with Broyles on revising the script, Burton brought in Lawrence Konner and Mark D. Rosenthal (*Mighty Joe Young*) last August for "a page-one rewrite," according to Konner. "The Broyles script has been radically changed," Zanuck says. "He came up with the characters pretty much as they are, but his script was impractical in many respects. It had monsters in it, all kinds of other things, half-horse—half-man. We wanted to go back to the basic element: the upside-down world." Konner and Rosenthal returned to the Pierre Boulle novel on which the original was based and watched the old movies. "I think it's fair to say we're a bit more faithful to the book and the original movie than Bill was," Konner says. "Tim felt very strongly that this needed to be the adventure of a guy on the planet of the apes."

Even as the story was being reconceived, work proceeded on the production. One of the first hires was six-time Oscar-winning makeup artist Rick Baker, who had already created realistic primates for such movies as *Gorillas in the Mist* and *Mighty Joe Young*. Baker and his crew were given just four months to create hundreds of ape makeups. "If they had asked me, I would have said I need, like, a year," Baker says. "If I hadn't had the experience on [*Dr. Seuss' How the Grinch Stole Christmas*] of doing 90 makeups a day for five months and not having enough lead time on that, I probably would have been afraid to do this."

Filming began on November 6. The shoot was scheduled to last 17 weeks, followed by a truncated postproduction period of 18 weeks. Toward the end of filming, Burton occasionally had three units shooting simultaneously and a mobile editing facility on location, which he would visit between setups. "He never compromised for a second," Wahlberg says. "It wasn't like we rushed for the sake of the short schedule." (According to Rothman, *Apes* "finished on schedule to the day and actually slightly under budget.")

The screenplay continued to be reworked throughout shooting, however. Burton has been criticized in the past for disregarding script and story, even as he has been lauded for his visual style. "They should read what the script *was*," he says of such comments. "I happen to think we're making it better." Baker, who came aboard on the strength of the title and the chance to work with Burton again (they also collaborated on *Ed Wood*), agrees. "When I finally read a script," he says, "I was not thrilled at all, which I probably shouldn't say. I even said to Zanuck,

'Why don't you throw this piece of shit out and get the [1968] Rod Serling script?' Fortunately [the story is now] much closer to what the first film was." Konner was often on the set reworking dialogue. "I read the first script, and then it was constant changes, so I would just read what was happening with my character in the mornings, while I was in makeup," says Roth. "I have no idea what's been going on, which will be good when I see the film."

For someone who has worked entirely within the studio system, and with consistent returns for the money spent (*Mars Attacks!* and *Ed Wood*, to a lesser extent, being his two blips), Tim Burton has remained remarkably (as Rothman observes) individualistic and iconoclastic. The 42-year-old director has always brought a personal connection to his movies, reflecting a childhood spent in suburban Burbank, finding solace in monster movies, Vincent Price, and cheesy '50s sci-fi cinema and indulging his affinity for outsiders, oddballs, and aliens. "There's an enthusiasm and an energy that is just refreshing," Roth says. "It reminds me of working with a young director on a very low-budget film." Says Wahlberg, "I look at this as an art film. The story itself, the way he's telling it, it's a very expensive art film."

"I've been very lucky," Burton says. "Making a movie is tough by nature, whether it's an independent film or whatever. As the world gets more corporate, you just want to protect that artistic feeling as much as you can. I don't want to create a me-versus-them, because that's not what it's about. It's a large operation—a lot of people, a lot of money—so I take that seriously. I feel like I'm in the army sometimes." For Burton, the joy is in the filming. He admits that everything else about making a blockbuster hasn't gotten any easier since 1989's *Batman*. "There's so much of this other crap," he says. "There's just this tiny ray of light where you're actually making the movie. Marketing, they're the ones now who decide which movies [get made]; it used to be agents, the studio." He's not frustrated with any studio per se but with the system as a whole. "It's ridiculous—it's like you're in the way of the marketing," he says. "I saw a teaser poster [for *Apes*] the other day and it said, 'This film has not yet been rated.' And I said, 'Why don't you put, "This film has not yet been shot"?' "

Dressed in his signature directing uniform of faded black Levi's and black combat boots, topped off by an array of predominately black shirts, Burton bounds around the set, an energetic, uncoordinated, oddly charismatic figure. His hair is an unruly mane of black, tangled curls, his gleeful face adorned with salt-and-pepper stubble and blue-tinted wraparound shades. "I call him the mad scientist," says Michael Clarke Duncan (*The Green Mile*), who plays Attar, Thade's right-hand gorilla. "When I first looked at him, I said, 'This guy is crazy-looking.' But you have to have that type of mentality to do a movie like this." Burton flits constantly to his actors between takes. "It's not because I'm paranoid," he says. "With this makeup, it's hard—I can't tell what's going on under there. I have to hand it to these people; it's like they're being buried alive every day."

"He's very solicitous and caring," Bonham Carter says. "Unfailingly, he will laugh after every take, even though it's not particularly funny. It's nice to have a compassionate heart in a director."

"Come day 60, 65, it gets a little old, getting up at five in the morning," Wahlberg says. "It would have been nearly impossible if it wasn't for the fact that I enjoyed being around him. I told him when we finished, 'Anytime, anywhere.'"

That's pretty much what Wahlberg said *before* they started as well. "We had a meeting that lasted all of two minutes," the actor recalls. "I went in and told him how much I liked him. I said I would be willing to do whatever he wanted. I was just hoping I wouldn't have to wear a loincloth [as Charlton Heston did in the original]. I like to keep my clothes on these days," adds the former Calvin Klein underwear model. "And I've got tattoos." For his stranger in a strange land, Burton says he needed someone who could "ground [the movie] against all this other weird stuff. All he has to do is look at something and it's like, 'Where the fuck am I? What's going on?' It's a kind of acting that is very hard to do."

Playing the human female who joins Leo in challenging the apes (the people on this planet are not mute, as they were in the original film) is Estella Warren (*Driven*), a Canadian model and former synchronized-swimming champion who is appearing in only her second movie. Her athletic background has come in handy during the film's more physical moments. "We were in Lake Powell [Arizona], in this freezing water, and I'm in my little outfit," she says. "Tim wanted to get a close-up of one of the actors coming out of the water on a horse. The trainers said,

'You can't have any of the actors riding the horses; they're for the stunt doubles.' And Tim's like, 'Can anybody [ride]?' So I get on the horse, and it was the biggest rush because I came pummeling out, neck-deep."

Burton says there was talk of using computer-generated imagery to create the apes, but the idea was swiftly discarded in favor of actors in makeup. "That's part of the energy of it, part of the mystery," he says. "There's something almost Shakespearean about it, like mask acting." That didn't mean, however, that they could scrimp on the quality of the performances. "There was one point where the studio felt we should drop down a notch because, after all, 'They're behind masks, all they have to be is actors,'" Zanuck says. "We wanted really *great* actors."

Bonham Carter was filming in Australia when Burton called, asking her to play a chimp, no audition required. "If you think about it, what am I meant to do, come in and eat a banana?" she laughs. "It was a straight offer, without even meeting me, which was very nice."

"I think it was a good stroke to get actors to play apes, as opposed to stunt guys or whatever," says Roth, who turned down the role of Snape in *Harry Potter and the Sorcerer's Stone* to play Thade. "All the performances are varied because of the worlds the actors come from."

"We're getting these performances because with Rick Baker's makeup, you see the actor come through," Zanuck says. Baker had first been contacted about the project back when Oliver Stone was involved. His vision for the apes was simple. "I wanted them to be more expressive than in the first one," he says. "You never saw the lips moving over the teeth. I wanted to be able to see teeth and have people move more like real apes." Applying the makeup takes between two and four hours. The actors' days begin at around 2:30 A.M., and despite the exceedingly long hours, there have been few complaints. "It's not hot, it doesn't irritate my face or anything," Duncan says. "I usually go into the makeup trailer, pop in a movie or go to sleep, and when I wake up, I'm Attar. The makeup is so beautifully constructed that the movements and the expressions of your own face work; it's just a matter of trusting it."

The female apes are less hairy and, from a human point of view, attractive. "I'm more evolved, I guess," sighs Bonham Carter. "I've got eyebrows. Apes don't have eyebrows. I wanted more hair." Lisa Marie, who says she plays "a sexy, glamorous chimpanzee," actually looks a bit like Mariah Carey. ("Have you told her that?" Burton asks me, laughing. "They were saying Ann-Margret yesterday," she says when I do.) Later, between camera setups, Burton carefully plants kisses on her chimp lips and neck. "It is a little strange," he admits, grinning. "But I know what's underneath." Even so, it could be disconcerting to see the actors without their makeup. "You go, 'Who the fuck is that?'" Burton says. "Michael Clarke Duncan walked onto the set the other day and it shocked me."

Despite his size, there's something almost cuddly about Duncan's Attar, like a teddy bear on steroids. Roth, however, is one intimidating primate, moving around "in a sharklike manner," he says, his slender frame encased in armor. Thade was originally written as a gorilla, until Baker informed Burton that chimps were the scarier apes. "You don't know whether they're going to kill you or kiss you," Burton says. "They're very open on some levels and much more evil in a certain way. They'll rip you to shreds." Roth was keen to exploit this unpredictability in his performance. "I wanted to do this thing where he would be across the room and then two inches away from you in a heartbeat," the actor says. "One moment they're your friend, the next they can tear your head off."

Before every take, Roth goes through a strange little routine, stretching, loosening his neck muscles, then uttering a loud noise. Sometimes it's a bark, other times a screech, most often a growl. Roth says it's less a case of Method Aping than boredom relief: "If you don't keep the movement going, you lose it in your head." He gets tips from Terry Notary, an ex–Cirque du Soleil performer employed to teach the actors how to move like apes (he's also Roth's stunt double). The primate performers also had to put in several preproduction weeks with Notary at Ape School. "They gave you a basic walk, and you adapted it to the kind of ape you were playing," says Giamatti (*Man on the Moon*). "Orangutans have a waddling kind of walk, and they hang from things, so there's a lot of me [doing that]." Bonham Carter found inspiration in childhood. "The most helpful image was to think of a nappy [a diaper] that was full between your legs, and you didn't want to spill it," she laughs.

If walking is complicated, eating is an ordeal. At lunch one day, in the parking lot of a defunct bank building across from the soundstage, Roth sits alone, grimly poking bite-sized pieces of food into his mouth with the aid of a small mirror on the table in front of him. "You need the mirror because you've got no idea where your mouth is," Bonham Carter explains. "It begins about an inch lower than where you usually aim for." Missing the mark could be a disaster. "The first day, I ate some beetroot," she says. "I thought we could just wash it off. And it was a nightmare because they had to repaint [my face]."

Of the many incongruous sights on the *Apes* set—gorilla extras singing a cappella off-camera; background apes sans masks, their eyes, mouths, and noses ringed in black, reading the *Los Angeles Times*—none is stranger than that of a chimp smoking. "The first time, I felt like one of those experiments, smoking beagles," says Roth, who, along with Bonham Carter, regularly steps out for a cigarette. Baker warned them about the flammable glues used to apply the makeup, as well as the makeup it-self. "He said, 'Be careful when you light the cigarette, you'll lose your face.' By that he meant our *real* face."

The only fire casualty, however, turned out to be Wahlberg, who was singed during a scene that had him being pelted by fireballs. "The stuntmen, of course, were seeing who could get closest to me, and who-ever hit me would get a hundred bucks," the actor says with a laugh. "After take ten, I got hit with a couple, but then they hit Helena, and I didn't like that much because she was very flammable." Bonham Carter says, "Mark was literally on fire. But we were next to a lake, and he went out pretty quickly."

Wahlberg also took a pounding one day from two real chimps that the actors spent time with during rehearsals. He greeted Bonham Carter with a hug, and the overprotective primates rushed in. "They were more familiar with me than they were with her, but I think she smells a little bit nicer than I do, so they got a little bit upset," he says. "They got over it."

The Internet has, inevitably, been abuzz for months with gossip and rumors about *Planet of the Apes*. "Of all [the Web's] wonderful uses, what seems to be sticking is the worst side of it," muses Burton. "Some crazy fucker making up weird things. Now you've got to spend all your time either confirming or denying." What about the report that George

Clooney plays an ape, for example? "That's a new one to me," the director laughs. "I didn't even hear that." The real burning question, however, has been this: Do Wahlberg's Leo and Bonham Carter's Ari consummate their mutual attraction? "It was in the early drafts," Konner says. "It preceded [our script]. What can I tell you? Mark and Helena express interest in each other. A physical sex scene? No." Why steer away from it? "Because I was told to."

"Interspecial love—we don't really go there," Bonham Carter says. "It's more platonic. It's not quite like dog and human, but there's definitely a special love that can't be categorized." For his part, Wahlberg insists, "I was in bed with a chimpanzee. You'll have to see whether it makes it into the movie. I've got a feeling it will." This is news to Burton, however. "I guess I wasn't there that day," the director laughs. "Maybe I was out getting coffee.

"Believe me, if I want to make a movie about bestiality, I'll do it without a major studio," Burton adds. "All we're trying to do is to deepen the characters a little bit, so it's more simple, emotional. I've seen much worse at the Central Park Zoo."

Other questions are more easily answered. As for what nods to the original fans can expect, parts of Burton's film were filmed at Lake Powell, where the spaceship crashes at the beginning of the 1968 version. Linda Harrison, the ex–Mrs. Zanuck, who played the beauteous Nova in the first two films, appears briefly as one of the humans brought into Ape City. And the biggest coup was nabbing Heston to play an ape. "He never wanted to do the sequel," says Zanuck, "and said to me at the time, 'I'll only do it on two conditions: One, you finish me in a week, and two, you kill me so we never have to have this discussion again.'" Thirty years later, Zanuck invited Heston to breakfast with a proposal. "I said, 'Chuck, it's unimaginable to me that we can make a picture called *Planet of the Apes* and not do some kind of homage to you. Obviously, you'll have to play an ape, because we killed you [in *Beneath the Planet of the Apes*] at your request.'"

Heston has just one scene, as Thade's dying father. Roth, who plays opposite him, admits he's no fan of the older actor's conservative, NRA-touting politics. "I have great disagreements with everything he stands for," Roth says. "I had to treat him with respect, as I would any actor, and so I did."

Wahlberg didn't work with Heston but made sure he came down to the set. "That was one of the few days I had off," he says, "but I had to see Chuck Heston. He had been in makeup for a good 12 hours and wanted to get out of it, but he was very polite and complimented me on my work. I said the feeling was mutual. Being from the hood, I've got my own views on guns."

Released during a turbulent period in U.S. history—the Cold War, Vietnam, the race riots—the original *Planet of the Apes* offered some social and political insight along with its sci-fi thrills. Those involved with this film are aiming for a bit of the same, but it's clearly not priority number one. "If we can make a little comment here and there without trying," Zanuck says, "and if it's amusing, that's fun." Says Konner, "Hopefully, it will say something about the condition of modern man without being as specific as that. Also about intolerance. We find apes saying things that people often say in racial ways, subtle and not so subtle." Yet Duncan, who earned an Oscar nod in the racially charged drama *The Green Mile*, doesn't see any such implications in the *Apes* story line. "Not to me," he booms. "When they asked me to do it, I just said, 'Yes, I'd be honored to,' because I remember Charlton Heston doing it. Nothing ever came into my mind about politics or race or anything like that. I'm an actor, and this is what we do to get paid."

As for the apocalyptic shock of seeing the ruined Statue of Liberty at the end of the original movie, the filmmakers are planning something different but, they hope, equally surprising. "We couldn't compete with the atomic bomb, which, in the '60s, was a concern of everybody's," Zanuck says. "But we have come up with an idea that we think is a lot of fun." Whatever that is, "it's not in writing anywhere," executive producer Ralph Winter said on the set in January. "There's no dialogue, so we'll give the actors direction that day." Says Wahlberg, "It was one of the last things we shot, and if people thought the Statue of Liberty was a cool ending, this is going to blow their minds."

It's now mid-April, and Burton is holed up in an editing suite in New York City, about to begin working on the music with composer Danny Elfman (*Batman, Edward Scissorhands, Sleepy Hollow*). "Everybody's got the answers, I guess, except me," says the director, who chortles at the idea of unwritten endings and the rumors that as many as four or five variations were filmed. "That's rubbish," he says. "Here's the thing: What the ending is, exactly, I can't tell you, 'cause I'm still working on it. [Fox] didn't pay for four endings. We've tried to leave ourselves a couple of options, like you do on anything, to see how things play." He sighs. "This is a tough one to maneuver. It sort of takes away from the process of doing it, and I'm trying to enjoy that brief moment as much as I can."

Playboy Interview: Tim Burton

KRISTINE McKENNA / 2001

It's odd that director Tim Burton keeps finding himself at the helm of big-budget studio blockbusters, because he's really not the type. Trained as a fine artist and described as a shy, withdrawn loner, he has indie filmmaker written all over him.

The potential blockbuster on his slate is *Planet of the Apes*, a "re-imagination," as Burton says, of the 1968 science fiction classic about an astronaut who lands on an alien world where apes talk and humans are second-rate primates. This upside-down simian society should be familiar territory for Burton, who has spent close to a decade exploring themes of social maladjustment in unconventional characters such as Batman, Edward Scissorhands, Beetlejuice and the Headless Horseman.

Burton creates quirky movies that rake in tons of cash for the studios. And his method is deceptively simple: He makes children's movies for adults. Burton combines the visual sophistication and complex narrative nuances adults demand of movies with a child's love of spectacle and mystery. His debut film, 1985's *Pee-wee's Big Adventure*—which he directed at the age of 26—was made for $6 million and grossed $45 million. The 1988 follow-up, *Beetlejuice*, cost $13 million and brought in $80 million, and the following year Burton broke box-office records with *Batman*. The film—along with Burton's sequel *Batman Returns*—became a billion-dollar business.

Born in Burbank, California, in 1958, Burton grew up in a lower-middle-class neighborhood he'd prefer to forget. He's been out of touch for more than two decades with his family—younger brother Danny

and their mother, Jean, who works in a gift shop. His father, Bill
Burton, died last year. Tim spent most of his time drawing, daydream-
ing, watching B movies and poring over issues of *Famous Monsters of
Filmland* magazine. The loneliness and isolation Burton felt as a
child—and his capacity to escape those feelings through fantasy—have
influenced almost all his movies, which often deal with outsiders and
estrangement.

Burton barely got through high school but on the basis of his
obvious artistic gift was admitted into the animation program at the
California Institute of the Arts, a school founded by Walt and Roy
Disney in Valencia, California. Burton foundered there as well, when he
discovered that animation isn't a good field for people who color outside the lines. But he was nonetheless hired by the Disney studio on the
strength of his brief exercise in pencil-test animation, called *Stalk of the
Celery Monster.* Disney put him to work on its 1981 film *The Fox and the
Hound.*

In his spare time Burton worked on a children's book that was an
homage to his childhood hero Vincent Price. The following year,
when Disney gave him $60,000 to create something, he adapted it
into a short film. The resulting six-minute film, *Vincent*, which he
completed in 1982, and *Frankenweenie*, a short film made in 1984 about
a young boy determined to revive his dead dog, launched Burton's
career.

After Burton left Disney, writer Stephen King recommended
Frankenweenie to a Warner Bros. executive, who screened it for Paul
Reubens. Reubens, whose television series, *Pee-wee's Playhouse*, was
hugely successful at the time, was looking for someone to direct him in
his first film. Together, Burton and Reubens created a charming, visually
captivating film. Contributing to the movie was composer Danny
Elfman, whose quirky music subsequently became an essential compan-
ion to Burton's visuals. Elfman scored Burton's next film, the offbeat
ghost comedy *Beetlejuice*, and followed that up with *Batman*. While he
was in England shooting *Batman*, Burton met German painter Lena
Gieseke, whom he married in February 1989.

Following the phenomenal success of *Batman*, Burton made *Edward
Scissorhands,* a modest fairy tale starring Johnny Depp. One of Burton's
most admired films and his most personal, it's the story of a misfit who

has scissors instead of hands and can't get close to people without accidentally hurting them.

A subtly observed, intimate film, *Edward Scissorhands* gave Burton a chance to catch his breath before diving into *Batman Returns*. By the time that film was released to mixed review in 1992, Burton's marriage to Gieseke was over, and he'd fallen in love with model Lisa Marie.

Burton cast Lisa Marie in a supporting role in his 1994 film, *Ed Wood*, a tribute to the Fifties cult filmmaker often described as the worst director of all time. Lisa Marie also appears in Burton's three subsequent films: *Mars Attacks!, Sleepy Hollow* and *Planet of the Apes*.

Although Burton assembled an amazing cast for *Mars Attacks!* that included Glenn Close, Jack Nicholson, and Annette Bening, the 1996 film was the most harshly reviewed of his career. *Sleepy Hollow* was praised for extraordinary art direction and broke the $100 million mark (a first for a film starring Depp).

Burton lives with Lisa Marie in the Hollywood hills, but freelance journalist Kristine McKenna—whose last *Playboy* Interview was with John Malkovich—tracked him down in New York City, where the 43-year-old filmmaker was holed up in the Brill Building, racing to complete a cut of *Planet of the Apes*. McKenna reports being surprised by the man she met. "Tim Burton has a reputation for being noncommunicative and remote, but I didn't find him that way at all. Though he invariably showed up for our meetings dressed in black—he has a goth–grunge thing going in terms of sartorial style—he was forthcoming, relaxed, and downright sunny.

"He's no slick glad-hander, and I imagine that he squirms a lot when he's in the studio boardroom. Talking with him, you can understand why those studio guys keep giving him the keys to the car. He really loves the things he loves, and when he talks about them he shows an enthusiasm that's contagious and charming."

PLAYBOY: *Do you have to be a good liar to survive in the movie business?*
BURTON: It's like being in the Army, in that you can't show people what you really think. I prefer not to think of myself as a liar and try to surround myself with people who can handle truth, but the truth is always subjective. In the movie business at the end of the day, it's all just people's opinions, because this isn't a precise science. Still, when

you're making something you're like a shark maneuvering through all these opinions. Movies are an out-of-body experience. I'm always amused when certain money people enter the movie business expecting truth, logic and a clear-cut return on their investment, because there's a surreal aspect to this entire undertaking that's impossible to control.

PLAYBOY: Planet of the Apes *is a cult classic. How much license did you grant yourself to reinvent the story? For instance, the previous* Apes *movies all could be interpreted as cautionary tales about nuclear war.*
BURTON: This one's a cautionary tale about trying to remake science fiction films from the late Sixties. Actually, we don't get into the nuclear thing too much because we weren't attempting to remake the original. The first *Apes* movie, directed by Franklin Schaffner, was such a classic that it wasn't ripe for remaking. The thing that may allow us to get away with this film is that we aren't trying to make it the same thing. Let's face it, you can't beat certain aspects of the original. They say you should try to remake only bad movies, and *Planet of the Apes* wasn't a bad movie. For many of us the film had a lot of impact, and for reasons I can't explain it was a weird idea that just clicked. I have done several films that involved elaborate makeup, but there's something really powerful in the simple premise of talking apes that's so eerie it's almost Shakespearean. Unfortunately, there were talking apes checking into the Beverly Wilshire and going shopping by the time the third *Apes* film came out in 1971. The apes dressed like car mechanics in the fourth and fifth films. We won't dwell on that though, because the first one was pretty great.

PLAYBOY: *You can't talk about the original* Planet of the Apes *without mentioning Charlton Heston. What do you think of his work?*
BURTON: I was a huge Charlton Heston fan when I was growing up—particularly during his *Planet of the Apes, Omega Man, Soylent Green* period—and he still fascinates me. Monster movies didn't scare me at all as a child, but Heston's films really did. Nobody ever mentions that *The Ten Commandments* is like a horror movie. Heston's character starts out like a normal guy and by the end of the film he's this weird zombie. There's tons of horrific imagery—it's like a monster movie and Heston has a presence in it that's terrifying. Because he communicated a belief

in what he was doing, he had this uncanny ability to make you believe whatever bullshit was going on, and in *Omega Man* he comes across as the most serious person who ever lived. Heston's like Vincent Price, who's an actor I love in a completely different way. Both of them seem tortured somehow, and there's something really personal about what they do on-screen.

PLAYBOY: *The makeup for the original* Apes *movies consisted of rubber masks and* Star Trek–*type outfits. How have you improved on that?*
BURTON: The problem is that if you strictly adhere to the basic premise and keep the apes naked and acting more like animals, it becomes another thing. We tried to get into ape behavior so it would feel like more than just people with ape masks on. The cast and crew spent a week at Ape School trying to get a feel for ape mannerisms. Some of what went on at Ape School was movement training, and some of it was interacting with live chimps. Being in Ape School was like flying on an airplane in that on some level everybody was terrified. There's an undercurrent of suppressed fear I feel on airplanes, and I sensed something similar at Ape School, which I think had to do with the fact that monkeys are completely unpredictable and intensely sexual.

PLAYBOY: *Sexual?*
BURTON: Yes. They fall in love with you, and they're jealous and possessive. They would start humping my leg, and if I didn't pay attention to them, they'd spit at me or throw shit at me. They'll grab you wherever. They're very interested in the inside of your nose and your mouth, and they try to groom you. They have an extra three feet to their reach, and they don't know their own strength. One day one of them jumped on me from a 10-foot platform and completely took me out. He was just playing, but it was like having an anvil thrown at you. I love animals, but with these monkeys I felt like I was gazing into the unknown. It's interesting that culturally we've come to regard them as cute, but they're capable of ripping you in half. They have an insane, psycho quality. One day I caught one of them staring at me and I thought, Man, if a human ever looked at me that way I'd run in the other direction. I felt like I was in some weird gay bar and some sleazy person was checking me out.

PLAYBOY: *Bill Broyles wrote the screenplay for your* Planet of the Apes.
*Then, at the 11th hour, you brought in the writing team of Lawrence Konner
and Mark Rosenthal to rework the script. Why?*

BURTON: I don't know why this is—it's something you should
probably ask the studios about—but with all the big movies I've done,
the scripts are never ready when it's time to shoot. Never. When I came
on board with the first *Batman* lots of people had been involved and
loads of money had been sunk into the thing. I don't know why there's
so much second-guessing in the movie business. I guess it's because
people with a lot of money tend to be concerned about what might
happen to their money, which is probably how they manage to accu-
mulate it in the first place. But this is a funny business to be in if you
want concrete answers. Movies are abstractions until they've been
completed—and that's the beauty of them. So, I hear myself saying OK,
we're going to start this film and we're going to get it into shape. I'm
like Ed Wood—Mr. Optimistic. Bill Broyles had been working on the
Planet of the Apes script for a long time before I got on it, and we worked
with Bill for a while longer, but I think it was starting to drive him
crazy. Sometimes you need a fresh perspective, and bringing in new
writers is like going to a doctor for a second opinion. Larry Konner was
on the set every day doing new pages as the shoot progressed, because
dialogue that might sound good in a story conference isn't necessarily
going to sound great when you get people in ape makeup saying it.
Budget also played a role in the script rewrite. If we had adhered to
Bill's script we'd still be shooting, and the film would have cost an extra
$200 million.

PLAYBOY: *What made Mark Wahlberg right for the lead?*

BURTON: Mark's a type of actor I really like. He's solid and there's not
a lot of bullshit about him. When you're doing a film like this you need
a person who can serve as an anchor, and Mark can do that. Before I
met him people were telling me he had all this baggage involving
music, Calvin Klein underwear ads, and so on. But the guy's good, so
people should give him a fucking break. You'll have an actor who never
shows up on time on one film, then he's right there like an angel on
the next one. It's all chemistry, so I don't pay too much attention to
people's reputations.

PLAYBOY: *Have you ever had to fire an actor?*

BURTON: No, partly because I'm not sure what good acting is. I strad-dle a fine line of knowing what's what. With *Pee-wee's Big Adventure* and *Beetlejuice* I was working with actors like Paul Reubens, Michael Keaton, and Catherine O'Hara. They're so good at improvisation that most of those movies wound up being improvised. I get excited by actors who can surprise you. The point is, I don't always assume I know best, par-ticularly when I'm working with a talent like Bill Murray, who was just great in *Ed Wood*. I love people I don't understand, and there's some-thing deeply puzzling about Bill. Prior to shooting he prepared for his character by having all the hair on his body waxed, and believe me, it looked extremely painful. I love him and that performance so much that I still day-dream about doing a music video of the scene of Bill with the mariachis.

PLAYBOY: *Do you have a sense if a movie is going to be a success?*

BURTON: I'm always surprised by how movies do. With *Batman,* I thought it had a shot at making a modest profit. But ultimately I don't have any clue, because you're dealing with things that are organic. I'm like Ed Wood in that I go into every movie with the same mixture of optimism, enthusiasm, and denial. You have to because you're devoting your time to it, so you get close to things and the movie becomes like one of your children. It may be ugly, but it's your child. Plus, there is no ultimate truth about the worth of a movie, and that's something I learned when *Pee-wee's Big Adventure* came out. It was on several lists as one of the worst films of 1985. Then when *Beetlejuice* came out in 1988, the same reviewers that gave *Pee-wee* minus 10 were talking about how great *Pee-wee* was and what a disappointment my new film *Beetlejuice* was. It's like high school the way critics trash you, then suddenly they're your best friend. I always think, Hey, you guys never talked to me in high school, so why start now?

PLAYBOY: *Directing a movie on the scale of* Planet of the Apes *is like being a general in the army—it demands leadership skills. Where did you acquire those?*

BURTON: Maybe all those endless hours spent watching movies where the Army attacks the giant insects taught me how to maneuver troops and destroy all monsters. As a kid I was always able to get other kids to do things. I once got some kids to help me set up a bunch of debris and weird footprints in a park, and we convinced these other kids an alien ship had crashed in Burbank. I would stage fake fights in the neighborhood so it looked like somebody was killing somebody, and I once convinced a kid that a killer had fallen into a neighbor's pool after they'd just cleaned it and doused it with acid and chlorine. I threw some clothes in there and told this kid the guy had dissolved.

PLAYBOY: *Now that you've done a few big movies, do you feel like you know the drill? Is it getting easier?*
BURTON: It's actually gotten harder. With the first *Batman* I was kind of flying below the radar, plus it was shot in England. I was eight hours away from the studio, the media and a lot of the pressure. At that point the pressures were just abstractions to me, but when the same things keep happening to you your tolerance goes down. I remember seeing people who looked like they were going to jump off a ledge and thinking, Gee, why is that person acting that way? After a few years you start climbing out on the ledge yourself. Working with a studio on a movie of this scale is an incredible journey because you don't have the option of not showing up. I plan to take a slightly deeper breath before I start the next movie, which will definitely be smaller.

PLAYBOY: *You've spoken about the terror you felt when you arrived in England in 1988 and saw the 95 acres of* Batman *sets that filled Pinewood Studios. How did you get through that experience?*
BURTON: Sometimes you get karmic lessons, and I guess that was one of mine. Throughout my life I'd never talked much or communicated well with people, and I think that's one of the reasons I like to draw and became an animator—you could show a picture instead of talking. Communicating with people was definitely one of the major challenges *Batman* presented. The first day of shooting I had an experience with Jack Palance that scared me to death—I literally saw white and left my body. It was the first shot and I figured we'd start simple with a shot of Jack Palance walking out of a bathroom. So he's in the bathroom and we're rolling camera, but when I call "action" nobody comes out. I say "cut" and walk over and say "OK, Mr. Palance, all you have to do is

come out." So we start again, I say "action" and he still doesn't come out. I walk back over and say, "OK, Mr. Palance, all you've got to do is come out," and he starts breathing heavy and grabs me and screams, "Who are you to tell me what to do? I've done over a hundred movies!" I absolutely freaked out and one of the producers had to calm everybody down. I don't know what was going on in Palance's mind, and he apologized later, but it scared me to death. That movie was a trial by fire on every level, and Jack Nicholson really helped me get through it, simply by being who he is and supporting me. Having somebody like him on my side was so helpful. I'll never forget that—Jack's a good man that way. It's also incredibly fun to watch him work because he has such an amazing command of his skills. He can come up with different approaches to a scene time after time, and I'd find myself wanting to do extra takes just to see what he'd do.

PLAYBOY: *What was your life like in 1989 when* Batman *was breaking box office records?*
BURTON: It was so surreal it didn't really affect me. If there were dancing girls throwing money around I might have had a stronger feeling about it. Right after I finished *Batman* I went to make *Edward Scissorhands*, which we shot in a small town east of Tampa, Florida. When you're staying in a mosquito-infested condo in a third-rate golf resort and there's a plastic fish hanging on your wall, it's hard to feel like you're king of the world.

PLAYBOY: *Unlike most directors, you're a recognizable personality. How do you like your celebrityhood?*
BURTON: Being a so-called public figure is a lot to adjust to and there are many layers to it. For instance, if somebody approaches me on the street and tells me he's been touched by something in one of my films, that makes me feel really good. On the other hand, when people come up and hand me scripts, I always want to say, "Hey, why are you handing me a script? Have you read any reviews of my films? Every reviewer says my scripts are terrible!" We live in a world where everyone's privacy is subject to invasion, but I like mystery in life. I prefer to look at people and wonder about them, as opposed to knowing every stupid detail about their lives. Of course I, too, occasionally have those

nosy feelings of wanting to know everything, but they aren't feelings I'm proud of and I don't think they deserve to be satisfied. Before I started making movies I used to go sit in the mall and draw, and I've always loved observing people. But that's not something I can do anymore. I've come full circle—now I am the observed and must reside in my own *Twilight Zone*. If I do something like this interview or go out to a dinner, it leaves me completely exhausted. I know I'm being looked at and I don't like it.

PLAYBOY: *Do you have a temper?*
BURTON: Unfortunately I have a quicker temper than I used to. We went on location in Hawaii and everybody showed up for work in Hawaiian shirts, like they were on the *Love Boat*. Maybe it's because I was tired, but it really bothered me and I yelled, "We're not on vacation yet!" Hawaii has a strong current of primal energy, and the first time I went there I thought I was dying because I felt a way I'd never felt before. Then I learned that what I was feeling was relaxation.

PLAYBOY: *What's the most widely held misconception about the lives of the famous?*
BURTON: One is that we all hang out together. I once went to a dinner where it was all famous people, and all I can remember is how uncomfortable everybody was. It was a weird evening.

PLAYBOY: *Is Hollywood a hard place to make friends?*
BURTON: I've read things about myself like, "Tim disappears on people," but I'm in a business where people disappear. I recently went to the doctor and the dentist, and I was surprised when they both told me that I hadn't seen either of them in a few years. I felt like I'd just seen them. Maybe as you get older the passage of time accelerates and the time machine gets put on full speed ahead. I've always felt like a friendly person, but I don't have that many friends, and I don't know if I can pin the blame for that on Hollywood.

PLAYBOY: *Which of your films has been the most personal and revealing of you?*
BURTON: *Edward Scissorhands*, which was self-generated way back. Alan Arkin was so good in that film that it was scary, because he really

reminded me of my dad. I feel very close to *The Nightmare Before Christmas* and *Ed Wood*, too.

PLAYBOY: *Several critics have noted you avoid dealing with sexuality in your films. Do you avoid sex?*
BURTON: I never thought of it that way—I consider Catwoman a sexual character, for instance. It's true, though, that I'm interested in manifestations of sexuality that are more subtle and difficult to define. Take Vincent Price. I always saw him as a heterosexual character, yet he was slightly ambiguous. That's one of the things that interested me about Ed Wood as well. He dressed in women's clothes but was neither gay nor heterosexual. He was something else that you couldn't quite define.

PLAYBOY: *What's the most difficult step in filmmaking?*
BURTON: I'm not good at business—in fact, I'm pretty bad at it. I'm a person who needs time to think and muse over things. Having a million things going on and constantly ringing cell phones don't bring out the best in me. The deal-making part seems to exist in a hermetically sealed world where people are prone to believe all kinds of crap, and I'm not comfortable in that environment and try not to spend too much time there. You feel at odds with yourself when you're making something, and if I'm looking out over a lake or at the ocean I often ask myself why I do what I do, because I don't get the pleasure from it that other filmmakers seem to get. The whole thing seems insurmountably difficult. I guess the thing that keeps me doing it is that I enjoy the people and I like the crew. They're not sitting around bullshitting in some boardroom, going over research about this or that—they're busting their asses to actually do something.

The most physically arduous part of the process is obviously the shoot itself, but that's also the best part, because there's movement. Emotionally you have to train like an athlete to shoot a big movie, and it's incredibly debilitating when the studio is still vacillating about giving the film a green light until you're halfway through shooting it—that really takes a lot out of everybody. This film was shot in 80 days, which is the fastest shoot I've ever done.

PLAYBOY: *Let's talk about your younger years. Did you do drugs in high school? You seem like the type.*

BURTON: A little, but I've never done acid or anything like that. When I was a child, I felt like I was already really old, so I never had friends my own age and never had access to drugs. I wasn't in the loop of social or cultural peer pressure to do what everyone else was doing, and I even left high school a semester early. I don't know what was up with the school system that I was able to get out early, because I was a lousy student. In fact, I was completely unable to write anything in my last year of high school because I'd gotten in a fight during a sporting event and broken my hand. When I left school early, people told me I was going to miss the best time of my life, but when I went back for the graduation ceremony, everybody looked like they'd just done life in prison.

PLAYBOY: *Did your parents support your creativity?*

BURTON: That's hard to say. My father actually liked to draw, but he didn't show that side of himself too much. He was an ex-baseball player, so I was kind of pushed into sports, though I was somewhat willing. I also played a musical instrument, and they tried to push me into the arts. The one thing they didn't push me into was drawing— and if they had, I probably wouldn't have gotten into it. My parents weren't particularly strict, but anyone who comes from suburbia can tell you that your parents don't have to be strict for you to feel strangled by that culture. We lived right by the Burbank airport and the planes flew so low that I could stick my ear right on the television set and turn it up as loud as it would go, and I still wouldn't be able to hear it. My parents tried to send me to church, but suburban religion is a bureaucratic setup where you're told things but you don't feel anything. I consider myself a spiritual person, but I don't place spirituality in any concrete form or place.

PLAYBOY: *Is it true your parents blocked out the windows in your bedroom?*

BURTON: Yeah, they covered them up for insulation, supposedly, and they put a little slit at the top of the covering so some light could get in. It was a suburban thing of keeping the heat in or something—they said the windows were letting in too much air. I thought, What the fuck? This is California for Christ's sake! That's probably why I've always related to Edgar Allan Poe, who wrote several stories revolving around the theme of being buried alive.

PLAYBOY: *Would you characterize yourself as a rebellious kid?*

BURTON: I was quietly rebellious. I never spent too much time in the principal's office, but my grandmother told me that before I could walk I was trying to crawl out the door. I just remember wanting to go. When I was 10 I went to live with my grandmother, and I lived with her until I got out of high school. My grandfather was dead by then. My dad understood my wanting to live with my grandmother, but my mom was really upset, which was kind of the reason I wanted to go. My grandmother gave me sanctuary and she really saved me. She made sure I had food and left me alone. I didn't hate my parents, but I just never felt socialized in that way. As a child I always had Italian friends. I didn't consciously do this, but I'd befriend these sweet, wonderful Italian families who'd give me food and take me in. My parents were much more reserved—so much so, in fact, that until around 10 years ago I always flinched whenever anyone touched me. Looking back on it now, it's pretty clear to me that my parents were depressed, and I always felt a deep, dark unhappiness permeating the air in their house. My dad was a baseball player who got injured, and he must have been unhappy about that. I don't know what was up with my mom, but she seemed real depressed. It's kind of scary, but I don't know much about them. I realized that when I was in my early 20s, so I tried to ask them about their lives, but they didn't really want to tell me. One of the things I love about traveling is that you get to see other cultures where people relate to one another in an open way. It's so beautiful I almost start to cry thinking about it, because it's something I never had.

PLAYBOY: *Are you in contact with your parents now?*

BURTON: My dad died last year. He had been ill for a while, and I made some little attempts to communicate with him and have some kind of resolution. His death wasn't a huge sense of loss, because I'd been grieving the absence of a relationship with him my whole life.

PLAYBOY: *Do you plan to have children?*
BURTON: I'm still so attuned to the feelings I had as a child that I
think I've resisted it so far. I'm kind of a late bloomer, probably because
there were a lot of issues I kept repressed for a long time. I don't know if
I've really dealt with those things yet. It's like seasons, and I think you
go through waves. You kind of think you've dealt with something, then
you find yourself regressing into it.

PLAYBOY: *Yes, but one likes to think that some things can be fully healed.*
For instance, you mentioned you no longer flinch when people touch you.
BURTON: Certain studio executives still make me flinch when they
touch me. If I were kissed by Jon Peters again I might flinch.

PLAYBOY: *Do you envision the day when you'll have worked through all the*
emotional and creative material generated by your childhood?
BURTON: Are you asking if I'm going to get tapped out? I don't know.
Maybe that will happen and I'll revert to some kind of amoeba state.
There is an element of catharsis to doing something creative—you can
work out certain things and move on. So if you were able to make
movies reasonably quickly, I guess they could work as some sort of therapy and you could use them to work through a lot of stuff. But the
problem with movies, especially these kinds of movies, is that they take
so long it's like a painful birth, a rough life and a bitter death, and the
whole experience winds up generating more psychological material.

PLAYBOY: *Is the world a better place now than it was when you were a*
child?
BURTON: It's hard to say if things get worse as we get older or if they
just seem worse. You read about people dying of leprosy at the age of 30
or having to have their fingers cut off, and you think obviously things
are better now. Nonetheless, there's so much overstimulation now that
I find myself longing for the time when you couldn't be contacted
every second of the day by cell phone. I have one and admit there's a
slight James Bond aspect to it that appeals to me, but I rarely use it and
Lisa is the only person who has the number. Seeing two people sitting
across from each other in a romantic restaurant having conversations
on their cell phones with other people is so freakish. I find the Internet

depressing, too, largely because so much of it is gossip. The Internet has amazing capabilities, but it also takes gossip, innuendo and the printed word and disseminates them at an incredibly rapid rate. It doesn't matter what's true because once it's out there gossip takes on a life of its own, and that's kind of evil. When somebody says something incorrect about an area of my life that is or was painful, that's not cool and it leaves me feeling as if I've been robbed.

PLAYBOY: *Back when you were learning to draw, who were your favorites?*

BURTON: Dr. Seuss was my favorite by far. His books are so beautiful and subversive, and they work on so many levels. Like any good folktale, Dr. Seuss' stories are timeless and they have cultural and sociological meaning that will always hold true. That work was so much of what he was, that I've always left it alone as far as trying to turn one of his books into a film. As far as the work that influenced me, I'm a child of television and I grew up on monster movies, *The Twilight Zone* and *The Outer Limits*. I still get a warm glow from a television set because for me it's always been the hearth, the parents, the womb and a friend, so I just like having it on. Now I mostly watch the movie channels and cooking shows like *Iron Chef*, but the main things I like are the soft waves of light and the sound a television gives off.

PLAYBOY: *What about books?*

BURTON: One of the problems of being part of the television generation is that I don't read much and it's not easy for me to read—in fact, in order to read a book I'd almost have to not do anything else. I spend a lot of time flying but I never read then. I can't do anything when I'm on a plane because the minute I start to focus on something there's turbulence, so I just stop everything and I sit there like my dog. I've tried drinking but that doesn't help. When you see a plane take off it just doesn't look like something that should be happening. The thing that drives me most crazy on planes is people who go up there and pull down the shade! As long as you're up there you might as well appreciate the view. You're in the heavens! You can see things! Why create more claustrophobia in a thing that's already a claustrophobic nightmare?

PLAYBOY: *What made you fall in love with Lisa Marie?*

BURTON: It was unexpected, which seems to be the way these things happen. I felt something on a level that was amazing to me, and I'll never forget it. It was kind of shocking, actually, because like a lot of people, I'd reached the point of believing it was never going to happen for me and that maybe I was expecting too much. Then I got this feeling that was bizarre and amazing—no matter what your intellectual mind tells you, when you experience a real feeling you know it, and it's a beautiful thing. It had additional meaning because it showed me I wasn't some kind of crazy monster incapable of having normal human feelings. I experienced a strong sense of connection the minute we met and it wasn't until later that I learned how much we had in common. Like me, she had left her parents' home at an early age, and the minute I saw her I sort of flashed on her as a young girl, as an old woman—I could see it all in her. It was like a weird special effect that felt really good and pure. She was someone I could share the things I do with, and I love working with her.

PLAYBOY: *She's had small parts in several of your films; do you plan to cast her in a leading role?*

BURTON: Oh yeah, I absolutely want to work with her in that way, but here's the problem. I've been trying to make kind of an independent movie since *Edward Scissorhands*, and I had to walk away from quite a few things to make that film. Once you've made a movie like *Batman*, people want to charge you $100,000 a month to rent you a house, and you wind up penalized for being associated with something you're not actually getting much benefit from. I'm not getting a financial benefit from *Batman*, and that's been one of the worst aspects of having done that film. When I did *Ed Wood* nobody believed I would work for scale, and I felt like I was being looked upon as kind of an idiot for doing it. The point I'm making is that you have to find a way out and I don't know what that way is.

PLAYBOY: *Was it a goal of yours to make big studio movies?*

BURTON: No, and I've always felt it's been one of my saving graces that it wasn't. I've never had one goal I was obsessed with, and having known people who have, I can see it's just a way to set yourself up for failure.

PLAYBOY: *Paul Reubens was a huge star when you directed him in your first feature,* Pee-wee's Big Adventure, *but he disappeared from public view for several years following his 1991 arrest for a sexual misadventure. Did the entertainment industry ostracize Reubens or was it his choice not to work?*
BURTON: That episode with Paul seemed to mark the beginning of a new era of "let's tear people down." America has a history of tearing people down and then resurrecting them, and it's a sick ritual that's a complete waste of time and makes me deeply angry. If a mobster did things that people in the movie business do every day, he'd be killed. Paul is talented, resourceful and creative, so he survived, but that entire episode was a waste of his time.

PLAYBOY: *What's the basis of the bond between you and Johnny Depp that enables you to work together so successfully?*
BURTON: I realized something about Johnny when he played Edward Scissorhands, which is that he has baggage too. He looks a certain way, but who he is goes far beyond his appearance. There's a lot going on with Johnny. I think I respond to the fact that he's perceived a certain way but isn't really that way, and I also love that as an actor he doesn't care how he looks—he has a real freedom in that regard. We've done three films together—*Scissorhands* in 1990, *Ed Wood* in 1994, and *Sleepy Hollow* in 1999—and he's been completely different in all of them. I'm excited by the possibilities with Johnny.

PLAYBOY: *Martin Landau won an Academy Award for his performance as Bela Lugosi in* Ed Wood. *What made you cast Landau as Lugosi?*
BURTON: I knew he'd understand the part. Here's a guy who's done all this great stuff and worked with Hitchcock, but he was also on *Gilligan's Island* with the Harlem Globetrotters. I knew he'd relate to Bela Lugosi's ups and downs, and he did. I was thrilled when he won the Oscar, but I've never gone to the Academy Awards and can't even be around that stuff. I like to be working when that's going on. This year I was in Hawaii, and although we finished shooting the day before the Awards, I stayed there an extra day to miss them. Have you ever seen that cheesy

movie from 1966, *The Oscar*? Unfortunately it's pretty close to the truth as far as what the Academy Awards are about. There's this weird current of politics and maneuvering that surrounds them. The whole thing feels like a high school popularity contest. Don't stand in line for hours to talk to Joan Rivers, then pretend you don't want to talk to her once you get up there.

PLAYBOY: *That's one aspect of Hollywood that you don't like. How about doing publicity—like this interview?*
BURTON: As far as promotion, I always question the value of doing press to help make a movie a success, because I really don't have anything to say. I'm basically an idiot and I don't have any funny stories about the set, so what good am I? Still, the studios make you feel like you're neglecting the movie if you don't do press. Generally I don't like reading about myself, and if I see my name in print or I see my picture I don't get anything out of it. I don't hold it against the studios that they "encourage" me to go out and promote the film, because they're just doing what studios do. Still, I've always found it odd that I ended up in this situation because I don't know what a hit movie is. Movies like *Planet of the Apes* are basically businesses, and they involve words like franchise and saturation that make my skin crawl. This one will be heavily merchandised, but that's not something I have any control over. They ask my opinion, of course, but sometimes I feel like the film gets in the way of the merchandising. There were people over in Taiwan making *Planet of the Apes* swords before we'd even shot the thing, and the film is being aggressively presold. Personally, I don't want to know too much about a movie before I go see it. When I went to see a movie as a kid I would know a little about it beforehand, and I'd go enter a world that surprised me. These days you know how much it cost and it's been picked apart in the press before audiences have seen it. It takes the humanity, the magic and the surprise out of the experience, and that's sad.

PLAYBOY: *Is the relationship between businesspeople and artists, writers, actors and directors an adversarial one?*
BURTON: At the end of the day, those relationships feel adversarial. With movies, businesspeople give artists a lot of money to make things,

and that's something I've never taken lightly. However, the thing they don't understand is that at the end of it all, they're asking me and everyone else on the film to put in incredibly long hours. We don't see our families, and regardless of how well everyone is being paid, we still need emotional support from the studio in order to do the job we're being paid to do. By the end of a lot of those meetings you feel bloodied, wounded and left for dead, and by the time you actually get down to making the movie, you feel like you've had the shit beat out of you and need to spend a few months recovering in a hospital.

PLAYBOY: *Do you think businesspeople are threatened by creative types?*

BURTON: Yes, I believe there is a subconscious jealousy that partly has to do with the fact that it's a very American thing to assume everybody else has it better than you do. People in independent film think people who get to make studio films have it easier, and if you work with studios you long to do an independent film. And listen, if I were in an office all day being tortured and feeling the pressure of a board and all that stuff, I'd go crazy too. Some of those studio gigs are difficult, thankless jobs and I'd be shocked if there weren't feelings of jealousy.

PLAYBOY: *Have your interests changed over the course of your life?*

BURTON: It's kind of sad, but I still love monster movies. I can watch them any time, and when they're actually on TV, as opposed to being on a video or DVD, there's a weird energy they give off. Maybe it's because you know other people are watching it at the same time, so it becomes this odd kind of shared experience. Monster movies are part of an age-old tradition that includes fairy tales and fables, and that tradition is not going to disappear.

PLAYBOY: *Who inspires you?*

BURTON: Lisa inspires me, so that keeps a certain heartbeat going in my life. I was lucky enough to work with Vincent Price, who was also inspiring. While he was working on *Edward Scissorhands* I got an idea to do a documentary called *Conversations With Vincent* that he agreed to narrate and was completely cool about. I felt like he got what it was about, that it was more than just a tribute to him, and it meant a lot to me. It was about the internal life of a child and how adults tend to overlook the fact that children are supremely intelligent in a unique way. They have instincts that should be taken seriously, and Vincent understood that. He was in his early 80s when we met, and it was great to meet someone so old who'd been through so much but was still so cool. The film has never been seen because it became a nightmare trying to get all the rights and clearances we needed. But it's not over yet. A little time has passed, and there are some great things in it—Vincent died in 1993, so it has some of his last footage. I haven't given up on it.

PLAYBOY: *What are you incapable of being sensible about?*
BURTON: I don't respond well to authority and have an aversion to anyone telling me what to do. Those kinds of seeds are planted early in life. I wasn't a good student, and I discovered in school that instead of reading an 800-page book, I could make a little Super-8 film and get by. I never wanted to do what people told me to do, and I've always tried to find my own way of doing things. As soon as somebody tells me what to do, my mind flip-flops to another place. To this day, when Sunday night rolls around, I get depressed because I feel like I have to go to school the next day, and if I walk onto any campus I feel that way. It's weird. Every month I get a letter in the mail saying I'm getting kicked out of the Directors Guild of America, and that brings up those anti-authority feelings, too. I paid my dues! I guess I got caught up in some form-letter cycle when I forgot to pay my dues one month, but getting that letter immediately throws me back to high school or to Cal-Arts, where I was fighting with authorities every day about this, that or the other thing.

PLAYBOY: *One would imagine that there aren't many authority figures ordering you around these days.*
BURTON: It still happens. I remember going to the premiere for *Pee-wee's Big Adventure*, and the security people didn't know who I was and refused to let me in. I still have a hard time getting on movie lots, and the studio guards always stop me. Scarily enough, I've been around long enough to see the studios change over five or six times, and when I drive onto the lots the guards always stop me, and I always have to ask the guard, "What's this studio called now?"

PLAYBOY: *Do you feel you're pigeonholed as an oddball, eccentric director?*

BURTON: School is your first taste of categorization and social hierar-
chies, and you don't have to do much to be put into a weird category.
I felt very lonely in school, and *Edward Scissorhands* was based on the
feelings of loneliness I experienced as a kid. I knew I wasn't a bad person and I didn't feel weird, yet that's how I was perceived. It was sad
and it made me feel like I was crazy. I can remember walking around
thinking, What's wrong with me? They tell me I'm weird so I guess I
must be, but I don't feel weird. In retrospect, I can see that it was the
people who had a strong quality of individuality who were ganged up
on and treated like freaks, probably because people who don't have
personal power like to torture those who have it.

PLAYBOY: *If you could change anything about the way you were raised,
what would it be?*

BURTON: I wouldn't change anything, because the more pain you
endure when you're young, the richer your adult life will be. I remember going to my 10-year high school reunion, and when I looked
around the room it was obvious that the people who'd done the most
with their lives were the ones who'd been troubled in school. People
who were satisfied with themselves in high school and thought they
had it all had stopped growing. Going to that reunion was a shock. The
one good thing about having that kind of childhood is that it gives you
time on your own. Because you're not popular you're not out socially,
so you have time to think and to be quietly angry and emotional.
And if you're lucky, you'll develop a creative outlet to exorcise
those feelings.

Big Fish: American Museum of the Moving Image

DAVID SCHWARTZ/2003

DAVID SCHWARTZ: *The film is based on a wonderful short book by Daniel Wallace. And it's almost like a sketchbook in style. It's got episodes, short chapters, and almost has a feeling of one of your sketchbooks. What I want to ask you about first is the ending, because in a way if you were doing a completely straight adaptation, you would've ended with the big fish in the river, when the son goes to the river. And then the funeral, the last section, I'm assuming was your invention. But could you talk about that?*

TIM BURTON: Yeah, I read the script before I read the book. And I was glad I did, actually, because I think it was a case of where John [August], the writer, actually helped focus the material. In some ways, it's good to not have a novel that's extremely well known—this big, thick, heavy thing everybody loves—just because I think it's easier to adapt into a film, somehow, a little less daunting. So I thought that John took what Daniel was trying to do and just helped focus it.

SCHWARTZ: *This is John August who wrote* Go *and* Charlie's Angels: Full Throttle, *I believe.*

BURTON: That's right. [laughter] Hard to believe, isn't it? Multitalented.

SCHWARTZ: *Versatile.*

BURTON: Yeah.

Moderated by David Schwartz, Chief Curator of Film. Published by permission of the American Museum of the Moving Image.

SCHWARTZ: *OK. But you read the script before the book.*

BURTON: Yeah. There was a freedom to what he did that just seemed to be not under the heaviness of a well-known novel.

SCHWARTZ: *It's such a personal film, such a deeply emotional film. I usually don't ask personal questions, but I'm sure this must have had some resonance, in terms of your relationship with your father.*

BURTON: Yeah, a little bit. But it had, actually, more to do with *Son of Godzilla.* [laughter] That was such a touching father and son movie that I never forgot, as a child. I think it's a thing where everybody loses a parent and, no matter what your relationship is, it's obviously cause for reflection. I found that even though I wasn't really close to him, that I still had lots of emotions that were all over the place. And I thought that this film, when I read it, was a good way of visually exploring those feelings, which are complicated and hard to actually put into words.

SCHWARTZ: *The film has a mythological feeling. It has the feeling of a classic story, a classic fable. And I'm just wondering if you could talk about your approach to the style and look. I mean, this film has such a great physical look to it.*

BURTON: I grew up loving movies. So I realize that I love the mythology, folk tale kind of thing . . . because that's basically what movies are, as well. So from *Jason and the Argonauts,* where you've got classic mythological representations of things, the magical town or city, all these sort of images. They were just variations on all the kind of classic imagery that way, and symbols.

SCHWARTZ: *One thing I love about the movie is the way you used the real locations. I know with* Sleepy Hollow *that was a case where you found you had to wind up building most of what we saw. But I think here, the landscape of Alabama, the rivers in Alabama, seemed to . . .*

BURTON: Yeah, it's nice to go to a place and just soak up the vibe of the place. I mean just talking to people and just . . . the light. You know, you do get a flavor of something that you can't get if you're shooting on a soundstage or in Los Angeles. So it was good to go down there and soak up the vibe and the chicken fat [laughter] and all the other stuff. Yeah. [laughs]

SCHWARTZ: *And apparently you were based in a sleepy small town?*
BURTON: Yeah, I think I was actually staying, it seemed like, where they shot *The Blair Witch Project.* I don't know, the trees looked awfully similar to me. But you're there working, so it's not like you're there to sightsee. You see it in a more under the surface way, which is always more interesting.

SCHWARTZ: *How involved were you in the production design area? The house . . .*
BURTON: We showed up a few days during the production of the film.

SCHWARTZ: *You built the . . .*
BURTON: Sorry . . .

SCHWARTZ: *It's your night, so, you know, just feel free. [laughter] Edward's house, the Bloom house was beautiful; and that was built, that's not something you found?*
BURTON: No, most of that was there.

SCHWARTZ: *Really?*
BURTON: We just added a little bit to it. Yeah, I mean, that was the thing. It was a film with a fairly quick schedule, so we were shooting very quickly, so we had to move sometimes three locations in a day. You know, it's like you would put on your baseball outfit and you'd do like four sports in one day. We were moving around a lot, and so we didn't have an opportunity to over-build a lot of stuff. We built Specter and all, but it was important to use as much live. I mean, we didn't do even a day of blue screen. It just needed a handmade kind of quality, because of the nature of it, and the stories. We tried to keep the effects as human as possible, doing them as live, and some in camera. I mean, we did do a little bit of stuff. But always kept it as real as we could.

SCHWARTZ: *Could you talk about your work with actors? Sometimes the visual style is what's talked about most with your films; but there are so many great performances in the movie.*
BURTON: Well, we were very lucky to get good actors. It was an interesting case, because in the case of Albert [Finney] and Ewan [McGregor] and Alison [Lohman] and Jessica [Lange], you couldn't quite think of just one person; you had to think in tandem. And so that was interesting

and difficult. I felt lucky every day, because they were really good. And we shot all out of sequence; it was a real puzzle that way. I like working with actors that don't care how they look. There's an openness to them, and they're more adventurous and open to trying things.

SCHWARTZ: *Some of the characters, or a lot of the characters, in your films are much more introverted. I mean, this is a real great extroverted character. I'm just wondering what it was like working with this character of Edward Bloom.*
BURTON: It was fun. That's why Albert's so great, because he . . . you know, someone either has that kind of thing in their personality . . . and when you're around somebody like that, you get the joy of that. You also get, from the son's point of view, the sort of positive and negative of the whole thing. So it was an interesting challenge to get the positive/negative between those two characters.

SCHWARTZ: *Was Albert Finney cast first?*
BURTON: Well, we had to do it together. That's the thing. We couldn't go out and get Albert, and then not think of Ewan. I remember seeing a picture of Albert Finney in *Tom Jones*. And it just struck us that it was very much like Ewan. And then we pulled out, from a couple years earlier, one of those *People Magazine* "Separated at Birth" type of things. And so we said, "See? *People Magazine* thinks it's a good idea, too." So . . . sanctioned-by-*People*-casting. Yes, thank you, *People Magazine*. That'll be the only thanks.

SCHWARTZ: *The dialect, there's a nice quality to it; it feels sort of old fashioned. It feels like Southern dialect, but it's not cliche.*
BURTON: Yeah. Well, that's the thing. I realized after deciding to do the film . . . I, quietly, to myself, one weekend shortly thereafter, I said to myself, "You know, I hate Southern movies." [laughter] There's a certain thing about it that I just don't like. I remember liking *To Kill a Mockingbird* and feeling like, well, there is a lyrical aspect to the language. And so we tried to go for what was a more poetic cadence, and a little bit less of the "Come on . . . tell-you-a-story-on-the-porch-with-a-mint-julep" type of thing that I always equate to it. So they were all very good at trying to capture that other type of slightly more lyrical, poetic cadence to it.

SCHWARTZ: *And how did this tie in with the way you shot the film? I mean, there's a poetic quality, I think, to the compositions, and there's a simplicity and beauty to the way the film looks. If you could talk a bit about how . . .*

BURTON: I don't storyboard as much. I mean, we do storyboard, but I don't pay attention quite as much. As you work with actors, you realize that's the fun. And so you get enough of an idea. When you're fighting with the weather and locations a lot, since we were outside a lot, you try to keep open to things. But the fun part of it is the shooting. It's the hardest part, but it's the most interesting. And, you know, just trying to find a balance from the stories to the reality. So it didn't really turn on and off like a faucet, but it was a bit more stream-of-conscious. We were always trying to be aware of that throughout.

SCHWARTZ: *What kind of production was it in terms of difficulty? There's an intimacy and simplicity to the story; but you have lots of animals and lots of sets . . .*

BURTON: Lots of animals [laughter] yeah. And we also were in a tornado zone. The scene where we were shooting Danny [DeVito] naked in the forest, the next day it was three feet under water. We had a whole circus that we shot. We were quite lucky. I mean, the tent almost blew away in a tornado—it was quite interesting weather, yeah. [laughter]

SCHWARTZ: *In your book,* The Melancholy Death of Oyster Boy, *there's a story called "Anchor Baby," which has an image of a naked woman coming out of the water and is very resonant to what we see in the film. And I'm just wondering sort of what . . .*

BURTON: Well, I love naked women in the water, I guess. I don't know. I mean, I guess you found me out. [laughter] Try to slip those in under the PG-13 banner, you know what I mean? It's not easy these days.

SCHWARTZ: *Ok, with that, I'm going to throw this open to the audience. [laughter] I'm afraid to ask another question, so, feel free to jump in if you have a question or comment.*

AUDIENCE MEMBER: *Have you given up on animation?*

SCHWARTZ: *Animator Bill Plympton. Have you given up on animation?*

BURTON: No, no, no. In fact, I'm doing another sort of stop-motion one in London. So I feel very excited . . . you know how long it takes.

So it'll be a couple of years, but it's a medium I love. And I love the puppet stop-motion, so far so good, but it's a couple years off.

AUDIENCE MEMBER: *Is there any film that you've made that you would've done differently?*
BURTON: You mean, like, not do it kind of thing? [laughter] Sure. I don't look at things that way. I think that you put a lot into it, whether it's good or a piece of crap; you know, I still put as much into it anyway. I think somebody once said they are like your children; they may have flaws, but you still are close to them. So, yeah, I always look at them more like little time capsules and things. So if it's got rough edges, which they do, that's OK to me.

SCHWARTZ: *And what was the decision process like to make this? You'd done two very huge productions before this, and . . .*
BURTON: Well, this was nice, because, again, it had a script before there was a release date, which was nice. [laughter] So chalk up one for that. [laughter] And it was a script that everybody liked, which again, whoa. When does that . . . [laughter] I can't remember that one happening. So it was amazing all the other stuff you go through when you don't have what should be the number one element right off the bat. So it was good for that reason.

AUDIENCE MEMBER: *Will* Batman *come to Broadway?*
BURTON: I think it's gonna go straight to an ice show. [laughter] No. I hung up my tap shoes many years ago. I don't know. I have no plans for that one.

AUDIENCE MEMBER: *Will* Batman *be released in a DVD special edition?*
BURTON: That's sort of a Warner Bros. thing. But I would imagine, now that they finally realize that DVDs are here for a while . . . yeah, so I think they might. I think they were holding out for a while to see how that was all going to go. I'd like to do that sometime.

AUDIENCE MEMBER: *Karl the Giant. Could you tell us about him?*
BURTON: I believe he was a bouncer in a Philadelphia nightclub, who I think trained as a lawyer. He's an amazing guy. When I met him, I . . . just something about him and his voice, and what he goes through all

day. He understood the part. [laughter] He just had a quality to him that I thought was really nice. You know, he's afraid of heights, which is kind of ironic. But really, he's an amazing, good guy.

AUDIENCE MEMBER: *Can you talk about Danny Elfman's score?*
BURTON: With Danny, it's like try to be a character. And it is like a character. So I always enjoy working with him. This was, I felt, something slightly different and new for him. And so I thought he did a beautiful, beautiful job on it.

AUDIENCE MEMBER: *Do you feel like your approach has changed over the years? Now in your career do you see yourself as more still working to please a studio or to please yourself?*
BURTON: Well, like I said, when I first started, it was storyboards and just real true to that. Well, I don't know, because I don't know how to really please anybody else. [laughter] Ask all my ex-girlfriends about that. [laughter] I mean, you want to do a good job. And it's a very personal thing. So it's hard to project what that is to other people. But I think probably the biggest thing is the storyboarding process.

SCHWARTZ: *The film ends with this beautiful passage about stories living on forever; and obviously, that's what filmmakers do, and hope to make movies that will last. Was there a sense when you were making this that this was going to be a movie that . . .*
BURTON: No, you never think that when you're making it. There's so many other things. Like I said, what I was saying earlier about a release date before a film is out, you know, before there's a script. It's like all that does, it cuts out the process of doing. When you're there on a set and you're . . . the weather and the actors . . . I mean, it's an immediate moment, which is so beautiful and important. And you never want that to get lost by thinking about what's going to happen or where it's going to go. It's just the joy of doing it.

AUDIENCE MEMBER: *[inaudible question about inserting deleted scenes onto DVD versions]*
BURTON: Yeah, I'm not a really big fan so much. The only time I'm doing it, when I'm not putting them into the movie is for the *Ed Wood*

DVD, where I'm going to put in some separate scenes, just because I thought they were interesting on their own, not integrated into the film. But I don't know. You also like a little bit of time. I think you just finish something; you like a little bit of distance to take it all in and soak it in. So hopefully, there'll be a little bit of time to assess and analyze what was out. You shoot, try to edit as we go, because schedules are so quick. The idea of shooting something and having a three-and-a-half hour film and looking at it the week after you finish it, having to cut an hour out—it's just too painful of an idea, to have it that quick. So you try to do it as you go along, and not shoot too much extra stuff.

SCHWARTZ: *What was the editing like on this film? Was there a longer version? It feels so perfect.*
BURTON: Well, we kind of cut quick. We'd see a cut, like a week after we finish shooting, and it's not way, way, way over. Even if you cut twenty minutes out, it's a lot of footage that you're cutting out, so . . .

AUDIENCE MEMBER: *[inaudible question about* Charlie and the Chocolate Factory*]*
BURTON: Well, we've got a tie-in with McDonald's, so I guess it's real. That's all we need. [laughter] The mark of reality. No, you know, again, we'll try to get a script and I've done enough where I've said yes to things where I get all into the drama of "Will we get a script? Will we, won't we before it comes out? I just feel like I got caught up in that. So I'm trying to watch that one in the future. [laughs]

AUDIENCE MEMBER: *Your films are very imaginative and sort of fearless. How did this evolve? Because from the very beginning, your films really do seem to spring some . . .*
BURTON: Well, I guess I feel lucky. Like, working at Disney, where it was probably the worst time in the company's history, allowed me the opportunity to do a couple of short films. If I had been there at the time when they were successful, I probably wouldn't have gotten the opportunity. So it's always been a weird dynamic, where they let me do whatever. So I've had the luck of being able to do what I wanted to do. And so once you get that, you don't want to go back. I don't think about it any other way, really.

SCHWARTZ: *You've talked about your childhood, growing up in Burbank, as being almost similar to Edward's, like, growing up in a small town and wanting to get out of it. I mean, did you relate to your childhood when making this film?*

BURTON: Well, yeah. I think you have to relate everything to what you do, just because that's your only reference of how to get something done and achieve something. I actually identify with every character on some level even if it's a dog or a woman or any kind of character. A bird or an ape or whatever. It's like you try to just relate to it.

AUDIENCE MEMBER: *This film seems like a real Tim Burton film, but very refreshingly different in a lot of ways.*

BURTON: You mean, like halfway decent, is that what you're saying? [laughter]

SCHWARTZ: *I don't think that's what he's saying. [laughter]*

BURTON: Well, I don't think about it. I don't think about that sort of thing. I guess, especially growing up in the Hollywood sort of system, you get labeled. And I've always resisted. I don't like to think too much about myself, really. I like to think about the material and think about what you're trying to do, but I don't try to think about myself so much, because I've been spending my whole life trying not to think about myself. [laughs] The point is to just keep fresh and not make yourself into a thing, you know? Just remain a human being and try to do the things that interest you and see what happens and all.

SCHWARTZ: *This is a sort of jump, but you became a father a little over a month ago. So how has that changed you?*

BURTON: It's like, you know, you grew up, and people call you weird, and it's actually the weirdest thing that you could ever do, this thing. [laughter] And we're all a result of it, you know? So . . . it's amazing. [laughter]

AUDIENCE MEMBER: *Do you have a desire to make a horror movie?*

BURTON: I don't know if I could be really, ultimately, really scary in that way. Because it's a real thing, to do that. And I think I have such a love of them, and they actually made me so happy that I never treated them as horror. I guess they're like my *Rocky* kind of movies, you know? The life-affirming . . . [laughter] you know, [hums]: Da-da-da-da-da-da. You know. Frankenstein up on the steps, [laughter] blaring music. I maybe come at it from a different way. I do love it, so I would always think about it, or entertain it, but . . . I would like to try it sometime. I just don't know if I could be quite scary enough.

AUDIENCE MEMBER: *Do you like working with actors that you've worked with before, or new people?*
BURTON: Well, both. You know, what's fun about working with somebody like Johnny [Depp], whom I've worked with three times, is that you get to see them do different things each time. And that's a real energy that's unique to that specific kind of thing. When you work with people that like playing characters, it's a lot of fun to see them change. And then it's fun to mix it up, because you meet somebody new, and you get a whole new energy with that. I've felt, for the most part, just very lucky. Because being around creative people, you know, it sounds stupid, but it's like that energy rubs off on everybody, and it's just a lot of fun.

SCHWARTZ: *Talk a bit about working with Ewan McGregor, because that's such a bold performance. And it had to be perfect to work, right?*
BURTON: Everybody had a particularly tricky job, and his was to play a sort of romanticized version of a character, so, to do that, while still keeping it a human being, was really, really, good. It was kind of a bad joke. It's like: OK, wrestle with the wolf today. There's a whole chasing of a pig, which is cut out. You know, there were more animals for the—yeah. Yeah, that's a good DVD, yeah. [laughter] No, but I mean, he's just got such an openness. And to do that kind of open-hearted stuff that he does in the film is very difficult, to be that open-hearted and to get the idealistic thing; to get the comedy, but also to keep it a human being. I mean, yeah. Very, very, good. Really good.

AUDIENCE MEMBER: *How do you choose the cinematographer and convey your vision to the cinematographer?*
BURTON: Well, the last couple times, I go with people that don't speak English very well. So that suits me just fine. [laughter] They say the

same of me. So it was good, you know. There's a few people that you have to like, because they're around you all the time, and it's part of your whole thing. So it's nice to like the director of photography and the art director and all. But you look a little bit at other people's work, but not too much. It's a little bit about how you relate to them. Philippe [Rousellot] was good, because he would like to work quick, and we needed to. And it keeps an energy going. And he got the feeling of trying to stream-of-conscious up, so it doesn't look . . . like I said earlier, about the stories and the reality stuff. So it's like making up a relationship quickly. You know, it's like that. Got to be that deep.

SCHWARTZ: *We have an exhibition of your artwork upstairs, and it's been said that you use your sketches and your drawings to convey ideas to your cinematographers.*
BURTON: It's good that way, because people that will look at something like that and not be literal about it—because they're obviously not sketches that can be translated literally—so somebody who gets it on that emotional level, that's the kind of person that I like.

SCHWARTZ: *I was wondering—this is another jump. I kept feeling like this film echoed* The Wizard of Oz *to me, and I wonder if that was conscious at all, or not.*
BURTON: No, it wasn't conscious. Those kind of movies . . . but you would also say any movie has an impact. That's one that has an impact, of course. All these movies. But no, we never consciously said anything about that.

AUDIENCE MEMBER: *[inaudible question about the film's budget]*
BURTON: Wait, hold on. My accountant is here with the receipts. Could you give it to him and tell him . . . [laughter] because I don't know. You mean in Alabama money? [laughter] What kind of currency are we talking? It cost fifty-five million and twenty thousand beer can tops. [Laughter] I don't know. It was up there in the fifties, sixty . . . drachmas.

AUDIENCE MEMBER: *This is your third film with an Edward as a main character.*
BURTON: The other two, I planned; this one was the name, and so I . . . yeah, no, I know. [laughter] I don't really like the name Ed, actually.

[laughter] It's like, I always have circus images, but I always hated the circus. [laughter] You know? So it's like, the Ed one, I don't get. I'll let you know in a couple of years, after some more therapy. [laughter]

SCHWARTZ: *You'll have a naked women named Ed.*

BURTON: Yeah, yeah, exactly. Whoa . . . [laughter] That'll be the last movie. [laughter]

AUDIENCE MEMBER: *How long did it take to shoot?*

BURTON: About sixty-five, sixty days, something like that.

AUDIENCE MEMBER: *You were very inspirational to me, growing up. I was wondering if you get called a hero a lot.*

BURTON: No, I don't. [laughter] No! No, no. [laughter] Other things, you know, starting with an A. [laughter] No.

AUDIENCE MEMBER: *[inaudible question about Albert Finney and Ewan McGregor working together]*

BURTON: It was interesting. They spent a little bit of time with each other. But it was interesting, because the challenge was Ewan playing it as a sort of romanticized version. So like I said, we had this weird schedule, where Albert shot and Ewan didn't. So it was more of a case of them spending a little bit of time. But it was not this overkill of them going, "Well, let's both do this or that." I felt they're both also intuitive actors. And I think they like to approach things, I sense, on a certain level. So there was some time spent, and little bit of that connection. And then I let them go, because it felt . . . you get enough rehearsal in, but not too much, because it's the joy of being there on the set and doing it was where they really want to go.

SCHWARTZ: *Again, I want to invite everybody to go upstairs and see the exhibition of Tim Burton drawings. And congratulations again, and thanks for . . .*

BURTON: Thank you.

SCHWARTZ: *. . . thanks for coming, thank you.*

[Applause]

INDEX

CONVERSATIONS WITH FILMMAKERS SERIES
PETER BRUNETTE, GENERAL EDITOR

The collected interviews with notable modern directors, including

Robert Aldrich • Pedro Almodóvar • Robert Altman • Theo Angelopolous • Bernardo Bertolucci • Jane Campion • Frank Capra • Charlie Chaplin • Francis Ford Coppola • George Cukor • Brian De Palma • Clint Eastwood • John Ford • Terry Gilliam • Jean-Luc Godard • Peter Greenaway • Alfred Hitchcock • John Huston • Jim Jarmusch • Elia Kazan • Stanley Kubrick • Fritz Lang • Spike Lee • Mike Leigh • George Lucas • Michael Powell • Jean Renoir • Martin Ritt • Carlos Saura • John Sayles • Martin Scorsese • Ridley Scott • Steven Soderbergh • Steven Spielberg • George Stevens • Oliver Stone • Quentin Tarantino • Lars von Trier • Orson Welles • Billy Wilder • Zhang Yimou • Fred Zinnemann